3D for iPhone® Apps
with Blender and SIO2

3D for iPhone® Apps with Blender and SIO2

**YOUR GUIDE TO CREATING 3D GAMES
AND MORE WITH OPEN-SOURCE SOFTWARE**

TONY MULLEN

Wiley Publishing, Inc.

Acquisitions Editor: Mariann Barsolo
Development Editor: Kathi Duggan
Technical Editor: Romain Marucchi-Foino
Production Editor: Rachel McConlogue
Copy Editor: Judy Flynn
Editorial Manager: Pete Gaughan
Production Manager: Tim Tate
Vice President and Executive Group Publisher: Richard Swadley
Vice President and Publisher: Neil Edde
Book Designer: Caryl Gorska
Compositor: Chris Gillespie, Happenstance Type-O-Rama
Proofreader: Nancy Bell
Indexer: Ted Laux
Project Coordinator, Cover: Lynsey Stanford
Cover Design: Ryan Sneed
Cover Image: The squirrel character on the cover is © copyright Blender Foundation | www.bigbuckbunny.org. Game images featured on the cover include images from Cerebrii © 2009 Richard Stoner, Shootin' Annie © 2009 Tony Mullen, Black Sheep © 2009 Rarebyte OG, Droploly © 2009 Inovaworks, Touch Ski 3D © 2009 Michael Perl, Naquatic, Ivory Tower © 2009 APC LLC (41games.com), Manic Marble © 2009 Rich Olson, Guns of War © 2009 Dumbgames.net, iPunch © 2009 iDev.com, iPentris © 2009 Rarebyte OG, and Meditation Garden © 2009 SIO2 Interactive.

Library of Congress Cataloging-in-Publication Data

Mullen, Tony, 1971-

3D for iPhone apps with Blender and SIO2 : your guide to creating 3D games and more with open-source software / Tony Mullen.

p. cm.

ISBN 978-0-470-57492-8 (paper/website)

1. Computer games—Programming. 2. SIO2 (Electronic resource) 3. iPhone (Smartphone)—Programming. I. Title.

QA76.76.C672M858 2010

794.8'1526—dc22

2009047260

Dear Reader,

Thank you for choosing *3D for iPhone Apps with Blender and SIO2: Your Guide to Creating 3D Games and More with Open-Source Software*. This book is part of a family of premium-quality Sybex books, all of which are written by outstanding authors who combine practical experience with a gift for teaching.

Sybex was founded in 1976. More than 30 years later, we're still committed to producing consistently exceptional books. With each of our titles, we're working hard to set a new standard for the industry. From the paper we print on to the authors we work with, our goal is to bring you the best books available.

I hope you see all that reflected in these pages. I'd be very interested to hear your comments and get your feedback on how we're doing. Feel free to let me know what you think about this or any other Sybex book by sending me an email at nedde@wiley.com. If you think you've found a technical error in this book, please visit http://sybex.custhelp.com. Customer feedback is critical to our efforts at Sybex.

Best regards,

Neil Edde
Vice President and Publisher
Sybex, an Imprint of Wiley

*For Yuka
and Hana*

Acknowledgments

I'm very grateful to everyone involved in the creation of this book and the software it deals with. In particular, I'd like to thank Romain Marucchi-Foino, author of the SIO2 game engine, for his efforts in creating such a useful set of tools for the game-programming community as well as for his great help as tech editor of this book. I'd also like to thank Ton Roosendaal and the Blender developers for their tireless work to make Blender the fantastic piece of software that it is. ■ In addition to the developers, I'd like to thank the many users and game creators who helped me directly or indirectly through their posts on the SIO2 forum. I'm especially grateful to the game creators who allowed me to use images from their games in this book. Their work provides a great showcase for the power of the Blender/SIO2 pipeline. ■ This book wouldn't have been possible without the collaboration of the editorial and production team at Sybex, and I'm very grateful to everyone who had a hand in bringing it to publication, in particular Mariann Barsolo, Pete Gaughan, Kathryn Duggan, and Rachel McConlogue. These are just the people I interacted with most regularly on this project; there are many other people whose contributions I am also grateful for. ■ I'd also like to thank my students and colleagues at Tsuda College, Tokyo, for their support. In particular I'd like to thank my colleague Associate Professor Akihasa Kodate for suggesting I take over teaching his computer graphics class. The deepening of my knowledge of OpenGL that I gained through preparing that class was a great help for me in coming to grips with SIO2 and game development for the iPhone. ■ Finally I'd like to thank my wife, Yuka, and our daughter, Hana, for their love, support, and patience!

About the Author

Tony Mullen is a college lecturer, programmer, animator, filmmaker, and writer living in Tokyo. In the past, he has worked as a newspaper cartoonist, graphic designer, and computer science researcher, among other things. Since discovering Blender, he has been involved in CG animation to the point of obsession, but he also maintains a keen interest in stop-motion and traditional animation techniques, notably as the lead animator and codirector of the 16mm film *Gustav Braüstache and the Auto-Debilitator* (winner of the Best Narrative Short award at the New Beijing International Movie Festival in 2007 and Best Filmstock Film at the San Francisco Frozen Films Festival in 2008) and other independent shorts. Along with his filmmaking partner, Rob Cunningham, he was short-listed for Seattle alternative weekly newspaper *The Stranger's* Genius Award for Film in 2008. He is an active member of the Blender community and one of the original members of the Blender Foundation's Trainer Certification Review Board. He is the author of numerous articles and tutorials on Blender and graphics programming for the Japanese magazine *Mac People* and of the Sybex books *Introducing Character Animation with Blender*; *Bounce, Tumble, and Splash! Simulating the Physical World with Blender 3D*; and *Mastering Blender*.

CONTENTS AT A GLANCE

Contents

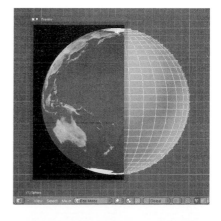

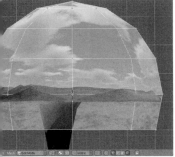

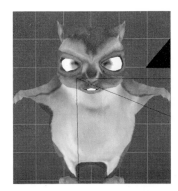

Foreword

When I first heard about the iPhone and its gaming capacities, I knew right from the start that it was going to be big; Apple has always been revolutionary in all its product lines. Knowing that the device would have support for OpenGL ES and OpenAL technology, I was excited to get the SDK.

I wanted to create a 3D engine built around it and provide a free, flexible, and scalable solution that users could start using out of the box. Being a fan for quite a while, when it came to which 3D editor I should use for the engine integration, Blender was the most obvious choice. Even after almost three years using it on a daily basis, Blender never stops impressing me, and I can't stop praising how much this software can do for the size of its download.

I grabbed my first copy of the iPhone SDK a day after its release and started spending all my free time building a game engine from scratch for the platform. Three months later, I released the first online version of SIO2—a version that ironically was actually never tested on a real device because the iPhone was not accessible in the country I was in. It took more than two revisions of the engine before I was able to test it on the device and the Blender/Xcode/iPhone game development pipeline that I had created.

Now a year later, SIO2 is one of the top 3D game engines used on the App Store, and it wouldn't have been possible without Blender and its community. I'm glad that I chose to use Blender since day one—using it as a world editor in order to provide a WYSIWYG interface for SIO2 was just a perfect match.

When Tony first contacted me, I was excited by the idea of creating this book, packed full of knowledge that will give a good kick start to anybody on their iPhone game creation learning curve with Blender and SIO2. I was honored to be able to participate in the creation of *3D for iPhone Apps with Blender and SIO2*, and I hope you will enjoy it and find it as useful as we do.

— *Romain Marucchi-Foino*

Author of SIO2, the free, open-source 3D game engine for
the iPhone and iPod Touch
Lead 3D Programmer at SIO2 Interactive
Shanghai, November 2009

Introduction

Congratulations! By cracking open this book, you have just taken the first step into the exciting, challenging world of interactive 3D content creation for the hottest handheld devices around: the iPhone 3G and its sleek sister, the iPod Touch. If you're coming from a related area of game design, programming, or 3D asset creation, you'll find the information you need here to transfer your skills to the realm of iPhone/iPod Touch development. If you are a complete newcomer to the technology, this book will give you the basis you need to begin creating games, visualizations, virtual worlds, and whatever interactive 3D content you can dream up and get them running on your iPhone or iPod Touch. You'll take advantage of the device's cutting-edge multi-touch interface technology, the physical sensitivity of its built-in accelerometer, and the brilliant clarity of its ultra-high resolution screen. By mixing in a little bit of hard work and ingenuity of your own, you will be able to develop your very own 3D applications to sell on the iTunes App Store, joining the growing number of budding entrepreneurs who are leading the way in innovation for the most exciting new game and application platform around.

What You Will Learn from This Book

This book introduces a powerful, straightforward pipeline for 3D content creation using Blender, the SIO2 game development application programming interface (API), and Apple's own Xcode and iPhone software development kit (SDK). With this combination of tools at your disposal, you'll quickly find yourself pushing the envelope of interactive 3D content creation for the iPhone and iPod Touch.

In this book, you'll learn how to create 3D assets and environments in Blender for use with the SIO2 engine, how to export them, and how to work with them using the SIO2 SDK. You'll learn how to use Blender's texture baking functionality to create convincing surface and lighting effects. You'll learn how to use the multi-touch interface to control

3D objects, camera movement, and characters. By the time you finish reading this book, you'll be in a good position to begin working on a 3D project of your own for the iPhone.

This book is not intended to replace the official tutorials and code samples that accompany the SIO2 SDK download. Those tutorials and code samples, which can be found in their respective project directories in the SIO2 SDK top-level directory, provide an indispensable sample of SIO2 functionality and cover much more material than is dealt with in this book. However, the information in the SIO2 code samples is dense, and diving right into reading the code can mean a steep learning curve for people who are new to the SIO2 engine. This book is an attempt to give a gentler introduction and to include some background information that will help you get more out of the tutorials and code samples. In Appendix C of this book, you'll find an overview of the content provided in the official tutorials. By the time you reach that appendix, you should be able to dive into the code samples with ease.

Why Blender/SIO2?

If you're reading this, you probably don't need to be told why somebody might want to create interactive 3D content for the iPhone or iPod Touch. Just the fact that you *can* is reason enough to want to! But there are a number of options for 3D content creation for the iPhone platform, and it's reasonable to wonder what the Blender/SIO2 pipeline has going for it.

For one thing, it's free. This is nice no matter what your budget is, but it's an even bigger deal when you consider that many of the most exciting and innovative projects available on the iTunes App Store are created by individuals or small studios. The iTunes App Store itself represents something of a revolution in software development and distribution, with many thousands of independent developers making their applications available to many thousands of users for very low prices. The path to success for such independent developers is a combination of solid programming skills, a killer concept, and low development overhead.

Blender is a free and open-source 3D content creation application that rivals applications costing thousands of dollars in terms of functionality and stability. A rapidly growing number of commercial animation and game studios have adopted Blender as their core 3D application for reasons of cost and flexibility. Likewise, SIO2 is free to use with only a minimal requirement of attribution, which is lifted for users of an inexpensive license. Like 3D applications, commercial game engines that offer iPhone compatibility also run into the thousands of dollars. For individual independent developers, the money saved can mean a lot of new hardware and some fancy dinners (or, for the frugal, it could just mean paying a couple of months of rent). For a studio, the savings is multiplied.

But being free isn't the whole story. In fact, the Blender/SIO2 pipeline isn't the only free solution to 3D development for the iPhone. The iPhone platform supports the OpenGL ES graphics API natively, the iPhone SDK comes with OpenGL ES built in, and there are numerous tools for developing and optimizing OpenGL ES code. It is possible to program games and 3D effects directly in OpenGL ES without using any high-level content creation tools at all. However, this is not the easiest or most intuitive way to work.

Modeling and animating are best carried out in a What-You-See-Is-What-You-Get (WYSIWYG) 3D environment such as Blender. The SIO2 API enables you to work directly with assets created in Blender and offers a high-level programming interface to greatly simplify the actual coding you have to do to obtain advanced effects. SIO2 also enables high-level functionality such as Lua scripting and networking.

There are also tools for working with 3D and Blender assets in the iPhone. The Oolong project in particular bears mentioning. Oolong is an open-source API with goals similar to the goals for SIO2. Like SIO2, it uses Bullet physics. It is also well integrated with the cross-platform Gamekit prototyping sandbox, which makes it worth investigating for advanced game programmers who are interested in cross-platform game development. As I write this, development is underway to add functionality to Oolong that will enable it to read Blender .blend files directly, which will be an exciting development for open-source game creators. Nevertheless, using Oolong requires a greater degree of game development experience and C++ coding skill to get started, and it is not as well supported by tutorials and code samples. For these reasons, I chose to focus on SIO2 for this book.

All in all, the combination of Blender and the SIO2 engine offers a powerful solution at a negligible fraction of the cost of the big commercial mobile 3D game pipelines while giving you WYSIWYG content creation and an accessible high-level programming environment.

What Else You Need to Know

Although a big part of their appeal is their apparent simplicity, the iPhone and iPod Touch are serious platforms, and the coding you learn about in these pages is serious software development. Creating complete applications for the iPhone and iPod Touch is itself an involved topic. At the same time, 3D programming in general has numerous challenges of its own.

For this reason, any background knowledge you have already about programming in C or OpenGL, computer graphics, 3D content creation, or iPhone development will be of great help to you as you work your way through this book. But because I can't assume you have *all* of this background, I'm going to proceed under the assumption that you have none of it. I'm going to do my best to explain everything in sufficient detail that it should at least make sense to even a completely inexperienced reader. If you find that the book progresses too slowly for you in some places, feel free to skip ahead. Likewise, if you start feeling like you're a bit in over your head reading discussions about computer graphics programming or Blender use, please refer to the appendices in this book, which I hope will function as quick tutorials to get you up to speed on the relevant topics. Throughout the book, I will give tips and references on where to find more in-depth information about a variety of topics. I strongly suggest that you follow these leads and track down as many supplemental resources as you can get your hands on.

The most important requirement for having success with this book, therefore, isn't any specific knowledge but rather an attitude. You may not know C or OpenGL ES, but you must be open to learning at least some of it. You may not be a hotshot at Blender modeling or animation, but you should be willing to be proactive about acquiring these skills. You may not have the slightest idea what a matrix is right now, but you must have enough faith in yourself to believe that you can learn the basic mathematical concepts that 3D game programming demands.

This book will get you well on your way. But it won't be the end of the story. Once you've worked your way through this book, you'll want to find other resources to fill in the gaps that remain in your knowledge. The official tutorials and code samples are an obvious next step. Appendix C offers an overview of what those tutorials contain, so you can get straight to learning the advanced functionality that interests you most.

Who Should Read This Book

This book is for anybody interested in creating 3D applications for the iPhone or iPod Touch. I think you'll find that following the tutorials in this book is the easiest and most direct path to learning what you need to know to create 3D content for the iPhone platform. That's not to say that the book is simple or a "beginner's book." If you don't have computer programming experience, you may find much of this book to be rough going. No single book can take you from 0 to 60 as a mobile game developer on its own; however, this book will at least get your foot on the pedal.

How to Use This Book

The best way to read this book is from beginning to end, all of the chapters in order. Several of the chapters follow explicitly and directly upon the preceding chapter, but there are also more subtle dependencies, and to avoid redundancy, the later chapters were written with the assumption that you have read the previous chapters.

I recommend working through each chapter's content from beginning to end, as it is described in the chapter, taking the SIO2 template project as the launching point. None of the tutorial projects are trivial, and the process of getting your project running based on what you read will give you ample opportunity to debug and double-check your code. At the end of each chapter, the code described in the chapter is printed in the context of the original template file. If you run into problems during the chapter, check this code to see where you might have taken a wrong turn. Finally, you can double-check everything by comparing your project to the corresponding project in the downloadable project archive that accompanies this book.

How This Book Is Organized

As I mentioned, the content of this book is roughly sequential, and concepts introduced early are referred to later. However, there are only a few strict dependencies. The first mid-sized project of the book is split over Chapter 3, Chapter 4, and Chapter 5, so those chapters should be read as a unit. The second mid-sized project is split between Chapter 6 and Chapter 7, and the third and final project is described over the course of Chapter 8 and Chapter 9, so those pairs of chapters should also be regarded as interdependent.

Here is a quick overview of what each chapter and appendix contains:

Chapter 1, "Getting Started with 3D Development for the iPhone," introduces the basics of iPhone development in Xcode and shows you how to build and run a project based on the SIO2 template.

Chapter 2, "Introducing Graphics Programming in SIO2," looks at some fundamentals of graphics programming in OpenGL|ES through the lens of SIO2 and the iPhone SDK.

Chapter 3, "Saying Hello to the Blender/SIO2/iPhone World," walks you through the creation of a simple Blender 3D scene featuring a model of planet Earth for use with SIO2.

Chapter 4, "Going Mobile with SIO2," picks up where Chapter 3 leaves off. This chapter shows you how to import the assets you created in Blender into the SIO2 development environment and add basic interactive functionality.

Chapter 5, "Extending Interactive Feedback with Picking and Text," builds upon the material in Chapter 4, showing you how to add even more sophisticated interactive functionality to your application.

Chapter 6, "Creating an Immersive Environment in SIO2," shows you how to use first-person camera movement and realistic physics to create an immersive 3D world for a player to explore.

Chapter 7, "Props and Physical Objects," builds directly on the project introduced in Chapter 6 by adding a variety of new objects to the scene. Material alpha blending, physics and collisions, and creating billboard objects are all covered here.

Chapter 8, "Animating a Character," turns to the Blender/SIO2 character animation functionality. In this chapter, you learn how to create simple animated actions for a rigged character in Blender and how to activate and control those actions in the SIO2 environment.

Chapter 9, "Working with Widgets," shows you how to use widgets to refine the interface of your app with splash screens and buttons.

Appendix A, "Blender Basics," gives an introduction to basic Blender use, suitable for people who have never used Blender before.

Appendix B, "Key Concepts for Graphics Programming," gives an overview of some key concepts in graphics programming to help deepen your understanding of the book's contents.

Appendix C, "SIO2 Reference," gives information on the official SIO2 tutorials and an overview of the SIO2 file format and functions.

Hardware and Software Considerations

Development for the iPhone platform is fairly restricted. You'll need a Mac running OS X 10.5 (Leopard) or later. You'll also need the iPhone SDK installed, which includes Apple's Xcode integrated development environment (IDE), the iPhone simulator, and other development tools. Getting your hands on the iPhone SDK doesn't cost anything but requires registration with the Apple Developers Connection. However, to make your applications available on the iTunes App Store or to compile your applications onto a physical iPhone or iPod Touch device, you will need to purchase a membership in the iPhone Developers Program, which costs about $100.

Some projects exist for making iPhone development possible on other operating systems. It's doubtful that such efforts will ever be sanctioned by Apple, as welcome as they would be to the developer community at large. The tutorials in this book assume that everything you're doing is carried out on a Mac with the official developer tools and an officially provisioned device. If you have any setup other than this, I wish you the best, but you're on your own.

The Book's Online Project Archive

The projects in this book are available for download in a zip file from the SIO2 website at http://sio2interactive.com/book/iphoneblendersio2 as well as from this book's Sybex website at www.sybex.com/go/iphoneblendersio2. Download and unzip the file, and then put the projects in this file into the main SIO2_SDK directory that is part of the official SIO2 package. The official SIO2 package is available for download at http://sio2interactive.com.

Contact the Author

You can contact the author at blender.characters@gmail.com.

CHAPTER 1

Getting Started with 3D Development for the iPhone

This chapter gives an overview of what you'll need to get started using Blender, SIO2, and Xcode to create interactive 3D content for the iPhone and iPod Touch. It also gives you a heads-up on what you can expect to learn over the course of the rest of the book and tips on where to look for further information on related topics. There's a lot to cover and a few hoops to jump through before you get to the real action, so you'll get right to business by downloading the software you need and setting up your development environment.

- Getting started
- Getting the software
- Setting up your SIO2 development environment

Getting Started

Welcome to the world of interactive 3D graphics programming for the iPhone and iPod Touch using Blender and the SIO2 game engine! I think you'll find that working with these tools is a fun and challenging experience.

Throughout this book, I will assume that you are working on a Mac computer running OS X Leopard (10.5) or later. The official iPhone Software Development Kit (SDK) is designed to run exclusively on Mac. There are some projects underway to create emulators and development environments for doing iPhone development on other platforms, but they are not officially sanctioned by Apple, so if you opt to try to make use of these alternatives, you're on your own. There's no guarantee you're going to be able to install and run your apps on a device or make them available to other iPhone and iPod Touch users.

As mentioned in the introduction, there are a number of areas of background knowledge that will be enormously helpful to you as you work your way through this book. A lot of the necessary information is dealt with in the appendices, but some of it will be up to you to fill in. A good print or online reference for C and C++ syntax will come in handy if you aren't already familiar with these programming languages. As a reference for OpenGL functions, the official *OpenGL Programming Guide (7th Edition)* by Dave Shreiner (Addison Wesley Professional, 2009)—also known as the Red Book—is indispensable.

It is not strictly necessary to have an iPhone or an iPod Touch of your own in order to learn the content of this book. Most (but not all) of the functionality described in this book can be run on your desktop using the iPhone simulator included with the iPhone SDK. However, some functionality, such as the accelerometer, requires the use of an actual device, and if you plan to make your app available to others, it will be necessary to test its performance on an actual device.

Getting the Software

There are a number of software tools you will need to have installed on your computer before you can proceed with this book. Some of what you will need is free and open source, some of it is simply free of charge, and some of it you'll have to pay for (although it won't break the bank). The rest of the chapter will focus on getting what you need and making sure it's working.

The iPhone SDK

If you're thumbing through this book in the shelves of your local bookstore wondering whether it's right for you, the one thing you should know immediately is that this book (like any book on iPhone development) is for Mac users only. The iPhone SDK 3.0 and development tools are available from Apple for Mac OS X 10.5.7 or greater, and it is not possible to develop for the iPhone on any other platform. If you're running an earlier version of Leopard, you should update your system using the Software Update tool in System Preferences.

The other thing you should be aware of, particularly if you are coming from a background of working with open-source software (as many Blender users are), is that there's nothing open about the iPhone development environment. Apple maintains strict control over how you use the iPhone SDK and how you are able to distribute the products you create with it. This isn't necessarily just because the folks at Apple are control freaks. The era of widely programmable mobile phone handsets has just begun, and there are many open questions about which directions the fledgling industry will take. Apple has erred on the side of caution in terms of security, and the success of the iTunes App Store and many of its contributing developers suggests that Apple is doing something right from a commercial standpoint as well. It remains to be seen how other, more open business models will fare in the arena of programmable handsets.

You can download the iPhone SDK at http://developer.apple.com/iphone/program/sdk/. The SDK includes Xcode, Apple's flagship integrated development environment (IDE) that includes a powerful editor and code browser, compilers, and a variety of debugging and testing tools. It also includes the Interface Builder, a separate but tightly integrated development application that enables you to create interfaces in a WYSIWYG manner, and the iPhone simulator, which enables you to test your iPhone software on your own computer via a graphical simulation of the iPhone displayed on your screen, as shown in Figure 1.1.

To download all these tools, you will need to register with the Apple Developer Connection (ADC). Basic membership is free of charge, but there are restrictions on what you can do with this level of membership. The most serious restriction on the free membership is that the SDK can compile iPhone software *only* to the simulator. If you want to compile your software for use on an actual physical iPhone or iPod Touch device, you will need to join the iPhone Developer Program, which costs $99. This membership also grants you the right to submit your software for possible inclusion in the iTunes App Store. Membership in the iPhone Developer Program is tightly controlled. Although it is open to anybody to join, there is a period of verification before the certification is issued, and any discrepancies in your application can result in annoying delays while your information is further verified. (Don't mistype your billing address on this one!)

Figure 1.1

The iPhone simulator

Throughout most of this book, I won't assume that you have iPhone Developer Program membership. The majority of examples in this book can be run on the iPhone simulator. A few features of the hardware are not present in the simulator, such as the accelerometer, which recognizes changes in the angle at which the device is being held. Any places in this book that deal with such functionality will be clearly indicated. If you're new to iPhone development, I recommend that you begin with the simulator. It's free to download, and you can get a good sense of what's involved in programming for the iPhone platform. Once you've decided to get serious, you can spring for the full iPhone Developer Program membership.

Installing the iPhone SDK will install Xcode, the iPhone simulator, Interface Builder, and some other tools on your computer. The installation should be straightforward and self-explanatory. There's a ton of documentation available on the Apple Developer Connection website, and you'll definitely want to delve into it.

Getting Blender

A great thing about mature, user-oriented free software like Blender is the relative ease with which you can download and install it. This book was written to correspond with Blender 2.49, which is the Blender version supported by SIO2 version 1.4.

You can download this version of Blender from the official Blender website. Since the latest Blender version may have changed by the time you read this, please download the software for OS X from the 2.49 archive page at `http://download.blender.org/release/ Blender2.49a/`.

Blender should run straight "out of the box." Clicking the Blender application's icon should open a session. If you're new to Blender, now might be a good time to run through Appendix A on the basics of working with it. There are tons of tutorials online as well as a growing number of books available covering a variety of specific topics. Obviously, if you plan to create 3D content in Blender, you're going to want to become as skilled as possible in working with the software.

A Python installation is also required, but you shouldn't have to worry about this because Python 2.5 is installed by default in Leopard.

In OS X, Blender-Python output and errors are displayed in the Console. To read any errors or output from Python scripts, you can run Console (`Applications/Utilities/ Console`) before starting up Blender.

Getting SIO2

The centerpiece of this book is the SIO2 engine. SIO2 is a set of software tools for exporting 3D assets from Blender and accessing them from within the Xcode development environment for inclusion in iPhone apps. This book was written to correspond to SIO2 version 1.4. The software is regularly updated and the released version changes regularly, but the version that corresponds to this book (as well as the tutorials used in this book) is available for download at the official SIO2 website: http://sio2interactive.com/DOWNLOAD.html.

As mentioned previously, SIO2 is available for free and its use is unrestricted except for one thing: If you use SIO2 to make a game or app available, you are asked to include the SIO2 splash screen at the start of the app. To bypass this restriction and use SIO2 without the splash screen, you are asked to purchase an inexpensive per-game Indie Certificate. The SIO2 Indie Certificate also gives you access to email technical support. SIO2 is not proprietary software, but purchasing the Indie Certificate is a big part of what keeps the project going, so I highly recommend doing so for any serious SIO2 projects. For now, though, simply download the ZIP file in the link and unzip it into a convenient location. I'll refer to this location from now on as your *SIO2_SDK directory*.

Setting Up Your Development Environment

Once you've downloaded the software and followed the steps for installing it, you can test your environment to make sure everything is working. In the following sections, you'll get your first look at the development environment that you'll become very familiar with over the course of the rest of the book. Building SIO2 projects in Xcode should be simple and straightforward, but if you're new to Xcode, there are a few things you might miss. If you hit any snags, skip forward to the troubleshooting section at the end of the chapter.

Building the SIO2 Template in Xcode

When you open your SIO2_SDK directory, you'll see a collection of directories. These include the code for the SIO2 engine, documentation of the API and .sio2 file format, a collection of tutorials in the form of sample projects, supplementary model and texture data for the tutorial projects, and a template for creating new projects. For the purposes of this book, you'll make very heavy use of the template. In fact, the template project will be the starting point for everything you do with SIO2, so it is a good idea to keep a backup copy of the entire directory. Right now you're not going to make any changes to the template—you're only going to build an executable from it to make sure your development environment is properly set up—so it is not necessary to make a copy.

Open the template directory and take a look at what's inside. You should see the directory listing shown in Figure 1.2.

Everything that your iPhone app needs resides in this folder. Some of the suffixes are probably familiar to you, but others may not be. Now's not the time to worry about these though. Any code files you need will be dealt with in the Xcode environment. So the only file you really need to bother with here is template.xcodeproj. As you might have guessed from the suffix, this file is an Xcode project file. You'll be working a lot with files like these.

Double-click template.xcodeproj to open the project in Xcode. The first time you do this, you should see a window something like the one shown in Figure 1.3.

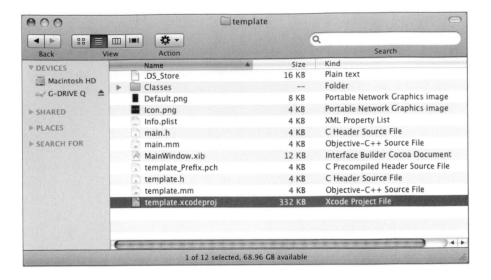

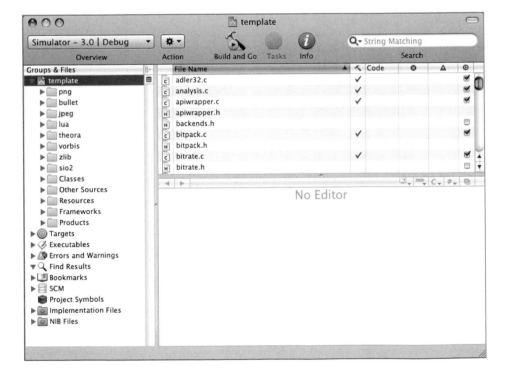

If all has gone smoothly so far, you should now be looking at the Template project in Xcode. This is the integrated development environment (IDE) that you will be working in for all of the coding parts of this book. The main area you see in the lower right (displaying the words *No Editor* in Figure 1.3) is where the code editor will open when a file is selected. Xcode's editor has a lot of powerful features that will help you code more quickly and accurately, and it's worth studying the online documentation available at the ADC website to get fully up to speed with what it has to offer. The window above the editor in the figure gives a listing of files in the project. This window is used for searching and navigating your project quickly.

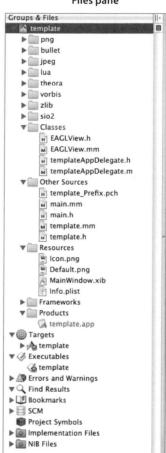

Figure 1.4

The Groups & Files pane

The drop-down menu in the upper left of the Xcode toolbar is important. This enables you to select the destination for your compiled app. The menu shown in the image is set to Simulator-3.0 | Debug, meaning that the app will be compiled to the iPhone simulator using the 3.0 version of the iPhone OS and with debugging information. Building the application with this setting will automatically start up the iPhone simulator and install and run the app there. If this drop-down menu selection is changed to Device-3.0, Xcode will attempt to install the app on your iPhone or iPod Touch handset. This is possible only if you have registered with the iPhone Developer Program and followed the necessary steps to certify your device.

The tall horizontal pane along the left of the Xcode window is the Groups & Files pane. This gives you a complete overview of everything in your project. Any data or code that your application has access to is listed here. You can click the little triangles to the left of the directory icons to open the directories. Figure 1.4 shows some of the most important files that you'll need to know about as you work your way through this book. Take a close look at those now.

The Classes directory lists some standard classes that are typically implemented in iPhone apps. These classes will come up again later in the book, but for now you can regard them as boilerplate code that sets up the viewing environment for the app. You should note, however, that the classes come in pairs of files. Each pair of files includes a header file with a .h suffix and a code file with either a .m suffix or a .mm suffix. The .m and .mm suffixes indicate Objective-C and Objective-C++ code, respectively. Other source code suffixes you will be likely to see when working with SIO2 and its associated libraries include .c for plain C code, .cpp for C++ code, and .cc for code that can compile as both C and C++.

The Other Sources directory includes, as its fiendishly straightforward name suggests, other source code files. The template_Prefix.pch file is a precompiled header that you will not need to deal with directly. The main.h and main.mm files contain the code that makes the top-level function calls for the application. You should take a look at this code, but you will not work much with it directly in this book.

By far, the file that you will work with most in the course of this book will be template .mm. This contains most (not all) of the SIO2 API code that accesses the 3D assets and implements the interactive behavior of your app. By the end of this book, you will know this file and files like it inside and out.

The `Resources` directory contains non-code data files that the app needs access to. As you can see, there are two PNG image files currently in the `Resources` directory. One of them is the app icon image, and one of them is the loading screen image.

The `MainWindow.xib` file is created by the Interface Builder application. If you go on to do more iPhone development, you will certainly learn about the Interface Builder and XIB files, but you won't need to deal with them directly for the purposes of this book. All of the official SIO2 tutorials and all of the code in this book are built using the default OpenGL ES template from Xcode, and there is no direct support for building OpenGL ES interfaces with the Interface Builder.

The `Info.plist` file is a property list. This is a table of property values for the app. You can change various things here about your app, such as which image is used for the icon.

The `Resources` directory will also be home to the `.sio2` files created when you export 3D assets from Blender. You'll learn about `.sio2` files in Chapter 3. Note that file extensions are case-sensitive in Mac, and the `.sio2` file extension is always formatted in lowercase.

The `Products`, `Targets`, and `Executables` directories hold the elements of your app. Mostly, you will not need to deal with these directly, except to change their names when creating your own project. The Target system in Xcode enables multiple related applications to be created within a single project, which is useful in large-scale development projects such as client-server applications. For iPhone development, however, it is unlikely you will ever need to deal with more than one target per project, so this functionality can be mostly ignored.

All those directories that I haven't mentioned in the upper half of the Groups & Files pane are important too, but you will mostly not need to access them directly. These are the libraries that provide the functions called in the application. The `sio2` directory contains the actual SIO2 code that implements the functionality you'll be using. The `bullet` directory contains the Bullet Physics Library. To learn about the implementation of these libraries, you can browse these directories.

Now that you've got some idea of what's in your project, you can go ahead and advance to the most anticlimactic part of this whole chapter: building the template app. Do this by clicking the Build And Go button at the top of the Xcode window. Wait a few seconds as Xcode builds the app and installs it on your iPhone simulator. The iPhone simulator should open automatically, the SIO2 loading screen should flash for a split second, and then, if everything has gone smoothly. . .nothing! The screen of your iPhone simulator should go completely black.

Of course, the reason nothing happened is that this is, after all, a template. The whole point of this book will be to teach you how to turn this nothing into something interesting. To stop the current app, click the round button at the base of the iPhone simulator, just as you normally would on your iPhone or iPod Touch to stop an app. You'll return to the buttons screen of the iPhone simulator, as shown in Figure 1.5, where you'll see, sure enough, the button for the template app alongside the other apps installed on the simulator.

If this has all gone as described, then you should be pleased. Your development environment is set up and SIO2 is building smoothly. You're ready to move on to creating actual 3D content for your iPhone or iPod Touch in Chapter 2.

Figure 1.5

The template app installed in your iPhone simulator

Nevertheless, I wouldn't blame you if you felt a little bit gypped after going through a whole chapter without getting to see any actual 3D action on your iPhone simulator. Fortunately, the SIO2_SDK directory is packed with ready-made code samples that you can dive into and explore right now. I highly recommend that you take a look at some of them. You can build and run them all in exactly the same way that you did the template, by opening the file with the filename extension .xcodeproj in the project's directory and clicking Build And Go. Figure 1.6 shows the results of the tutorial02 project, featuring every Blender artist's favorite digital monkey. Have fun exploring the other tutorial files. Don't worry if they seem over your head. After you have made your way through this book, you will have the background you need to dive in and pick them apart. Chapter 9 gives an overview of their contents, so you can go straight to the tutorial that has the advanced information you need.

Figure 1.6

Suzanne in your iPhone

Troubleshooting

If Xcode does not open when you double-click a file with the filename extension `.xcodeproj`, it means there is a problem with your Xcode installation. You will need to go back to the instructions at the Apple Developer Connection website and make sure you correctly downloaded and installed the iPhone SDK.

The first time you build an app, it is important to have the build destination and the SDK version set correctly. Make sure the drop-down menu in the upper-left corner of the Xcode window is set to the version of the SDK you are using. Furthermore, make sure the application itself is set to compile using the correct version of the SDK. You can check this in the project settings under Project → Edit Project Settings. If you have trouble, refer to the iPhone Reference Library at `http://developer.apple.com/iphone/library/navigation/index.html` and search for "running applications" for more details about how to set the Project Build settings correctly.

If you are enrolled in the iPhone Developer Program and are compiling to a device, be sure you have read all the relevant documentation on certifying and making your device available to Xcode. If you have done this and have trouble compiling some of the tutorials, it may be due to discrepancies in code signing. If the apps are code-signed to another developer, you will need to change the code-signing value to build them yourself. Code-signing information for a project is found in the Project Settings properties list, and code-signing information for the target application is found in the Active Target properties list, which can be accessed under Project → Edit Active Target `target_name` (where `target_name` is the name of your target). Code-signing information must be set correctly for both the project and the target. You can find more information about this on the same "Running Applications" iPhone Reference Library page mentioned previously.

You will get a lot of use out of the iPhone Reference Library if you continue with iPhone and iPod Touch programming, so it's a good idea to bookmark it. If you've read this chapter and the pertinent iPhone SDK documents and iPhone Reference Library resources and you're still having problems, go to the SIO2 forum at `http://forum.sio2interactive.com` and run a search on your problem.

In the next chapter, you'll learn more about the fundamentals of OpenGL ES graphics programming in the iPhone.

CHAPTER 2

Introducing Graphics Programming in SIO2

In this chapter, you'll get your first taste of programming graphical content for your iPhone or iPod Touch screen using SIO2. This chapter will also give you an introduction to some of the OpenGL ES graphics programming concepts that you will encounter throughout the book. OpenGL ES is the mobile specification of OpenGL and provides the foundational 3D programming functionality upon which SIO2 is built. SIO2 code works hand in hand with OpenGL ES code to create an exceptionally flexible game programming environment. In this chapter, you'll see how OpenGL ES calls integrate seamlessly with higher-level SIO2 functions. You'll also get a closer look at how easy it is to work with input from the iPhone's sophisticated hardware interface. You won't be working with 3D content quite yet. The fancy 3D stuff will come in the next chapter when you fire up Blender to create your first 3D scene.

- ■ **The SIO2 template**
- ■ **A simple OpenGL demo**
- ■ **Introduction to interactivity**
- ■ **The Complete Code**

The SIO2 Template

The SIO2 engine provides a powerful, high-level programming environment for interactive 3D development on the iPhone. A lot of that power comes from the fact that SIO2 brings together a variety of different libraries and technologies. One of the most important technologies you will be using is the OpenGL ES application programming interface (API) for graphics programming. OpenGL ES is a widely used variant of OpenGL specified for mobile embedded systems such as the iPhone and iPod Touch as well as numerous other mobile platforms. OpenGL ES plays a big role in this chapter and in all subsequent chapters. If you're already conversant with OpenGL, then you will mainly be interested in seeing how its functions are used in the context of the SIO2 environment. If you don't have any experience with OpenGL or graphics programming, then now would be a good time to read through Appendix B, which is an overview of some key concepts that will help you better understand what's going on in the code.

Setting up the SIO2 environment to work within the iPhone SDK framework and to make use of all the necessary tools is not trivial. Fortunately, you don't have to. As you saw in Chapter 1, in addition to a wide array of in-depth, heavily annotated example projects, the freely downloadable SIO2 package comes with a ready-made Xcode template project for you to begin work with right away. All of the SIO2 code in this book takes this template as its starting point.

In Chapter 1, you got an overview of the files in the Template project. Here, you'll take a closer look at the contents of the main files you'll be working with throughout this book. In this chapter, you will be making changes to the code to create some simple graphical content, so you should first make a copy of the entire template directory. Do this by right-clicking the directory in the Finder and selecting Duplicate. Rename the new directory project1. Don't move this directory anywhere though. It needs to stay in your SIO2_SDK directory so that the various libraries and resources it uses are accessible. Once you have created the new project directory, go into the directory and open the project in Xcode by double-clicking on the template.xcodeproj file.

Although there are several files in the template project, the one that you will spend the most time working with is template.mm. This can be found in the Other Sources directory in the Groups & Files area of the Xcode interface. Navigate to the file and click on it to bring it up in the Xcode text editor. The rest of this section is devoted to a line-by-line description of the template.mm file.

The first few lines contain boilerplate descriptive comments and copyright information:

```
1  /*
2   *  template.mm
3   *  template
4   *
```

```
5    *  Created by SIO2 Interactive on 8/22/08.
6    *  Copyright 2008 SIO2 Interactive. All rights reserved.
7    *
8    */
```

Objective-C enables comments to be written in the C style: Multiline comments are delineated by a preceding /* and a following */. Anything between these strings is a comment and is ignored by the compiler. Single-line comments can be written using // at the beginning of the line.

The next two lines of code ensure that the necessary header files are included:

```
10 #include "template.h"

12 #include "../src/sio2/sio2.h"
```

The convention for iPhone development is to have functions' prototypes placed in a header file and their definitions written in a source code file with the same name as the header.

> Prototypes tell the compiler about functions that will be defined elsewhere, making it possible to organize your code in a sensible way without causing trouble for the compiler. You don't need to worry too much about that for the purposes of this book as long as you know where things are located.

The template.h file contains the prototypes for all the functions defined in the template .mm file. You will need to edit that file only if you add new function definitions to template.mm. The ../src/sio2/sio2.h file is the initialization header for the entire SIO2 engine. This file contains include directives for all the other SIO2 header files and for those of other necessary directories. In addition to this, the sio2.h file defines several important constants, contains prototypes for functions, and defines the structure of the sio2 object that you will access often when you use the SIO2 engine. There is a single sio2 object created for an application, and this object acts as a container for all the data you will need to access while the application is running. You'll begin to see the sio2 object in action later in this chapter. In short, the sio2.h file contains the guts of the whole SIO2 engine.

The next chunk of code is where most of the action will occur in your programs. This is the templateRender function:

```
15 void templateRender( void )
```

This function loops as the game progresses, rendering the screen fresh for each frame. Because this function executes repeatedly in rapid succession, it is important to keep it as lean as possible. Be sure not to call initialization functions here, or anything else that can be done just once. This function is only for code that needs to be executed anew for each frame of the game.

The default contents of templateRender are minimal, just a few standard OpenGL calls. OpenGL functions can be called directly in the code. The first function called is glMatrixMode(GL_MODELVIEW), which sets the current matrix mode to GL_MODELVIEW (see Appendix B to find out what this means if you're not sure). The next function called is glLoadIdentity(), which sets the active transformation matrix to the identity transformation (also covered in Appendix B). Finally, the glClear(GL_DEPTH_BUFFER_BIT | GL_COLOR_BUFFER_BIT) function is called, which clears the depth buffer and the color buffer. It is usually necessary to clear the content of the previous frame before rendering the next frame so that the effect is animation rather than simply a stack of images rendered one on top of the next. This is not always necessary though. For example, when a background or sky box is used so that the screen is redrawn in its entirety each frame, you don't need to clear the color buffer. As with anything, if it's not necessary, you shouldn't do it because it requires time and resources.

The color buffer contains information about the color of each pixel and the depth buffer contains information that is used to calculate which elements should be rendered in front of or behind other elements. This information is used to determine which pixel-sized image fragments are ultimately rendered. As you can see from the comment on the next line, the rendering code specific to your app will generally follow these lines:

```
16 {
17      glMatrixMode( GL_MODELVIEW );
18      glLoadIdentity();
20      glClear( GL_DEPTH_BUFFER_BIT | GL_COLOR_BUFFER_BIT );
22      // Your rendering code here...
23 }
```

The next function is the templateShutdown function. This is an important function, but it's not something you will usually need to monkey with. This function frees the resources that SIO2 has been using and shuts down the engine:

```
26 void templateShutdown( void )
27 {
28      // Clean up
29      sio2ResourceUnloadAll( sio2->_SIO2resource );
31      sio2->_SIO2resource = sio2ResourceFree( sio2->_SIO2resource );
33      sio2->_SIO2window = sio2WindowFree( sio2->_SIO2window );
35      sio2 = sio2Shutdown();
37      printf( "\nSIO2: shutdown...\n" );
38 }
```

The last three functions deal with the interactive functionality of the iPhone/iPod Touch. They are templateScreenTap, templateScreenTouchMove, and templateScreenAccelerometer. Their names are indicative of what they handle, namely screen taps (the state argument distinguishes between the tap down event and the tap up event), moving touches on the screen, and tilting or shaking of the device itself, as sensed by the built-in accelerometer. No functionality is defined for any of these functions:

```
41 void templateScreenTap( void *_ptr, unsigned char _state )
42 {
44 }

47 void templateScreenTouchMove( void *_ptr )
48 {
51 }

54 void templateScreenAccelerometer( void *_ptr )
55 {
58 }
```

That's it. The template is a syntactically correct, complete app that does nothing at all. The necessary functions to render frames and to handle interaction are all defined. In the next sections you'll see how to make changes to this template to make something happen on the screen.

A Simple OpenGL Demo

In the following sections, you'll look more closely at how to run OpenGL code in SIO2. The code introduced here is based on the SIO2 Tutorial 1, which in turn is based upon the iPhone OpenGL ES demo provided by Apple. If you are knowledgeable in OpenGL, this will all be very straightforward. If not, pay close attention and don't be afraid to experiment with variations on the code to get a firsthand feel for how things work. The material in Appendix B is also pertinent here. If you're new to graphics programming, you should definitely read Appendix B. If you're inexperienced with C, you should be prepared to look up some terms online or in a C reference book. These sections and much that follows assume that you are familiar with some common basic concepts in programming, such as what data types are. If you aren't sure what things like floating-point numbers or unsigned chars are, be prepared to spend some time with Google.

Creating Graphical Content in OpenGL ES

The first thing to do is to create a graphical object. Ordinarily, SIO2 will do this automatically, by reading data exported from Blender, but in this example you will create an object by hand by defining a vertex array. The object you'll create is a simple square. The array that will represent its vertices is created like this:

```
const GLfloat squareVertices[] = {
    -100.0f, -100.0f,
     100.0f, -100.0f,
    -100.0f,  100.0f,
     100.0f,  100.0f,
};
```

This code should be the first few lines in the templateRender function, so insert it between lines 16 and 17 in the original template code. The elements of the array represent the *x* and *y* values for each vertex in the square, resulting in a 200×200-pixel square. The name of the array is squareVertices, and later you will be able to render the square by creating an OpenGL vertex array using this data. The elements are of type GLfloat, which is the OpenGL implementation of floating-point numbers.

You'll color the square vertex by vertex using a color array. In a color array, the first four elements represent the color values for the first vertex, the next four elements represent the color values for the second vertex, and so on, with four array elements for each vertex. Colors on the iPhone are always expressed with four values: R, G, B, and A. Some graphical programming environments also allow colors to be represented with three values, dropping the alpha value, but not the iPhone. The elements represent the red, green, blue, and alpha values. When using unsigned char data types, as in this example, the range of values for each color channel is from 0 to 255. The fourth value, alpha, is used to represent opacity when blending is enabled, but in this example the alpha value is not used. Take a look at the following code and see if you can predict what color each vertex of the square will be. Include this code right after the previous code with the vertex array:

```
const unsigned char squareColors[] = {
    255, 255,   0, 255,
    0,   255, 255, 255,
    0,     0,   0,   0,
    255,   0, 255, 255,
};
```

You've now defined the data for use in a color array and stored it in a variable called *squareColors*.

The next chunk of code is for rendering. It should follow the OpenGL lines in the original template, starting at the point where the your rendering code here comment is. It will extend to the end of the templateRender function. To keep it simple for now, this example is not in 3D, so you'll use SIO2's 2D rendering mode. You'll need to enter 2D mode first and then leave it later. Use the following functions to do that:

```
sio2WindowEnter2D( sio2->_SIO2window, 0.0f, 1.0f );
{
//insert the following code here
}
sio2WindowLeave2D();
```

The arguments to sio2WindowEnter2D represent the SIO2window object itself and the depth of the ortho projection in GL units.

Between the functions to enter and leave 2D mode, curly brackets delineate a block of code with the comment insert the following code here. That's what you'll do. The remaining code described in this section will be inserted between those curly brackets, and will specify how to render the square.

The first line creates the actual vertex array:

```
glVertexPointer( 2, GL_FLOAT, 0, squareVertices );
```

The first argument tells OpenGL how many coordinates are to be used for each vertex. The example is a 2D square with only x- and y-coordinates defined, so the value is 2 in this case. For 3D data, a value of 3 would be appropriate. A value of 4 is also possible, which enables access to the fourth coordinate in the homogeneous coordinate system (see Appendix B for more information on this). The next argument tells OpenGL what type to expect from elements of the array. The array was made up of floating-point numbers, so GL_FLOAT is the appropriate label. The next argument is the *stride* of the vertex array, which determines whether the vertex array's elements are densely packed or interleaved. In this example, the stride is 0, so there is no interleaving. Finally, the array of floating-point numbers previously defined is passed to the function to supply the actual data. The next line of code is required to tell OpenGL to use the vertex array when it comes time to render:

```
glEnableClientState( GL_VERTEX_ARRAY );
```

The next two lines set up and enable the color array:

```
glColorPointer( 4, GL_UNSIGNED_BYTE, 0, squareColors );
glEnableClientState( GL_COLOR_ARRAY );
```

The arguments for glColorPointer are analogous to those of glVertexPointer. Notice that the size value is 4 because the color values for each vertex are described using four values. You might wonder why four values are used in this example despite the fact that the alpha values are not being used. Indeed, this is an example of a place where your options are somewhat more limited in OpenGL ES than in standard OpenGL. Although you have some options in OpenGL, in OpenGL ES this value is required to be 4. Don't worry too much about these GL function calls though. When you get to using SIO2, you will generally not have a need to work with these functions directly because they will all be called behind the scenes by SIO2.

In the next few lines of code, the sio2 object finally makes its appearance!

```
glTranslatef( sio2->_SIO2window->scl->x * 0.5f,
              sio2->_SIO2window->scl->y * 0.5f, 0.0f );
```

In this example, it's being used to place the square at the center of the screen with the glTranslatef function. The glTranslatef function adds a translate transformation to the modelview matrix, determining where the center will be when the scene is drawn. You want this to be in the middle of the screen, so it is necessary to translate the center point half the screen width along the x-axis (from left to right) and half the screen height along the y-axis (from top to bottom). No translation is necessary along the z-axis because this is all taking place in 2D. The way these dimensions are accessed should give you a sense of some of the things that have been initialized automatically with the sio2 object. The sio2 object includes a _SIO2window object as one of its properties, which in turn has scl (scale) values for the x and y axes. The x scale is accessed with sio2->_SIO2window->scl->x and the y scale in a corresponding manner. To get half the distance across and down the screen, both values are multiplied by 0.5.

To get a sense of the looping nature of the templateRender function, you'll incorporate animation into this example also. A simple example of animation is to rotate the square by a small increment each frame. There are several ways to accomplish this effect, but in this example you will once again turn to the sio2 object and its _SIO2window, which has a property called d_time that returns the amount of time that has passed since the application began running, based on an internal chronometer. The next line declares the variable *rotz* and initializes it to 0.0:

```
static float rotz = 0.0f;
```

The next line of code rotates the transformation matrix:

```
glRotatef( rotz, 0.0f, 0.0f, 1.0f );
```

The glRotatef function's first argument is the rotation value, and the next three arguments represent how much influence the rotation value has on each of the three axes. In this case, x- and y-axes are unaffected while z is rotated the full amount of the rotation value. The next line sets the *rotz* value by multiplying the d_time value (the change in the chronometer value from the previous frame) by 90.0, so that the *rotz* value increases with each frame:

```
rotz += 90.0f * sio2->_SIO2window->d_time;
```

The static identifier before the declaration of *rotz* ensures that the initialization to 0.0 occurs only once and the value is retained over repeated calls of the function.

The last line renders the scene using the currently enabled arrays with the glDrawArrays function. The first argument, GL_TRIANGLE_STRIP, tells OpenGL which drawing mode to use:

```
glDrawArrays(GL_TRIANGLE_STRIP, 0, 4);
```

With OpenGL ES, the options are limited to drawing modes that work with points, lines, and triangles. Other polygons must be constructed out of triangles. The second argument tells OpenGL which index of the arrays to start with, and the third argument determines how many vertices will be drawn. Using triangle strips is a faster way to render triangles, but there are some cases in which they shouldn't be used. They don't work well when physics simulation is used on an object, which you'll read more about in Chapter 6.

You're ready to build and run your application now. Follow the same steps you followed in Chapter 1 to build and run the example in the section "Building the SIO2

Template in Xcode." You should see a multicolored square appear and rotate counterclockwise on your screen as shown in Figure 2.1.

Looking Closer at Transformations

In this section, you'll go through a few further examples that will help you form a fuller sense of how transformations work. If you are already fluent in OpenGL, you can skim this part. If you're just getting the hang of it though, you'll want to follow this section closely because OpenGL transformations play an important role in programming with SIO2.

To see some more transformations in action, you'll create another square. It's not necessary to use a different vertex array—the one you already created is fine. However, you'll use different colors for the second square. To do this, create another array called `primaryColors`. The 1st vertex will be red, the 2nd vertex blue, the 3rd green, and the 4th white. Remember, the 4th, 8th, 12th, and 16th elements here are basically going to be ignored because alpha blending is not used. Add the following code just after the place where the previous vertex and color data arrays were defined:

```
const unsigned char primaryColors[] = {
    255,   0,   0,   0,
      0, 255,   0,   0,
      0,   0, 255,   0,
    255, 255, 255,   0,
};
```

This square will be a small square that orbits the larger square in a clockwise direction. Because the direction of its rotation is opposite that of the first square, you need to rotate the matrix −2 times the value of *rotz* in order. The next line adds a translation along the x-axis, which will offset the square away from the center of the screen. The next line adds a scaling transformation to reduce the square's size. The last two lines render the square just as before, except using the new color data for the color array:

```
glRotatef(-2.0f*rotz, 0.0f, 0.0f, 1.0f);
glTranslatef(125.0f, 0.0f, 0.0f);
glScalef(0.2f, 0.2f, 0.2f);
glColorPointer(4, GL_UNSIGNED_BYTE, 0, primaryColors);
glDrawArrays(GL_TRIANGLE_STRIP, 0, 4);
```

If you build and run now you'll see what was just described: a large square with yellow, cyan, maroon, and black corners rotating counterclockwise and the primary-colored smaller square orbiting it clockwise, as shown in Figure 2.2.

Figure 2.1

A rotating square created in OpenGL

Figure 2.2

A small square orbiting the large square

Transformation Order

The order in which matrix transformations are performed makes a difference. This is due to the fact that matrix multiplication is not commutative (AB≠BA), as described in more detail in Appendix B. You can see that here by reversing the order of the translate and rotate operations. In the preceding code, reverse the order of these lines:

```
glRotatef(-2*rotz, 0.0f, 0.0f, 1.0f);
glTranslatef(125.0f, 0.0f, 0.0f);
```

They then appear like this:

```
glTranslatef(125.0f, 0.0f, 0.0f);
glRotatef(-2*rotz, 0.0f, 0.0f, 1.0f);
```

When you build and run the project, you'll see that the effect has changed. The small square now follows the large square, clinging to one side while rotating around its own center, as shown in Figure 2.3. It shouldn't be too hard to grasp why this is. In the first case, the rotation happens first, so the axis along which the translation happens has already changed direction. In the second case, the translation of the small square occurs before the clockwise rotation (but of course after the original counterclockwise rotation) so the translation is completed first, after which the rotation happens around the new center point.

Figure 2.3

The small square's location follows the large square's rotation.

Using the Matrix Stack

Now, what if you want to render both of those small squares simultaneously, one rotating counterclockwise with the large square and the other rotating clockwise in the opposite direction around the large square? You might be tempted to simply write the code for rendering both squares in order, like this:

```
glRotatef(-2*rotz, 0.0f, 0.0f, 1.0f);
glTranslatef(125.0f, 0.0f, 0.0f);
glScalef(0.2f, 0.2f, 0.2f);
glColorPointer(4, GL_UNSIGNED_BYTE, 0, primaryColors);
glDrawArrays(GL_TRIANGLE_STRIP, 0, 4);

glTranslatef(125.0f, 0.0f, 0.0f);
glRotatef(-2*rotz, 0.0f, 0.0f, 1.0f);
glScalef(0.2f, 0.2f, 0.2f);
glColorPointer(4, GL_UNSIGNED_BYTE, 0, primaryColors);
glDrawArrays(GL_TRIANGLE_STRIP, 0, 4);
```

But if you do this, you'll see that it does not yield the results you're looking for. If you use this code, you will find that the second small square is smaller still than the first one, tiny in fact, and it is riding piggyback on the first small square rather than rotating around the large square, as shown in Figure 2.4. The reason for this is clear enough when you recall that all of the transformation operations on the model/view matrix are cumulative (if you're not sure what the model/view matrix is, please refer to Appendix B). You've already scaled down once, so scaling again will make the next square even smaller. Likewise, the rotations and translations acting on the third square are all with respect to where the matrix was when the second square was rendered. Clearly something else is needed.

The solution to this is to use the *matrix stack*. The matrix stack enables you to set a point in the sequence of transformations, add new transformations, and then jump back to the previous point. This is done by *pushing* the matrix onto a stack, adding transformations, doing what you want to do with them, and then *popping* the matrix stack to return to the previous state of transformations. The data structure of a stack is something

Figure 2.4

A tiny square riding on the small square

like a PEZ candy dispenser if you were to load it piece by piece through the character's mouth—as you push more objects onto the stack, the first objects you pushed on are pushed further and further down the stack. To take objects from the stack, you pop them from the top of the stack (like a PEZ dispenser used in the ordinary way). Objects are popped from the stack in first-in/last-out order.

In this case, you will want to push the matrix onto the stack before transforming and drawing the first small square, then pop the matrix to return to the transformations of the larger square, and then do the same thing for the second small square, like this:

```
glPushMatrix();
    glRotatef(-2*rotz, 0.0f, 0.0f, 1.0f);
    glTranslatef(125.0f, 0.0f, 0.0f);
    glScalef(0.2f, 0.2f, 0.2f);
    glColorPointer(4, GL_UNSIGNED_BYTE, 0, primaryColors);
    glDrawArrays(GL_TRIANGLE_STRIP, 0, 4);
glPopMatrix();

glPushMatrix();
    glTranslatef(125.0f, 0.0f, 0.0f);
    glRotatef(-2*rotz, 0.0f, 0.0f, 1.0f);
    glScalef(0.2f, 0.2f, 0.2f);
    glColorPointer(4, GL_UNSIGNED_BYTE, 0, primaryColors);
    glDrawArrays(GL_TRIANGLE_STRIP, 0, 4);
glPopMatrix();
```

When you build and run the code now, it will behave as expected, with one small square rotating clockwise around the big square and the other following the counterclockwise rotation of the big square and rotating clockwise around its own center, as shown in Figure 2.5. Experiment with changing these transformations on your own. Can you set it up so that a tiny square orbits the small square? What happens if you call the glLoadIdentity function inside the stack?

Introduction to Interactivity

In the final part of this chapter, you'll see how simple it is to work with the iPhone's touch screen and accelerometer interfaces with the SIO2 engine. User interactivity with the iPhone and iPod Touch comes from touching the multi-touch screen with one or more fingers and by accessing the accelerator by moving or shaking the device. In this section, you'll look at callback functions for the whole screen, but SIO2 also enables you to have local callbacks on components or part of the screen, so it is not necessary to always put all your code in these functions. You'll read more about local callbacks in Chapter 9 during the discussion of widgets.

Figure 2.5

The three squares rotating as expected

There are two basic types of touch input: screen taps and screen touch moves. The first type, taps, can be in one of two states, tap down and tap up. The tap-down event is triggered when a finger initially makes contact with the screen. The tap-up event is triggered when a finger that is touching the screen separates from the surface. Therefore, quickly tapping the screen once will result in two tap events: a tap-down event followed by a tap-up event. Screen-touch move events occur when a finger touching the screen changes location without leaving the screen. All touch move events are preceded by a tap-down event and followed by a tap-up event.

You should recall from the first section of this chapter that there are already functions defined to handle these events. Here, you'll add some code to those functions to access and print out the information they return. First, write the templateScreenTap function as follows:

```
void templateScreenTap(void *_ptr, unsigned char _state)
{
    if( sio2->_SIO2window->n_touch )
    {
        printf("templateScreenTap >> state:%d tap:%d x:%f y:%f\n", _
state,
                sio2->_SIO2window->n_tap,
                sio2->_SIO2window->touch[0]->x,
                sio2->_SIO2window->touch[0]->y );
    }
}
```

The first line here is simply a conditional to ensure that the screen has been touched in at least one place for the print statement to be executed. Note that once again you are accessing data held by the sio2 object, and specifically its _SIO2window property. The value being accessed is n_touch, which holds the number of simultaneous touch points at any given time. There's no point trying to print out touch data if the screen hasn't been touched.

Inside the conditional block is the printf function, which is the C command for printing formatted data to the standard output. If what's between the quotes there looks cryptic to you, do a Google search for "printf" to find a primer on what the percent symbols mean. For the moment, suffice it to say that the quoted string in the first argument of printf will include the data from the second, third, fourth and fifth arguments, inserted into the appropriate points in the string. So what are the other arguments? The second argument is the _state value, which will be either 2 (tap down) or 1 (tap up). The third argument is the n_tap value, which tells how many times the screen has been tapped in rapid succession. This is often used to register simple double taps, but it can actually count an arbitrarily high number of quickly struck taps. A pause between taps will reset this value to 0. The fourth and fifth arguments of printf are the x and y values, respectively, of the first touch point. This simple code doesn't exploit the full multi-touch capacity of the iPhone. You access data from subsequent multi-touch points by the index on the touch array: 0 is the first finger to touch the screen, 1 is the second finger to touch the screen simultaneously, 2 is the third, and so on.

So this code will print this data to the standard output. But where is the standard output? That's an important thing to know about when developing anything, and in this case, the standard output is written to Xcode's console. To see the console, select Console from the Run menu. Build and run your project. If you are building on the simulator, you can test the function by clicking your mouse on the simulator's screen. The console should register the touches, as shown in Figure 2.6. If you're building to your device, then touching the screen will have the same effect. Experiment with touching different places on the screen and note what the corresponding x and y values are. Try tapping quickly and seeing how the tap count changes. Tap down and hold for a while before lifting your finger to see the difference between tap-down and tap-up events.

Figure 2.6

Monitoring touches in the console

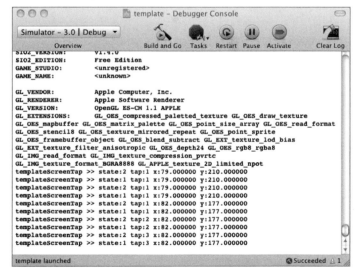

Implement the `templateScreenTouchMove` function as shown here:

```
void templateScreenTouchMove(void *_ptr)
{
    if( sio2->_SIO2window->n_touch )
        {
            printf("templateScreenTouchMove >> x:%f y:%f\n",
                    sio2->_SIO2window->touch[0]->x,
                    sio2->_SIO2window->touch[0]->y );
        }
}
```

This is simpler than the tap function because there's less data to retrieve. There are no states and nothing is counted. The function simply prints the changing x and y values. You can build and run again to see how this works when you drag your finger around the screen.

The last function can be used only if you have a provisioned device and are a registered member of the iPhone Developer Program because the simulator is not able to work with accelerometer data. The accelerometer senses the position in space of the device, and the 2D interface of the desktop iPhone simulator isn't well suited to mimicking it.

The code here won't cause any problems if you run it on the simulator—it just won't do anything. If you do have a registered device to use as a build destination, then you can access accelerometer data by implementing the `templateScreenAccelerometer` function as shown here:

```
void templateScreenAccelerometer(void *_ptr)
{
    printf("templateScreenAccelerometer >> x:%f y:%f z:%f\n",
            sio2->_SIO2window->touch[0]->x,
            sio2->_SIO2window->touch[0]->y,
            sio2->_SIO2window->touch[0]->z);
}
```

Build and run, and move your device around in the air to see the values printed to the screen. The x, y, and z values here define a 3D vector that represents the direction that the iPhone is pointing in space.

The Complete Code

In case you've run into any snags and need to double-check your work, here is the complete code for the `template.mm` file of this project:

```
/*
 *   template.mm
 *   template
 *
 *   Created by SIO2 Interactive on 8/22/08.
```

```
 *   Copyright 2008 SIO2 Interactive. All rights reserved.
 *
 */


#include "template.h"
#include "../src/sio2/sio2.h"


void templateRender( void )
{
    const GLfloat squareVertices[] = {
                    -100.0f, -100.0f,
                     100.0f,  -100.0f,
                    -100.0f,  100.0f,
                     100.0f,   100.0f,
                     };

    const GLubyte squareColors[] = {
                    0,   255,  255,  255,
                    255,  0,   255,  255,
                    255, 255,   0,   255,
                    0,   0,    0,    0,
                    };

    const GLubyte primaryColors[] = {
                    255,  0,    0,    0,
                    0,   255,   0,    0,
                    0,    0,  255,    0,
                    255, 255, 255,  255,
                    };

    glMatrixMode( GL_MODELVIEW );
    glLoadIdentity();

    glClear( GL_DEPTH_BUFFER_BIT | GL_COLOR_BUFFER_BIT );

    sio2WindowEnter2D( sio2->_SIO2window, 0.0f, 1.0f );
    {
        glVertexPointer( 2, GL_FLOAT, 0, squareVertices );
        glEnableClientState( GL_VERTEX_ARRAY );
        glColorPointer( 4, GL_UNSIGNED_BYTE, 0, squareColors );
        glEnableClientState( GL_COLOR_ARRAY );

        glTranslatef( sio2->_SIO2window->scl->x * 0.5f,
                      sio2->_SIO2window->scl->y * 0.5f, -0.0f );

        static float rotz = 0.0f;
```

```
            glRotatef( rotz, 0.0f, 0.0f, 1.0f );
            rotz += 90.0f * sio2->_SIO2window->d_time;

            glDrawArrays(GL_TRIANGLE_STRIP, 0, 4);

            glPushMatrix();
                glRotatef(-2*rotz, 0.0f, 0.0f, 1.0f );
                glTranslatef(125.0f, 0.0f, 0.0f);
                glScalef(0.2f, 0.2f, 0.2f);
                glColorPointer( 4, GL_UNSIGNED_BYTE, 0, primaryColors );
                glDrawArrays(GL_TRIANGLE_STRIP, 0, 4);
            glPopMatrix();

            glPushMatrix();
                glTranslatef(125.0f, 0.0f, 0.0f);
                glRotatef(-2*rotz, 0.0f, 0.0f, 1.0f );
                glScalef(0.2f, 0.2f, 0.2f);
                glColorPointer( 4, GL_UNSIGNED_BYTE, 0, primaryColors );
                glDrawArrays(GL_TRIANGLE_STRIP, 0, 4);
            glPopMatrix();
        }
    sio2WindowLeave2D();
}


void templateShutdown( void )
{
        // Clean up
        sio2ResourceUnloadAll( sio2->_SIO2resource );
        sio2->_SIO2resource = sio2ResourceFree( sio2->_SIO2resource );
        sio2->_SIO2window = sio2WindowFree( sio2->_SIO2window );
        sio2 = sio2Shutdown();
        printf("\nSIO2: shutdown...\n" );
}


void templateScreenTap( void *_ptr, unsigned char _state )
{
    if( sio2->_SIO2window->n_touch )
    {
        printf("templateScreenTap >> state:%d tap:%d x:%f y:%f\n",
                _state,
                sio2->_SIO2window->n_tap,
                sio2->_SIO2window->touch[ 0 ]->x,
                sio2->_SIO2window->touch[ 0 ]->y );
    }
}
```

```
void templateScreenTouchMove( void *_ptr )
{
      if( sio2->_SIO2window->n_touch )
      {
            printf("templateScreenTouchMove >> x:%f y:%f\n",
                    sio2->_SIO2window->touch[ 0 ]->x,
                    sio2->_SIO2window->touch[ 0 ]->y );
      }
}


void templateScreenAccelerometer( void *_ptr )
{
      printf("templateScreenAccelerometer >> x:%f y:%f z:%f\n",
              sio2->_SIO2window->accel->x,
              sio2->_SIO2window->accel->y,
              sio2->_SIO2window->accel->z );
}
```

You now have a pretty good idea of how the SIO2 template works to quickly get you started creating interactive graphical content on the iPhone and iPod Touch. You've also learned something about how OpenGL code is integrated into the SIO2 programming environment. But you haven't yet seen anything happening in 3D. You can probably tell already, though, that entering floating-point numbers into vertex arrays by hand is not how you want to be creating sophisticated 3D models for your virtual worlds. In the next chapter, you'll put Xcode aside and take a brief detour through the world of creating 3D content the way it ought to be created—with Blender! The chapter after that will bring the threads together and show you how to work with 3D content from Blender directly in SIO2.

CHAPTER 3

Saying Hello to the Blender/ SIO2/iPhone World

In this chapter, you'll get down to the business of creating 3D content for the iPhone using Blender. First, you'll take a quick look at where Blender fits into the Blender/SIO2/Xcode game development pipeline. Then you'll get straight to the first part of a relatively simple hands-on example, putting a new 3D spin on the classic Hello World program.

- The Blender/SIO2/Xcode workflow

- An overview of SIO2

- Hello 3D World! Creating your world in Blender

- Exporting to the SIO2 format

The Blender/SIO2/Xcode Workflow

Programming games for a specific platform such as the iPhone can be relatively easy or relatively difficult, depending very much on the tools you have at your disposal for game creation and their ability to compile the game to the appropriate platform. On the easy end of the spectrum for game creation, you have graphical game logic editing tools such as those in the Blender Game Engine (BGE), which can be used to create sophisticated interactive environments with minimal programming knowledge. However, if you take this route to create your game, you will be very restricted in terms of how and where you deploy your game. There's currently no way to compile a BGE game directly to the iPhone, or any other mobile platform for that matter. On the other end of the spectrum lies low-level game programming in a language like C using a graphical library like OpenGL ES. If you can do this, you'll have a great deal of flexibility in terms of the platforms you can develop for. However, even for people who know these technologies well, modeling, texturing, animation, and other aspects of content creation are not best approached from a programming standpoint. These are things that should be done with the appropriate content creation program. Furthermore, the logic that underlies graphics libraries like OpenGL ES is quite different from the way high-level game designers tend to think about things. Bridging this conceptual gap can be challenging, and tools that help to make the relationship between game design and game programming more transparent are always welcome. That is exactly what SIO2 is.

An Overview of SIO2

The SIO2 engine comprises several components. There is the .sio2 file format specification, an exporter written in Python to export 3D data from Blender to the .sio2 format, and a library of classes and functions written in C and C++ to enable you to access and work with data from the .sio2 file format in the iPhone SDK environment.

The way these tools work together with Blender and Xcode is illustrated in Figure 3.1. The first step in the process is to create your scene in Blender. In general, a scene created for use with SIO2 is created in the same way as any other Blender scene, but there are a number of crucial differences that will be discussed when they arise throughout this book. Some Blender settings have a specific meaning when exported to the .sio2 file format, which is not the same as their meaning within Blender. One obvious and drastic example of this is that sound files are exported as texture channels. Notwithstanding a few such quirks, though, the scene you create in Blender is very much like the scene you will eventually be working with in the iPhone development environment.

Once the scene is ready to be exported, the SIO2 exporter script is run from within Blender. You'll see how to do this later in the chapter, but if you've used scripts in Blender before, it will be straightforward. The output of running this script is an .sio2 file. This file contains all the 3D data that will be accessible to the iPhone app.

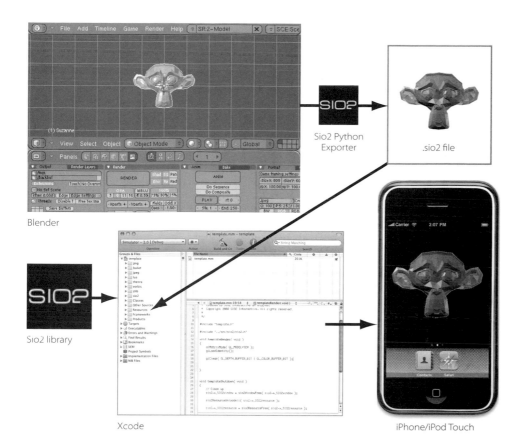

Figure 3.1
An overview of the Blender/SIO2/Xcode workflow

Sio2 Python Exporter

.sio2 file

Blender

SIO2 library

Xcode

iPhone/iPod Touch

After the .sio2 file is created, it is placed in the Resources directory of your Xcode project so that its data can be available to the app. You'll recall from Chapter 1 that the Resources directory is where data other than code is placed so that it can be accessed by the app. Once the .sio2 file is in the Resources directory, you will be able to access the 3D assets within Xcode using the tools provided by the SIO2 library.

As you can see from the diagram of the workflow, the first step toward implementing your 3D application is to create the 3D assets you will need in Blender and export them. The rest of the chapter will be devoted to showing you how to do that. In the next chapter, you'll begin with the 3D content you created here and see how to work with it using SIO2 in Xcode.

Hello 3D World! Creating Your World in Blender

In the following sections, you'll model the planet Earth and a simple background. You'll place the camera and some lights, and export the whole scene for use in your iPhone app later. Although all the steps are described, it's assumed you know the basics of Blender. If you don't feel confident that you do, this would be a good time to take a detour and read through Appendix A. The material in that appendix is the bare minimum you should know in order to make the most of the Blender tutorials in this book.

If you *do* know the basics of Blender, please pay close attention anyway. Creating content for SIO2 in Blender is not identical to other things you might do in Blender. As you'll see in detail in the following sections, there are subtle things you must keep in mind, such as quirks about naming objects and restrictions on texture image size. There are also a number of attributes and settings that have a different meaning to SIO2 than they are taken to mean either in Blender or in the BGE.

Modeling and Texturing the World and Background

Modeling the planet Earth for this exercise will be pretty simple. An unmodified textured sphere will do fine. The texturing will be done simply as well: no bump mapping or normal mapping, no cloud cover or specularity adjustment—just a simple planet Earth color map like the one from NASA's Visible Earth project (`http://visibleearth.nasa.gov`) illustrated in Figure 3.2, which you will find in the downloadable archive that accompanies this book.

Figure 3.2

A color texture for planet Earth

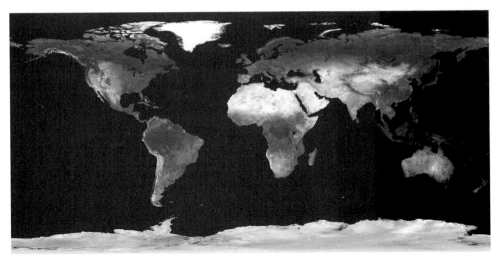

NASA GODDARD SPACE FLIGHT CENTER IMAGE BY RETO STÖCKLI (LAND SURFACE, SHALLOW WATER, CLOUDS). ENHANCEMENTS BY ROBERT SIMMON (OCEAN COLOR, COMPOSITING, 3D GLOBES, ANIMATION). DATA AND TECHNICAL SUPPORT: MODIS LAND GROUP; MODIS SCIENCE DATA SUPPORT TEAM; MODIS ATMOSPHERE GROUP; MODIS OCEAN GROUP. ADDITIONAL DATA: USGS EROS DATA CENTER (TOPOGRAPHY); USGS TERRESTRIAL REMOTE SENSING FLAGSTAFF FIELD CENTER (ANTARCTICA); DEFENSE METEOROLOGICAL SATELLITE PROGRAM (CITY LIGHTS).

There are a few things you'll have to do before the scene is ready for export to SIO2. First, follow these steps to create your planet:

1. Fire up Blender and delete the default cube. Do this by right-clicking the object to select it and then clicking the X key to delete it. Press Enter or left-click on the dialog box shown in Figure 3.3.

2. Add a UV sphere by pressing the spacebar to bring up the floating menu and selecting Add → Mesh → UVsphere, as shown in Figure 3.4.

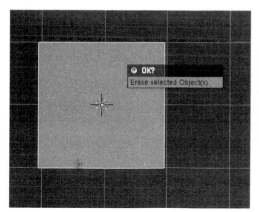

Figure 3.3
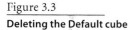
Deleting the Default cube

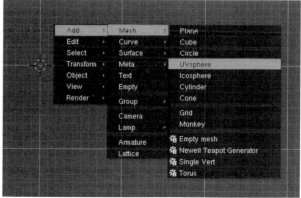

Figure 3.4
Adding the UV sphere

3. Leave the default values at 32 rings and 32 segments, as shown in Figure 3.5, and click OK.

4. The resulting sphere is shown in Figure 3.6. The object's location will be wherever the 3D cursor was when you added the object. In case you added the object some-where other than the center of the space, press Alt+G to move it to the center of the space. Depending on your user preferences, the object may also be rotated. Press Alt+R to remove any rotations.

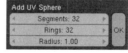

Figure 3.5
Default values for the UV sphere

Note that the default values of 32 rings and 32 segments result in a fairly dense mesh. In a lot of cases, particularly for use in mobile graphics, you will not need such a dense sphere and should use lower values for rings and sections. In this case, however, this denser mesh is appropriate for two reasons. The first is that there will be almost no more vertices in the scene (aside from four more in the background). So a some-what detailed object isn't going to slow anything down too much. The second reason is that this example will eventually make use of dynamic lighting. Lamps in the scene act on vertices, and the effect is much bet-ter on denser meshes. If dynamic lighting is not needed, it's better to use lower poly meshes and get your

Figure 3.6
A UV sphere

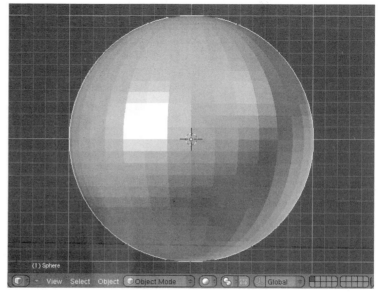

lighting effects by using static textures, as you will do in other tutorials later in this book.

5. With the sphere selected, go to the Link And Materials tab, shown in Figure 3.7, select Set Smooth, and then add a material by clicking New in the Material button panel. This material will hold the image texture for the object.

6. Add a texture in the Texture tab of the Material buttons (F5), shown in Figure 3.8, by clicking Add New.

Figure 3.7

Adding a material in the Link And Materials panel

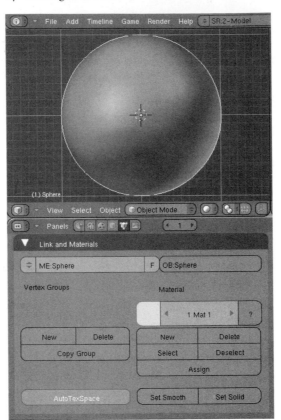

Figure 3.8

Adding a texture to the material

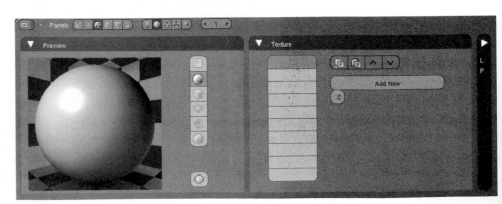

7. In the MA field in the Links And Pipeline panel of the Material buttons area, rename the material **MatEarth**.

Blender has two distinct ways to apply textures to objects. For ordinary animation and rendering, textures are associated with materials on objects. Alternately, you can use only *texture faces* without a material, which can be viewed in the BGE. Texture faces are automatically created whenever an object is UV mapped with a texture, whether a material is present or not. UV textures are present on materials only if they have been explicitly added to a material and set to UV mapping. This can be a confusing distinction, but it is important to understand. When you work with SIO2, the relationship becomes even muddier. SIO2 uses material textures (the first two texture channels of a material, to be specific) but is restricted to using only UV mapped image textures. Furthermore, SIO2 also takes several important settings from the Texture Face panel values. You'll learn more about this in Chapter 6, when you read about using billboard textures.

8. Enter the Texture buttons area (F6) and select Image for the texture type, as shown in Figure 3.9.

Figure 3.9

Setting an image texture

9. Click the Load button on the Image panel to open a file browser and find the planet Earth texture you downloaded previously. Load it so that it appears as shown in Figure 3.10. This kind of rectangular texture can be mapped onto a sphere shape using the Orco mapping coordinates and Sphere mapping.

10. Set those values on the Map Input tab, as shown in Figure 3.11.

Figure 3.10

Loading the Earth surface texture

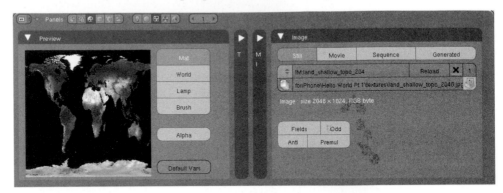

Figure 3.11

Sphere mapping the texture

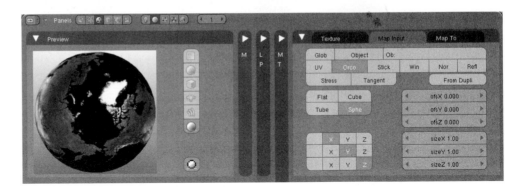

11. If you render the image now or preview it in the 3D viewport using Shift+P, you will see that the texture is correctly applied, as shown in Figure 3.12. Note that Shift+P must be pressed in Object mode; after that you can switch to Edit mode to see the mesh structure, as shown in the figure.

12. If you were only interested in rendering the planet Earth with a color texture, this would be sufficient. However, SIO2 requires UV textures, and the mapping for this texture is a spherical texture mapping, not a UV mapping. To get SIO2 to recognize the texture, it is necessary to bake the current texture to a UV map. To do this, you need to unwrap the sphere and create a UV texture on it. Select the edge loop around the equator of the sphere by pressing Shift+Alt and right-clicking on one of the edges in that edge loop (see Figure 3.13).

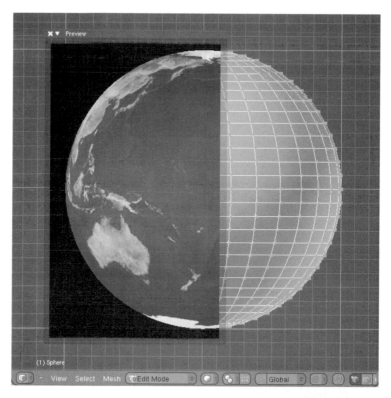

Figure 3.12

The sphere-mapped texture

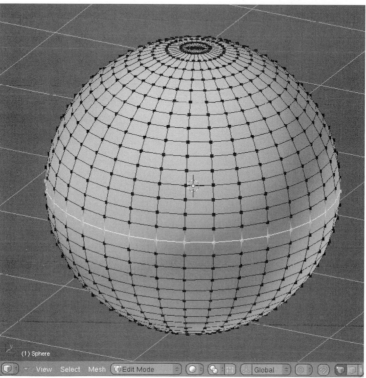

Figure 3.13

The equator edge-loop selected

13. Press Ctrl+E to bring up the Edge Specials menu, and from there choose Mark Seam, as shown in Figure 3.14.

14. Add a UV texture to the mesh by clicking the New button next to the UV Texture label on the Mesh panel in the Editing button area (F9) (Figure 3.15).

15. Select all faces of the object using the A key, and then open up a UV/Image Editor window and press the E key over the mapping area to unwrap the sphere (Figure 3.16). The resulting unwrapped mesh should appear in the UV/Image Editor window as two spiderweb-patterned circles, as shown in Figure 3.17.

Figure 3.15

Adding a UV texture

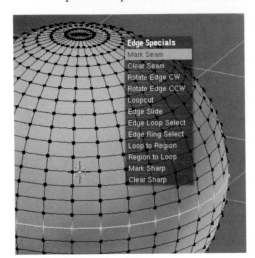

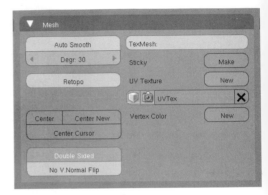

Figure 3.14

Marking the seam

Figure 3.16

Unwrapping the sphere in the UV/ Image Editor

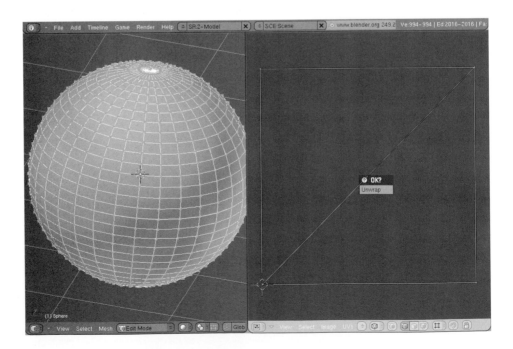

Figure 3.17

The unwrapped mesh pattern

16. Create a new UV texture image by choosing New from under the Image menu in the header of the UV/Image Editor window as shown in Figure 3.18. Leave the Width and Height values at 1024, and select UV Test Grid as shown in Figure 3.19. When you've done this, you can see the texture on the object, as shown in Figure 3.20, by viewing the object using the Textured Draw Type option from the 3D Viewport header.

Figure 3.18

Creating a new UV texture image

All graphics that you plan to use in SIO2 need to be sized according to powers of two. Images can have 64, 128, 256, 512, or 1,024 pixels per side, but images with dimensions that are not powers of two will not be rendered by OpenGL ES in the iPhone. This is an easy mistake to make, and no error will be raised at any point; your objects will simply fail to appear. For this reason, it's a good thing to bear in mind and to double-check if you have a problem viewing your objects in the iPhone. You should always use the smallest image size that you can without sacrificing the quality of the final image.

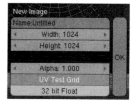

Figure 3.19

Values for the UV texture image

17. You are now working with two textures. One of them is the sphere mapped texture
on the material you created previously; this is the texture that will render if you
render the scene. The other is the UV map on the texture face, which is visible in
Textured Draw Type view mode. This is the texture that can *receive* rendered information in the form of texture baking. To see texture baking in action, go to the Bake
tab in the Scene buttons area (F10) and set the bake value to Textures, as shown in
Figure 3.21. Then go ahead and click the BAKE button. When you do this, you will
see the UV test grid image transform before your eyes into the UV-mapped Earth
surface texture shown in Figure 3.22. Be sure to *save the image* by selecting the Save
As option from the Image menu in the UV/Image Editor header. Baked images are
not automatically saved to distinct image files, and if you close Blender without saving the baked image, it will be discarded when you reopen Blender. Save the file as
earthUV.jpg. Select Jpeg from the drop-down menu on the File Browser header when
you save. JPEG files do not have an alpha channel, so it is not possible for them to
carry transparency information. In this example, you won't be using transparency,
so the smaller size of a JPEG is a good option. Saving video memory is critical when
programming for mobile devices, so any way you can conserve is worthwhile.

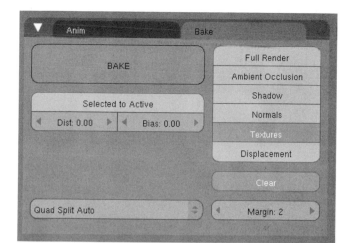

Figure 3.21

The Bake tab

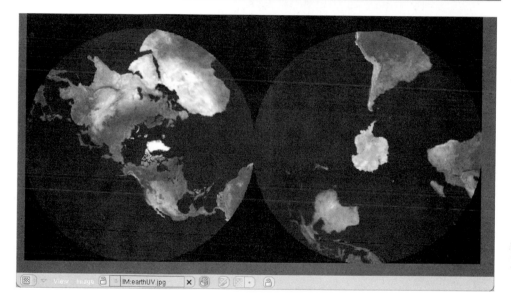

Figure 3.22

The baked UV-mapped Earth surface texture

18. Now you have a properly UV-mapped Earth texture. You must now replace the sphere-mapped texture on the material with the UV-mapped texture you just created. First, you need to replace the image associated with the image texture by selecting the new image from the drop-down menu in the Image tab in the Texture buttons area, as shown in Figure 3.23. Then you need to change the Map Input values in the Material buttons area from Orco and Sphere to UV and Flat, as shown in Figure 3.24. If you pre-view the render now, using Shift+P, you will see that the UV-mapped image is now set as the image to render, as shown in Figure 3.25.

Figure 3.23

Selecting earthUV .jpg as the texture image

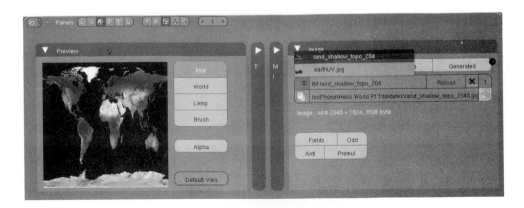

Figure 3.24

Changing the Map Input values to UV mapping

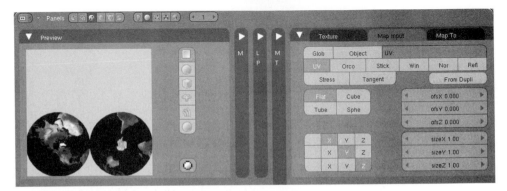

Figure 3.25

Previewing the UV mapped model

19. Aside from UV textures, the settings on the Blender materials themselves have minimal effect on how the object will look in SIO2. There are a few places where they do. Changing the specular and diffuse reflection colors will change them in the SIO2 file also. The Hard value on the Shaders tab of the Material buttons will affect the shininess value of the SIO2 file output. For this example, the results look better with a low shininess value, so set the value of Hard to 5.

You're now finished with modeling and texturing the planet Earth for this example, but the scene is not quite finished. You still need to set up the camera, and adding some lights and background will make the scene look nicer.

Lights, Camera, and Background

As in the BGE, using lights and real-time shading is optional. You can create a scene that uses no lights at all and have all of your shadows and lighting effects represented by textures. In many cases, this is the best way to go for static objects because real-time lighting requires processor resources to calculate and because meshes lit with real-time lights require a higher vertex density to look good. In this example, however, you'll use real-time lights. For one thing, the scene complexity is limited, and a reasonable mesh density can be used on the sphere. For another thing, you will later make the sphere spin, and dynamic objects cannot be lit convincingly using static textures only.

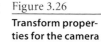

Figure 3.26

Transform properties for the camera

Placing the camera is simple. Select the camera in Object mode and press the N key over the 3D viewport to bring up the Transform Properties window. Set the values as shown in Figure 3.26. The location along the x- and z-axes is **0**, and the location along the y-axis is **−3.5**. Rotation around Y and Z is **0**, and rotation around X is **90**. There's nothing special about these values—they simply place the camera in a position to get a nice straight shot of the planet Earth model you created. You don't need to make any other changes to the camera for this exercise. The camera won't be moving in this example, so you don't need to worry about gimbal lock, which can arise when an animated camera points straight down with 0 rotation on all axes.

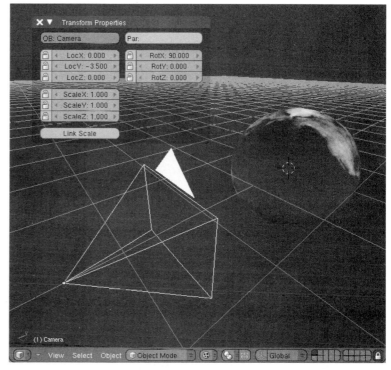

For this example there will be two lights: one for key lighting and one for a slight backlight from the opposite direction. By default there is a single light of the omnidirectional Lamp type. Select this lamp and change it to a Hemi light in the Lamp buttons area, as shown in Figure 3.27. Give it an Energy value of **1.24**. Finally, change its Object name to **Hemi**.

Once again, in the 3D viewport press the N button to bring up the Transform Properties window, if it isn't already up. Enter the rotation and location values shown in Figure 3.28 (LocX: **5.052**, LocY: **−4.15**, LocZ: **1.17**, RotX: **81**, RotY: **−17.5**, RotZ: **55.5**).

Figure 3.27

Lamp values for the Hemi lamp

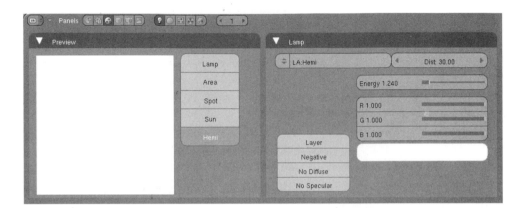

Figure 3.28

Transform values for the Hemi lamp

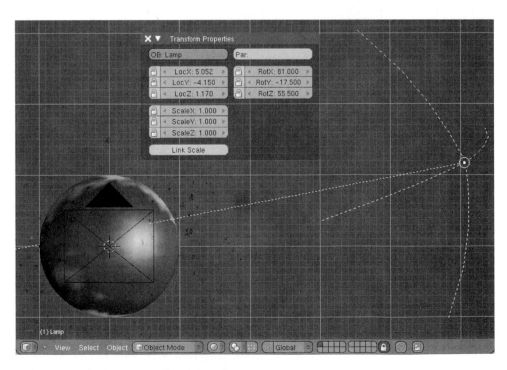

Create the second lamp by copying the Hemi lamp with Shift+D. Switch the lamp type to Spot and rename the object **Spot**. Renaming objects when you copy them is important because the .001 object suffix format has a specific meaning in SIO2. It indicates pseudo-instancing, which you'll learn about later. This is a convenient feature when you want it, but it means that you must be careful not to accidentally have object names with that suffix. Set the Spot light's values as shown in Figure 3.29. Specifically, set the Energy at around 1.12 and push the blue value up to 1 while leaving red and green at 0.8. Set the Transform values for the Spot light in the same way you did for the camera and the Hemi light, with values as shown in Figure 3.30 (LocX: **–2.55**, LocY: **4**, LocZ: **–0.005**, RotX: **90**, RotY: **–12**, RotZ: **–147**).

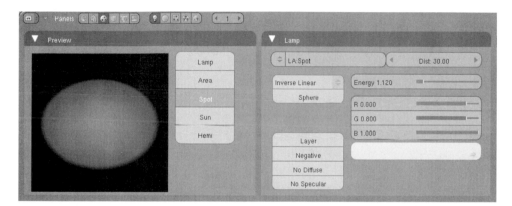

Figure 3.29

Lamp values for the spot light

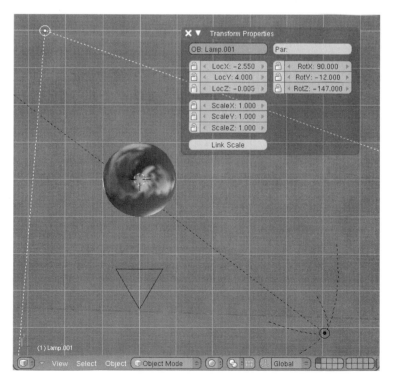

Figure 3.30

Transform values for the spot light

Now that you've got the lights and camera set up as they should be, follow these steps to create a simple, glowing background that will appear as a kind of halo or aura around the planet:.

1. In Object mode, press the spacebar and select Add → Mesh → Plane to create a new plane, as shown in Figure 3.31. Depending on how you have your defaults set, you may automatically enter Edit mode. If you are in Edit mode, reenter Object mode. In case you added the plane somewhere other than the center (origin) of the 3D space, press Alt+G to clear the location of the object, and then press Alt+R to clear the object's rotation. The result should look like Figure 3.32.

Figure 3.31

Adding a plane

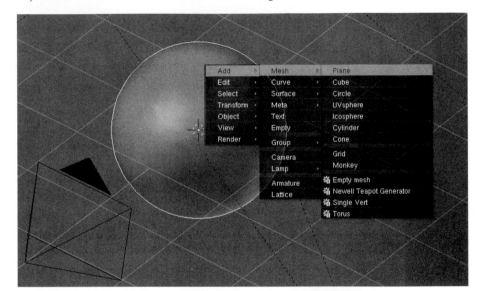

Figure 3.32

The plane at the origin

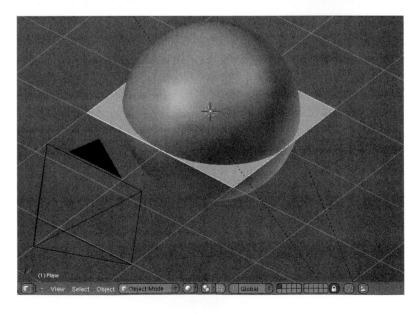

2. Set the location, rotation, and scale as shown in Figure 3.33. All the axes are scaled up by a factor of 3.35. The object is moved 5.9 units along the y-axis and rotated 90 degrees around the x-axis. Later, once you've seen the results, you can adjust these values to see how the background effect changes. The important thing is that the face normal must be pointing toward the camera; otherwise the face will not be visible by default.

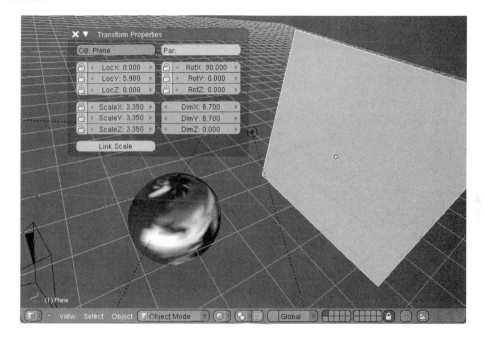

Figure 3.33

Positioning the plane

3. Add a new material to the plane and add a texture to the material. Make the texture a blend type texture with values as shown in Figure 3.34. Set the type to Halo and use the Colorband on the Colors tab to create a gradation from black (R: **0**, G: **0**, B: **0**) to white (R: **1**, G: **1**, B: **1**) with both colors having an Alpha (A) value of **1**. Set the Map Input values as shown in Figure 3.35. The mapping type should be set to Orco and the XYZ texture mapping matrix at the lower-left corner of the Map Input tab should be set as shown.

4. Just as you did for the sphere mapping of the planet Earth model, you will bake this blend texture to a UV mapped image texture. Follow the same steps to add a UV texture to the plane, and then create a new image with the UV Test Grid pattern, except that this time you should create the new image to be 512×512 pixels. Unwrapping isn't necessary this time because the object is just a single face. In Texture Draw Type view, the plane will look like it does in Figure 3.36.

Figure 3.34

A blend texture
for the plane

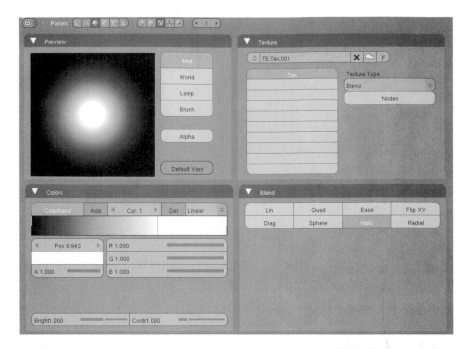

Figure 3.35

Mapping the
blend texture

Figure 3.36

The new UV image
texture on the plane

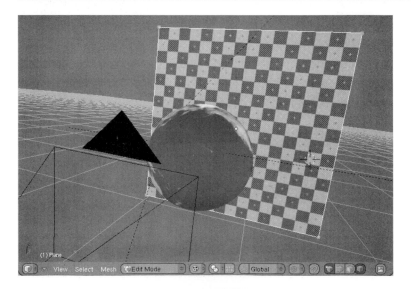

5. With the plane selected, go to the Bake panel in the Scene buttons area (F10) and once again select the Textures option and click the BAKE button. The halo blend texture will be baked onto an image, as shown in Figure 3.37. As you did with the planet Earth model in step 9 of the previous procedure, go back and replace the current material texture (in this case the Blend texture) with an Image texture using this newly baked image. Just as you did with the planet Earth model, select UV in the Map Input tab. Don't forget to save the image as a JPEG file!

6. This background isn't intended to reflect light, so turn the specularity and hardness values way down on the material. When you look at the result in the preview, the textured plane should provide a glow around the edge of the Earth model as shown in Figure 3.38.

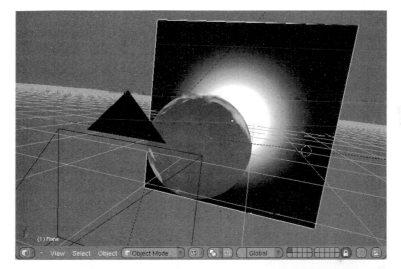

Figure 3.37

The baked UV texture on the plane

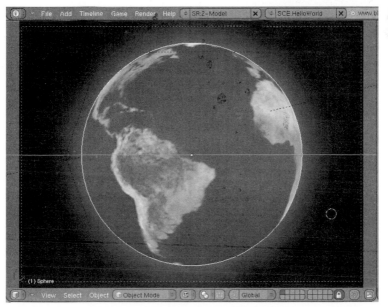

Figure 3.38

The final scene in preview

You're finished with the main modeling and texturing of the scene. It is now necessary to export the scene to the SIO2 file format using the Python export script bundled with SIO2. Before you do that, there's one more thing you should do with both of the mesh objects you've created. You should convert them both from quads to triangles. This step is optional because the SIO2 export script also has an option to convert from quads to triangles, but it is a good idea so that you don't forget or get confused about the state of your meshes. To convert a mesh from quads to triangles, select the mesh, enter Edit mode by pressing Tab, and select the entire mesh by pressing the A key. Finally, press Ctrl+T to convert the entire mesh to triangles. Your UV mapping values will be preserved. If you don't convert your quads to triangles, and forget to choose that option in the exporter, your quads will all show up with one blacked-out triangular half when you run your application on the iPhone.

Exporting to the SIO2 File Format

To make your 3D objects accessible to the SIO2 library in the Xcode environment, you must export them to the SIO2 file format. This is simple to do, but there are a few important points to keep in mind and some subtle details to be aware of that will help things go more smoothly.

The Exporter Script

For exporting Blender assets, a Python exporter is included with the standard SIO2 distribution. You can find this in the `SIO2_SDK/exporter` subdirectory. The script itself is called, intuitively enough, `sio2_exporter.py`. You run `sio2_exporter.py` in Blender just as you would any other standard Python script. You can either run it directly from the Blender Text Editor or install it in the `.blender/scripts` directory. If you install it, you will be able to access it from the main File → Export menu. Installing scripts in the `.blender/scripts` directory is not as straightforward on Mac OS X as it is on other platforms due to OS X's tendency to conceal important files from the user in the GUI. If you want to install scripts for Blender in OS X, you will need to copy them into the appropriate directory via the terminal command line. If you have installed Blender in the ordinary way in your applications directory, the location to copy the script to is `/Applications/Blender 2.49/blender.app/Contents/MacOS/.blender/scripts`. It's beyond the scope of this book (and unnecessary for the book's purposes) to get into the details of how to navigate the file system and move files around via the command line. However, bear in mind that the contents of `blender.app` can be accessed only by the command line and that the `.blender` directory is a hidden "." directory, as distinct from the `blender` executable found in the same subdirectory. You can find basic Unix command-line documentation on the Web. For the time being, it is fine to simply run the exporter directly from the Text Editor.

To do this, you need to open up a new Text Editor window area as shown in Figure 3.39. From the Text menu, select Open and navigate to the location of the sio2_ exporter.py file on your hard drive, as shown in Figure 3.40. Select the file and click Open Text File.

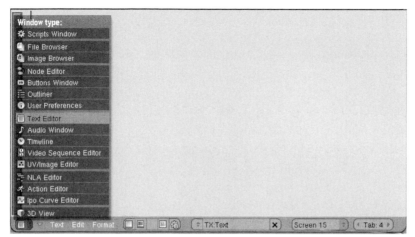

Figure 3.39

A Text Editor window area

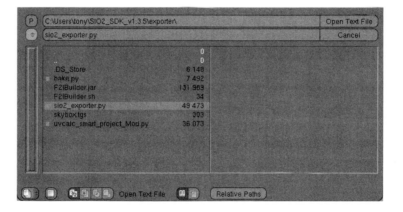

Figure 3.40

Opening the exporter script

The script will appear in the Text Editor window as text. To run the script, you can select Text → Run Python Script from the header menu, or simply press Alt+P with the mouse over the Text Editor area. When you run the script, the Text Editor area will be replaced by the Scripts Window area and the script's interface will appear in that area, as shown in Figure 3.41.

Figure 3.41

The interface of the exporter script

The Exit button halts the script, and the Export button executes the export. Before exporting, you must select the destination for your .sio2 file in the Output Directory field. The ellipses (…) button to the right of the field will enable you to browse the file system to select the directory you want. Keep in mind that this field is for the directory *into which* the .sio2 file should be placed. In general, you will probably want to choose your project directory so that you can keep all the necessary files for your project in one place. Because you haven't yet created a project directory for this project, you can export to whatever directory you choose—just be sure it's someplace you'll remember. Another important thing to keep in mind is that the exporter will also create a new directory with the same name as the .sio2 file (you'll read more about this in the next section). When you have to export multiple times, be sure you don't accidentally start exporting into this subdirectory. A few confusing things can happen when you export repeatedly (as you will no doubt do, because you will want to continue to work with the Blender content as you develop your application). Normally, when you export multiple times, the same output directory will appear by default, so you won't have to set this by hand afresh each time you export. However, when you export repeatedly and delete multiple export files by moving them to the trash, the exporter sometimes gets confused and defaults to the trash directory. In these cases, you'll have to set the output directory again by hand.

The five buttons along the left have the following meanings:

UP updates a previously exported .sio2 file. This speeds up the process of exporting but should be used only when updating objects that have already all been exported. If you are exporting for the first time, or if you have added objects to the scene that have not yet been exported for a first time, you should leave this button unselected.

N enables the export of normal direction information. In order for real-time lighting to be calculated, SIO2 must know about the direction of the normals of all the faces. If you do not select this option, real-time lighting will not be calculated correctly. In the present Hello3DWorld example, you need to export with this option.

O enables mesh optimization. This option automatically splits quads into triangles, converts triangles to triangle strips, and removes doubles. If you did not split the quad faces into triangles in Blender in advance, you should use this option.

V bakes the current lighting conditions onto the mesh by setting the appropriate vertex colors. Vertex colors are one way to get simple, static lighting effects on a mesh.

IP ensures that all Ipo curves are exported rather than just the ones that are linked to objects that are exported.

Exporting the World

To export a scene, you need to take the following steps:

1. Make sure all the objects you want to export are on Layer 1 of the Blender layers. If you created all the objects on Layer 1, you don't need to do this, but if you don't know, it can't hurt to be sure. To do this, select all objects with the A key in Object

mode, press the M key, select the farthest left square on the top row of the layer buttons (see Figure 3.42), and then click OK.

Figure 3.42
Sending all the objects to Layer 1

2. Make sure the scene name is the name of the file you want to export. Do this by editing the name in the SCE field of the User Preferences header at the top of the default Blender screen, as shown in Figure 3.43. The default scene name is Scene, and this is fine to use, but it will become confusing to have all of your .sio2 files named Scene.sio2. It's better to give the scene a name. For this example, name the scene **Hello3DWorld**.

Figure 3.43
The SCE field with the name of the scene

3. Make sure all the objects you want to export are selected in Object mode by pressing the A key if necessary. Select the N option on the exporter script interface to export normal directions, and click Export. Check your output directory to make sure that the file Hello3DWorld.sio2 and a new directory with the same name (minus the .sio2 suffix) have been created there.

The *.sio2* File Format

You have now finished exporting your Blender scene to a format that can be read and used by the SIO2 library in the Xcode environment. Before you go on and actually start working with it directly in Chapter 4, it's a good idea to take a closer look at what you've just created.

When you export your Blender scene using the SIO2 exporter script, the 3D data is saved as a file with the suffix .sio2. This is the file format that the SIO2 library reads. In fact, you can read it too. The .sio2 file format is simply a zip file containing a directory tree with plain-text files to encode the 3D data. If you want to, you can uncompress the .sio2 file yourself by simply changing the suffix to .zip and uncompressing the archiving in the same way you would uncompress any other ZIP file. This isn't usually necessary though, because by default the exporter writes the .sio2 file and an uncompressed version of the data to the same directory. The name of the directory, like the name of the .sio2 file, is the same as the name of the Blender scene that was exported. If you open this directory, you will see eight subdirectories: camera, image, ipo, lamp, material, object, script, and sound. These subdirectories contain the data you would expect. In each subdirectory are files corresponding to the 3D assets from the Blender scene. Each asset, such as a mesh object, is represented by a separate text file with the same name as the object itself. You can see the subdirectories of the exporter output in Figure 3.44. The top-level output was to the template directory introduced in Chapter 1. The Hello3DWorld directory is the uncompressed content of Hello3DWorld.sio2. The exported scene includes the Sphere object and the plane, which are found in the object directory. The files that represent the meshes themselves are plain-text files.

Figure 3.44

The contents of
Hello3DWorld.sio2

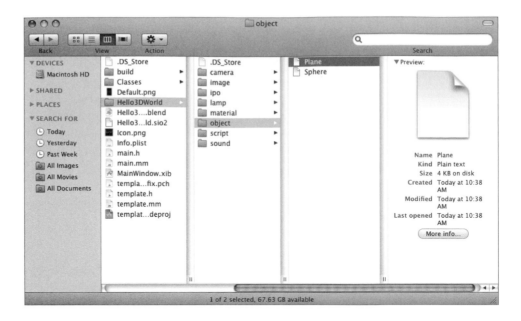

The text of these files gives SIO2 the information it needs to build the assets in OpenGL ES. As an example, here are the contents of the Camera file created in the camera directory that was generated by the script:

```
camera( "camera/Camera" )
{
        l( 0 -3.5 0 )
        r( 0.0 0 0 )
        d( 0 1 0 )
        f( 49.134 )
        cs( 0.1 )
        ce( 100 )
}
```

The syntax used here is similar to the C syntax, and the information is mostly straightforward, although some details are different from what you would find in Blender. The l attribute is directly from the corresponding location value in Blender. The r attribute is the rotation value, which is also directly from Blender. The d attribute, however, is the normalized direction vector of the camera, which is not an explicit Blender value but rather is calculated from the camera's position and rotation. Likewise, the f (field of view) represents the angle of view and is calculated from the Blender camera lens value. The lower the lens value, the wider the f value. The cs and ce values are the start and end clipping values, respectively, taken directly from the Blender values. These values determine the area within the field of view that the camera can see. Things farther away from the camera than the cend value are clipped from the scene and therefore not visible to the camera, and things closer than the cstart value are also clipped.

The kind of information contained in the SIO2 file about each type of 3D asset is specific to the type of object. The Camera file, therefore, contains information about the field of view and clipping values, whereas the file for a Mesh object contains information pertinent to meshes. You can see a simple example of this in the following code, which was generated to describe a simple UV-textured plane that has been divided into two triangles (the text to describe a cube is already fairly long to be displayed on the page of a book, so an example with fewer vertices is more suitable here):

```
object( "object/Plane" )
{
        l( 0 5.9 0 )
        r( 90.0 0 0 )
        s( 3.351 3.351 3.351 )
        ra( 4.739 )
        di( 1 1 0 )
        vb( 128 0 48 96 0 )
        v( 1 1 0 )
        v( -1 1 0 )
        v( -1 -1 0 )
        v( 1 -1 0 )
        n( 0 0 1 )
        n( 0 0 1 )
        n( 0 0 1 )
        n( 0 0 1 )
        u0( 0 1 )
        u0( 1 1 )
        u0( 1 0 )
        u0( 0 0 )
        ng( 1 )
        g( "null" )
        mt( "material/Material" )
        ni( 6 )
        i( 0 1 2 )
        i( 0 2 3 )

}
```

The first line, l, is the same as for other objects. The object's pivot point is located at the origin in Blender, so the values are 0. The ra and di values are used in physics simulations to determine the collision boundaries of the object. The vb attribute determines the offset value for the OpenGL vertex buffer object that will hold the vertex data for this 3D object. (For more information about vertex buffer objects in OpenGL ES, see Appendix B.) The v attributes show the x, y, and z values for each vertex, and the u0 values represent the UV mappings for each vertex for the first UV layer (two are possible). The n attributes represent the direction of the normals. These were exported because you had the N option selected in the exporter. The ng value is the number of vertex groups defined on the mesh, and the g value contains their names. Finally, the i value represents the number of indices necessary to assemble the full polygon mesh from the vertices, and the ind attributes list the indices in the order necessary to do that. Depending on the mesh and its features, other attributes may be present. In general, you will not need to work directly with this data because the SIO2 library provides an API for accessing the data in a convenient way. Nevertheless, it is good to have a basic idea of what information the data files contain and how they are formatted. The complete SIO2 file format specification is included in the SIO2 installation directory and is reprinted in Appendix C.

Now you've created and exported the scene, and you have a basic knowledge of what is in the files you'll be working with from here on. In the next chapter, you'll finally get down to putting these files to use to create content that you'll be able to run directly on your iPhone!

CHAPTER 4

Going Mobile with SIO2

In this chapter you'll use the SIO2 library to access and work with the 3D data you created in Chapter 3. You'll see how assets are loaded and how data is accessed through the sio2 object. You'll also take the next step in creating interactive content, using touch input to interact directly with the 3D scene. By the end of the chapter you will have compiled and run your Hello 3D World application on your iPhone simulator or device, and you'll know all the basics of how to get your 3D content from Blender to your iPhone or iPod Touch screen.

- Initializing SIO2 and loading assets
- Rendering
- Touch screen interaction
- The Complete Code

Initializing SIO2 and Loading Assets

In Chapter 3 you created a 3D scene in Blender and exported it to an .sio2 file using the SIO2 Python exporter. You also took a brief look at the contents of that file to get an idea of the kind of data that the SIO2 engine will have at its disposal to work with. Now, the scene you created will serve as the basis of an SIO2/OpenGL ES 3D environment for your iPhone.

To make this happen, first create a new Xcode project. In your SIO2_SDK directory, right-click the template directory and select Duplicate, as you did in Chapter 2. Rename the directory **project2**. To keep things organized, move the Hello3DWorld.sio2 file that you created in Chapter 3 into this directory also. Fire up Xcode by double-clicking the template.xcodeproj file in this directory.

Headers and Prototypes

As discussed previously, most of your SIO2 programming will be focused on the template .mm file. There are some occasions where other files also need to be modified, and this is one of them. For this project, you're going to create a new function in the template that will handle one-time loading and initialization tasks to avoid a lot of heavy resource use inside the render loop. This function will be called templateLoading and it will be defined, like the other functions, in template.mm. However, like the other functions, it must be prototyped in the corresponding header, template.h.

Find template.h in the Other Sources directory in Groups & Files and click it to bring it up in the text editor. Below the comments, the file looks like this:

```
#ifndef TEMPLATE_H
#define TEMPLATE_H

void templateRender( void );
void templateShutdown( void );
void templateScreenTap( void *_ptr, unsigned char _state );
void templateScreenTouchMove( void *_ptr );
void templateScreenAccelerometer( void *_ptr );

#endif
```

The #ifndef, #define, and #endif preprocessor commands ensure that the content of this file is included only once. The code between the conditionals consists of function prototypes. You probably recognize the names of these functions from Chapter 2. These are the functions defined in template.mm. Add another line to this list someplace after #define and before #endif to prototype the templateLoading function, like this:

```
void templateLoading( void );
```

That's all that needs to be done in template.h, but there's still one more file that needs to be edited slightly. In the Classes directory in the Groups & Files list in Xcode, find the file EAGLView.mm. Line 129 of that file looks like this:

```
129        sio2->_SIO2window->_SIO2windowrender = templateRender;
```

This executes the `templateRender` function. However, because you will be adding a different function to handle the initialization, you will need to ensure that the initialization function is executed first. To do that, change the function called here to `templateLoading`, like this:

```
129         sio2->_SIO2window->_SIO2windowrender = templateLoading;
```

Later, within the code of `templateLoading` itself, you will assign `templateRender` back to the `SIO2windowrender` callback function and the rendering will continue as it was originally intended.

You can now turn your attention to `template.mm`. This of course is the default template source file that was explained in its entirety in Chapter 2. Recall that the `.mm` suffix indicates that the file will be interpreted by the compiler as potentially containing C, C++, or Objective C code. In general, `template.mm` will almost always contain C/C++ code, although you will see an example in Chapter 6 where a small amount of Objective-C code is also used in this file.

The *templateLoading* Function

Now that you've added the prototype for the `templateLoading` function, you'll define what the function actually does. In `template.mm`, add the function definition after the end of the `templateRender` function definition. For now, you can just add an empty definition, like this:

```
void templateLoading ( void )
{
}
```

The remaining code in this section will go between these two curly brackets.

The purpose of the `templateLoading` function is to load assets from the `.sio2` file into the SIO2 iPhone programming environment. This entails converting the `.sio2` file assets into OpenGL ES v1.1 content, although this is somewhat behind the scenes. SIO2 does this by associating an `.sio2` file with an `SIO2resource` object, which in turn is associated with the top-level `sio2` object.

The main `SIO2resource` structure will hold the contents of the `.sio2` file in a dictionary data structure so that they can be accessed and used to populate other structures. To initialize this dictionary structure, use the `sio2ResourceCreateDictionary` function, with the `SIO2resource` structure belonging to the `sio2` structure as the function's argument, like this:

```
sio2ResourceCreateDictionary( sio2->_SIO2resource );
```

---

void **sio2ResourceCreateDictionary**(SIO2resource *resource*)

This function initializes the dictionary structure of the SIO2resource object *resource* with the keys object, material, lamp, camera, ipo, and action.

You then need to open up the appropriate .sio2 file and associate it with the SIO2resource object. This is done as follows:

```
sio2ResourceOpen( sio2->_SIO2resource, "Hello3DWorld.sio2", 1);
```

void **sio2ResourceOpen**(SIO2resource *resource*, const char *fname*, unsigned char *rel*)

This function opens the file named *fname* and associates it with SIO2resource *resource*. The *rel* value determines whether the relative path is used. If *rel* is nonzero, it is assumed the file is located in the project directory; otherwise an absolute path must be given.

Note that Hello3DWorld.sio2 is the name of the .sio2 file you exported from Blender in Chapter 3. At the beginning of this chapter, you placed the file in the same directory with the rest of the project files, but this is not quite enough to make the file accessible to the project in Xcode. Any files used by an iPhone application must be placed into the project itself from within Xcode. Do this now by dragging the icon for the file Hello3DWorld.sio2 from the Finder into the Groups & Files area in Xcode, as shown in Figure 4.1. This is very important. If you try to run a program that accesses files that haven't been placed into the project in this way, you will get an error. When you have placed the file in Groups & Files, you'll see the dialog shown in Figure 4.2. Check the box next to "Copy items into destination group's folder (if needed)."

Figure 4.1

Dragging the .sio2 **file from the Finder to Groups & Files**

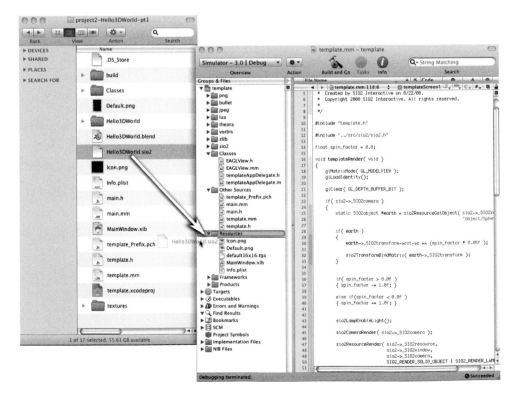

The next step is to extract the contents of the SIO2resource object.

```
unsigned int i = 0;
while( i != sio2->_SIO2resource->gi.number_entry )
{
        sio2ResourceExtract( sio2->_SIO2resource, NULL
);

        ++i;

}
```

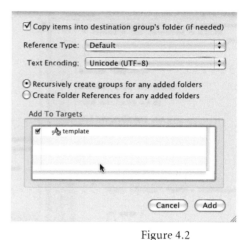

Recall that the sio2 file is basically a ZIP file, so its contents need to be uncompressed before use. The details of this block are not really important to understand completely, but you should know that it's a necessary step for putting the content of the SIO2resource into usable form.

Figure 4.2

Dialog for adding items to Groups & Files

```
void sio2ResourceExtract( SIO2resource *resource, char *password )
```

This function extracts the archived contents of the SIO2resource *resource*. The *password* value is NULL by default.

Now that the content of the .sio2 file has been extracted, you can close the file. Do that with the next line of code:

```
sio2ResourceClose( sio2->_SIO2resource );
```

```
void sio2ResourceClose( SIO2resource *resource )
```

This function closes the .sio2 file associated with the SIO2resource object *resource*.

Now you need to bind the resources. In OpenGL terminology, to "bind" an asset or property means to set it to be used in subsequent function calls. This is what you are doing here. Binding the images, materials, and matrices makes them active as the program runs. This is done with the following lines of code:

```
sio2ResourceBindAllImages( sio2->_SIO2resource );
sio2ResourceBindAllMaterials( sio2->_SIO2resource );
sio2ResourceBindAllMatrix( sio2->_SIO2resource );
```

```
void sio2ResourceBindAllImages( SIO2resource *resource )
void sio2ResourceBindAllMaterials( SIO2resource *resource )
void sio2ResourceBindAllMatrix( SIO2resource *resource )
```

These functions set the images, materials, and matrices associated with the SIO2resource *resource* to be affected by relevant subsequent function calls.

The next line generates OpenGL ES ID values of the appropriate type for all of the assets in the SIO2resource object (ID generation is discussed in Appendix B):

```
sio2ResourceGenId( sio2->_SIO2resource );
```

The next two lines are some basic initialization code for the sio2 root object. The first of the two lines resets the state of the sio2 root object. This involves setting the sio2 root object's 3D property objects to null values. This does not change the sio2->_SIO2window value. The next line assigns the content of the templateRender function to the actual render function, which itself is a property of the SIO2window object (recall how you changed a similar line in the original template's EAGLView.mm file):

```
sio2ResetState();
sio2->_SIO2window->_SIO2windowrender = templateRender;
```

---

void **sio2ResetState(void)**

This function sets the SIO2camera, SIO2object, SIO2lamp, SIO2vertexgroup, SIO2material, SIO2font, SIO2ipo, SIO2ipocurve, SIO2action, and all SIO2image structures associated with the sio2 root object to NULL.

The camera asset from SIO2resource is assigned to the SIO2camera value of the sio2 root object like this:

```
sio2->_SIO2camera = sio2ResourceGetCamera( sio2->_SIO2resource,
                                           "camera/Camera" );
```

Now the project has a camera. With the camera information from the .sio2 file and the scale information from sio2->_SIO2window, you can build the perspective view volume (as described in Appendix B) using the sio2Perspective function. This function was not called in the example in Chapter 2 because 3D rendering was not used in that example. To adjust the projection matrix, the function needs the camera's field of view (sio2->_SIO2camera->fov), which represents the camera's lens angle measured in degrees, the aspect ratio of the window (calculated by dividing the x scale of the window by the y scale: sio2->_SIO2window->scl->x / sio2->_SIO2window->scl->y), and minimum and maximum clip values (cstart and cend, respectively).

```
sio2Perspective( sio2->_SIO2camera->fov,
                 sio2->_SIO2window->scl->x / sio2->_SIO2window->scl->y,
                 sio2->_SIO2camera->cstart,
                 sio2->_SIO2camera->cend );
```

---

void **sio2Perspective("oat fovy, "oat *aspect*, "oat *zNear*, "oat *zFar*)**

This function adjusts the projection matrix with size and angles determined by the arguments to the function. The *fovy* argument is the camera's field of view. The *aspect* argument is the width over height ratio of the view window. The *zNear* and *zFar* values are the front and back clipping panes, respectively; that is, the nearest and farthest z-axis values to be rendered.

This wraps up the loading and initialization portion of the program. You can now turn your attention to setting up the render loop.

Rendering

Now it's time to write the render loop, which is the code that will be executed for each frame as your application runs. As you should recall from Chapter 2, this code goes in the function `templateRender`. The default template implementation of that function looks like this:

```
void templateRender( void )
{
    glMatrixMode( GL_MODELVIEW );
    glLoadIdentity();
    glClear( GL_DEPTH_BUFFER_BIT|GL_COLOR_BUFFFR_BIT );
    //Your rendering code here...

}
```

For the most part, this section of the function will remain unchanged, except for one small thing. If you remember the scene you created in Blender, you'll recall that the background of the scene is a solid, opaque textured plane. Each frame that renders will completely overwrite all pixels in the window. Because of this, there's no need to clear the color buffer for each frame. On mobile platforms such as the iPhone, processing resources are at a premium, and it's best to eliminate all unnecessary processing steps. To stop the color buffer from being cleared each frame, delete the `GL_COLOR_BUFFER_BIT` label from the `glClear` function call, changing the line to this:

```
glClear( GL_DEPTH_BUFFER_BIT );
```

The depth buffer still needs to be cleared to properly calculate hidden face removal when faces move in relation to each other, so you can't remove this line entirely.

The remaining render code should execute only after the `sio2` root object has been populated with a camera, which happens in `templateLoading`, as you saw previously. To ensure this has happened, use a conditional statement to check that the `sio2->_SIO2camera` structure is pointing to an existing handle, like this:

```
if( sio2->_SIO2camera )
{

}
```

The rest of the rendering code should all be placed between the two curly brackets of that conditional. Because you'll eventually be using real-time lighting, you need to declare a variable to represent the color of the ambient light. You want a weak uniform light for this, so declare the variable `ambient_color` like this:

```
static vec4 ambient_color = { 0.1f, 0.1f, 0.1f, 1.0f };
```

Making the World Go 'Round

To access a 3D object for the purpose of transformations, you have to assign the appropriate resource to an SIO2object structure. In this example, the model of the planet Earth will rotate, so you must create a variable of the type SIO2object and use sio2ResourceGetObject to assign the Sphere object from the Blender scene to the variable. I've chosen the name *earth* for the variable name. Assign it the appropriate value like this:

```
        static SIO2object *earth = sio2ResourceGetObject( sio2->_
    SIO2resource,


    "object/Sphere" );
```

The next block of code will rotate the world around the z-axis:

```
        if( earth )
        {
            earth->_SIO2transform->rot->z += 15.0f*sio2->_SIO2window->d_time;
            sio2TransformBindMatrix( earth->_SIO2transform );

        }
```

First check to make sure the object is pointing to a valid handle to avoid errors that can arise from trying to access properties of uninstantiated objects. Objects of type SIO2object have _SIO2transform properties, which in turn have rotation values for each axis. The x-axis rotation value for this object is accessed with *earth->_SIO2transform->rot->z*. The first line in the conditional statement increases this value with each frame. You should never use a hard-coded value for animation on the iPhone. Using the sio2->_SIO2window->d_time as a factor for animation values makes them independent of the frame rate because it associates them directly with the delta time value of the window.

The next line binds the transformation matrix to ensure that the transformation is actually applied at render time.

---

void **sio2TransformBindMatrix**(SIO2transform *transform*)

This function sets the transform function to be calculated for use in subsequent functions in the program. This function recalculates the new matrix based on the location, rotation, and scale transformations in the corresponding SIO2transform structure. It is necessary to call this before rendering an object that has been operated on with an SIO2transform.

On the following line, add a comment to indicate where to include the interactive spin factor code:

```
        //spin factor code
```

This will be discussed in the next section, on touch screen interactivity, and you'll want to come back to this point in the program to include the pertinent code.

Before you code in the touch screen interactivity, you'll finish the basic render code so that you can run the application and see some preliminary 3D results. To do this, the only thing missing now is light.

And Then There Was Light

The last few lines of the render code enable lighting and then complete the rendering process. Set the ambient light value and then enable real-time lighting with the following function calls:

```
sio2LampSetAmbient( &ambient_color );;
sio2LampEnableLight();
```

void **sio2LampSetAmbient**(vec4 color)

This function sets the ambient lighting to the color described by the *color* variable. Assigning full white color will yield maximum ambient lighting.

void **sio2LampEnableLight**(void)

This function enables the OpenGL ES states required for lighting to be calculated.

The next few lines of code call the sio2CameraRender function, which calculates the placement of the camera, and the sio2ResourceRender function, which renders the resources indicated by the bit mask in the fourth argument. In this case, SIO2_RENDER_SOLID_OBJECT and SIO2_RENDER_LAMP tell the SIO2 engine to render solid 3D objects and lights:

```
sio2CameraRender( sio2->_SIO2camera );
sio2ResourceRender( sio2->_SIO2resource,
                    sio2->_SIO2window,
                    sio2->_SIO2camera,
                    SIO2_RENDER_SOLID_OBJECT | SIO2_RENDER_LAMP);
```

void **sio2CameraRender**( )

This function calculates the placement of the camera.

```
void sio2ResourceRender( SIO2resource *resource, SIO2window *window, SIO2camera
*camera, int mask )
```

This function renders the resources associated with SIO2resource *resource* to the SIO2 window *window*. The camera information is passed via the *camera* parameter. The types of resources rendered depend on the value or values of the bit mask *mask*. The possible values are SIO2_RENDER_IPO, SIO2_RENDER_LAMP, SIO2_RENDER_SOLID_OBJECT, SIO2_RENDER_TRANS-PARENT_OBJECT, SIO2_RENDER_ALPHA_TESTED_OBJECT, SIO2_RENDER_CLIPPED_OBJECT, SIO2_RENDER_EMITTER, SIO2_EVALUATE_SENSOR, SIO2_EVALUATE_TIMER, and SIO2_UPDATE_SOUND_STREAM. Multiple *mask* values can be entered, separated by the vertical pipe symbol, representing Boolean disjunction (or).

Figure 4.3

Running the application on the simulator

At this point you can build and run the application. You should see the planet Earth appear on your screen with a black background and a white glow, as shown in Figure 4.3, just as you saw in your Blender render. You should also see that the planet is rotating slowly around the z-axis.

It's good to be aware that real-time lighting in the iPhone is extremely demanding on the graphics processing unit and can have a serious effect on performance. The SIO2 engine allows a maximum of eight lights to be set up, but you should normally not try to light a whole scene using GL lighting. In most cases, real-time lighting is not necessary, as you will see in Chapter 6 when you learn to bake lighting patterns to textures in Blender. Doing that can enable you to get well-lit scenes in your iPhone with no real-time lighting at all.

Troubleshooting

As is always the case with programming, there are a virtually infinite number of places where small things can go wrong and cause problems for successfully executing your code. If you have managed to get this far in the book without errors, my hat is off to you! If you do run into problems at this point, here are some general tips for tracking them down.

Syntax errors are the most common problems you'll have. You've forgotten a semicolon somewhere or mistyped a keyword. Xcode's code completion and syntax highlighting is a great help in preventing many potential syntax errors, but errors get past it. In these cases, the application will usually not compile successfully. If there are errors compiling, Xcode will highlight the line where the error occurred with a red icon with a little white *x* in it, as shown in Figure 4.4. Always focus your attention on the first error that comes up because subsequent errors are often a result of the first one.

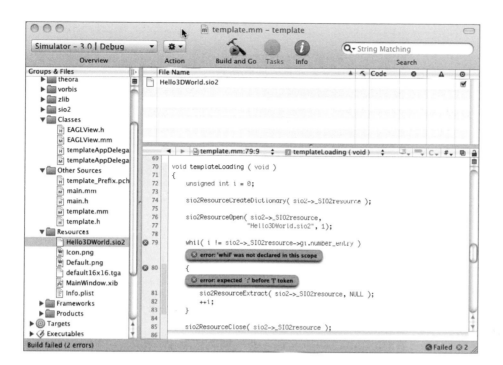

Figure 4.4

Syntax error highlighting

There are more insidious bugs that can occur at runtime, after a successful compile. For an inexperienced C/C++/Objective-C programmer, collecting diagnostic information from the debugger can be a challenge, and it's beyond the scope of this book to get into hard-core C debugging. In any case, if you're sticking with code from this book for the time being, this shouldn't be necessary. If you're having runtime crashes, a very likely cause of the problem is that data files are missing from the project's resources. Any files accessed by the code *must* be included in the Groups & Files area. Check the Resources directory here to make sure everything is in place. Double-check the filenames to make sure they are the same as the ones you're calling in the code.

If your screen is simply black when you run the application, it's likely the problem has to do with either the .blend file or the .sio2 file you exported from it. Check the .blend file again to make sure the normals are pointed outward and all the lamps and objects you want to render are on a selected layer (see Appendix A if you're not sure how to do these things). Try reexporting the .sio2 file to the project directory, being careful to have all the objects that you want to export selected in the Blender 3D view. Objects that are not selected will not be exported!

When you're reexporting, the export directory will be removed and re-created if the UP toggle button is not toggled. However, note that if you are updating an export with UP toggled and you change an object's name, the previously exported object information will not be removed, so if you ever need to delete or rename exported objects, delete the previous .sio2 file and the corresponding directory. This is not always strictly necessary, but sometimes it is, and it's important to know that not deleting a previous .sio2 file and directory can be the source of some problems. If you are having persistent problems, you should also try deleting the build directory that the compiler places in your project directory. This will force a completely fresh build.

You can run your program with the debugger by starting the application with Run → Debug.

Touch Screen Interaction

Now that you've run the application and seen the 3D content in action in your iPhone/iPod Touch or on your iPhone simulator, it's time to add some interactive functionality and take advantage of what makes the iPhone platform so exciting in the first place!

Spin Control

The goal here will be to control the spin of the planet using a swipe of your finger on the touch screen rather than simply watching it go round and round. To do this, you'll modify the speed it spins in an interactive way. This will require a variable. You'll use a floating-point number for this, and the variable will be called *spin_factor*. Declare it at the beginning of the program, before the definition of templateRender, like this:

```
float spin_factor = 0.0;
```

This variable is going to be used as a multiplier for the change in rotation. In template Render, find the line where the change in rotation is determined:

```
earth->_SIO2transform->rot->z += 15.0f * sio2->_SIO2window->d_time;
```

Then change the line to include the spin factor value, like this:

```
earth->_SIO2transform->rot->z += (spin_factor * sio2->_SIO2window->d_time );
```

If you build and run the application now, the globe will be completely still because *spin_factor* is initialized as zero and has not been changed. You'll deal with giving the variable a nonzero value shortly. But first, there are a few more lines to add to template Render. In the case where *spin_factor* is not zero, you want to gradually bring it back to zero so that when you spin the planet it eventually slows down and stops spinning, just as a real globe would do. The following code does this by checking to see if the globe is spinning in a positive or negative direction and, if it is, slowing it down incrementally. Place this code at the same point where you inserted the //spin factor code comment in the previous section:

```
if( spin_factor > 0.0f )
    { spin_factor -= 1.0f; }
else if(spin_factor < 0.0f )

    { spin_factor += 1.0f; }
```

Handling the Screen Tap and Touch Move

The `templateScreenTap` and `templateScreenTouchMove` functions are where the touch screen magic really happens. But before you get into defining the functions themselves, you need to declare another variable. This variable will be used inside the functions, but it must be defined outside of the functions so that it will be global and its value will be available across function calls. You can declare the variable anywhere in the code prior to the function definitions, but to minimize confusion, it's a good idea to declare it close to the functions where it will be used. For that reason, declare the variable right above the definition of `templateScreenTap`. The variable is of type vec2, which represents a two-dimensional vector. Call the variable *start* and declare it like this:

```
vec2 start;
```

The next thing to do is to fill in the definition for `templateScreenTap`:

```
void templateScreenTap( void *_ptr, unsigned char _state )
{
    if( _state == SIO2_WINDOW_TAP_DOWN ){
        start.x = sio2->_SIO2window->touch[ 0 ]->x;
        start.y = sio2->_SIO2window->touch[ 0 ]->y;
    }
}
```

All that needs to be done here is to register the x and y positions of the point where your finger makes contact with the screen. That way, when you swipe your finger, SIO2 can calculate which direction the swipe went. Because you're only interested in the tap down case, include a conditional to ensure that the state of the tap is SIO2_WINDOW_TAP_ DOWN. Then assign the *x* and *y* values of the 0 touch (the first finger to hit the screen) to the *x* and *y* values of the *start* vector.

The `templateScreenTouchMove` will finally give *spin_factor* its nonzero value:

```
void templateScreenTouchMove( void *_ptr )
{
    if( sio2->_SIO2window->n_touch )
    {
        spin_factor = 2*(sio2->_SIO2window->touch[ 0 ]->x - start.x);
    }
}
```

This is calculated depending on the difference between the current position of your finger and the start position so that a longer swipe will increase the speed of the spin more than a short swipe. This gives a pretty good approximation of the kind of behavior you'd expect when spinning an object with your finger.

You won't be using the accelerometer in this example, so the default empty function definition of `templateScreenAccelerometer` remains unchanged. You can build and run your application now and you'll see that you can spin the globe by swiping your finger to the right or left.

The Complete Code

Here is the complete code for template.mm:

```
/*
 *  template.mm
 *  template
 *
 *  Created by SIO2 Interactive on 8/22/08.
 *  Copyright 2008 SIO2 Interactive. All rights reserved.
 *
 */


#include "template.h"

#include "../src/sio2/sio2.h"

float spin_factor = 0.0;
void templateRender( void )
{
    glMatrixMode( GL_MODELVIEW );
    glLoadIdentity();

    glClear( GL_DEPTH_BUFFER_BIT );

    if( sio2->_SIO2camera )
    {
        static vec4 ambient_color = { 0.1f, 0.1f, 0.1f, 1.0f };
        static SIO2object *earth =
                    sio2ResourceGetObject( sio2->_SIO2resource,
                    "object/Sphere" );

        if( earth )
        {
            earth->_SIO2transform->rot->z +=
                    (spin_factor * sio2->_SIO2window->d_time );
            sio2TransformBindMatrix( earth->_SIO2transform );
        }

        if( spin_factor > 0.0f )
            { spin_factor -= 1.0f; }
        else if(spin_factor < 0.0f )
            { spin_factor += 1.0f; }

        sio2LampSetAmbient( &ambient_color );
        sio2LampEnableLight();
```

```
        sio2CameraRender( sio2->_SIO2camera );
        sio2ResourceRender( sio2->_SIO2resource,
                            sio2->_SIO2window,
                            sio2->_SIO2camera,
                            SIO2_RENDER_SOLID_OBJECT |
                            SIO2_RENDER_LAMP);


    }
}


void templateShutdown( void )
{
    // Clean up
    sio2ResourceUnloadAll( sio2->_SIO2resource );
    sio2->_SIO2resource = sio2ResourceFree( sio2->_SIO2resource );
    sio2->_SIO2window = sio2WindowFree( sio2->_SIO2window );
    sio2 = sio2Shutdown();
    printf("\nSIO2: shutdown...\n" );
}


void templateLoading ( void )
{
    unsigned int i = 0;
    sio2ResourceCreateDictionary( sio2->_SIO2resource );
    sio2ResourceOpen( sio2->_SIO2resource,
                      "Hello3DWorld.sio2", 1);

    while( i != sio2->_SIO2resource->gi.number_entry )
    {
        sio2ResourceExtract( sio2->_SIO2resource, NULL );
        ++i;
    }

    sio2ResourceClose( sio2->_SIO2resource );
    sio2ResourceBindAllImages( sio2->_SIO2resource );
    sio2ResourceBindAllMaterials( sio2->_SIO2resource );
    sio2ResourceBindAllMatrix( sio2->_SIO2resource );
    sio2ResourceGenId( sio2->_SIO2resource );
    sio2ResetState();

    sio2->_SIO2camera = sio2ResourceGetCamera( sio2->_SIO2resource,
                                               "camera/Camera");
    sio2Perspective( sio2->_SIO2camera->fov,
                     sio2->_SIO2window->scl->x /
                         sio2->_SIO2window->scl->y,
                     sio2->_SIO2camera->cstart,
                     sio2->_SIO2camera->cend );
```

```
        sio2->_SIO2window->_SIO2windowrender = templateRender;
}

vec2 start;

void templateScreenTap( void *_ptr, unsigned char _state )
{
    if( _state == SIO2_WINDOW_TAP_DOWN ){
        start.x = sio2->_SIO2window->touch[ 0 ]->x;
        start.y = sio2->_SIO2window->touch[ 0 ]->y;
    }
}

void templateScreenTouchMove( void *_ptr )
{
    if( sio2->_SIO2window->n_touch )
    {
        spin_factor = 2*(sio2->_SIO2window->touch[ 0 ]->x - start.x);
    }
}

void templateScreenAccelerometer( void *_ptr )
{
}
```

CHAPTER 5

Extending Interactive Feedback with Picking and Text

In this chapter, you'll pick up from where you left off with the previous chapter and explore several more ways of adding interactivity to your application. You'll begin by taking an in-depth look at how SIO2 enables you to easily implement 3D picking so the user can select objects simply by touching the screen. After you've seen how to incorporate picking into your Hello3DWorld application, you'll learn how to implement text-based feedback on the iPhone screen. Finally, you'll see how to package your application with its own name and icon.

- Object picking

- Working with text and fonts

- Using multi-touch functionality

- Packaging your app

- The Complete Code

Object Picking

The word *picking* refers to identifying a point in a virtual 3D environment based on a 2D point indicated by the user. With picking, a user can select an object in the 3D world with a mouse click or a touch screen tap. This is a crucial function for many 3D games and interactive environments because it grants the user a high degree of interactivity with the virtual world.

There is more than one way to do picking. You can find several common approaches using OpenGL functions in OpenGL literature online and in books such as the *OpenGL SuperBible* by Richard S. Wright and Benjamin Lipchak (3rd edition, Sams, 2004) and *OpenGL Programming Guide: The Official Guide to Learning OpenGL, Versions 3.0 and 3.1* (often referred to as "The Red Book") by Dave Shreiner and the Khronos OpenGL ARB Working Group (7th edition, Addison-Wesley Professional, 2009). In SIO2 specifically, there are also several ways to do picking. One method that I will not discuss in depth in this book involves using the Bullet physics library to calculate a ray from the view plane to the 3D object being picked. You can learn about this method by studying Tutorial 6.1 in the SIO2 package. The method I cover in this chapter follows the approach taken in Tutorial 6.2 and is both computationally less expensive and a little bit easier to understand than the physics-based method.

The method of picking here works by first assigning each object a unique solid color and then rendering a frame to the OpenGL color buffer with the objects in these colors, without lighting or materials. When the frame has been rendered, an OpenGL function is called to return the color value of the pixel that has been tapped. Because each object has been rendered in a solid, unique color, the color of the pixel is all that's needed to pick the correct object.

A Simple Picking Example in Blender

Before you apply picking to your Hello3DWorld application, it's a good idea to look at a more stripped-down example so you can easily see exactly how the picking code is working. This example will give you a little bit more practice creating 3D scenes for SIO2 and will show you how to dig deeper into the SIO2 code to find out how things work on your own. Being able to quickly navigate from function calls to function definitions is a fundamental skill in Xcode that you'll find comes in very handy when debugging.

To begin, create a new project by duplicating and renaming the `template` directory, just as you have done in previous chapters. Give it the name **picking**. Now fire up Blender and save the `.blend` file in the project directory. Follow these steps to create a simple scene for use in this project:

1. Select the cube and the lamp objects and delete them both by pressing the X key. For information about navigating the 3D space and selecting objects, refer to Appendix A.

2. Select the camera and press Alt+G to clear the location. Press the N key over the 3D viewport to bring up the Transform Properties floating panel (Figure 5.1). Input the rotation values RotX: **90**, RotY: **0**, and RotZ: **0** as shown in the figure.

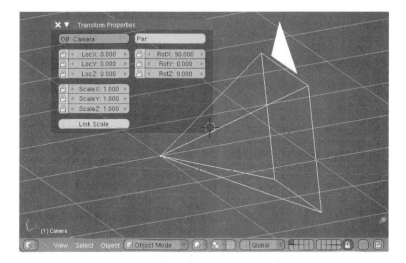

Figure 5.1

Setting the location and rotation of the camera

3. Press the spacebar and choose Add→ Mesh→Plane to add a plane, as shown in Figure 5.2. If you are using default settings, the plane should appear as shown in Figure 5.3, at the origin of the space facing upward. If it looks different from this, tab into Object mode and press Alt+G and Alt+R to clear the rotation and location.

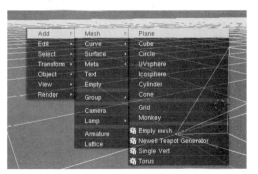

Figure 5.2

Adding a plane

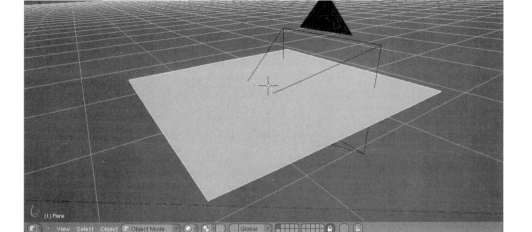

Figure 5.3

The resulting plane

4. Look at the Transform Properties panel (N key) and enter the values LocX: **0**, LocY: **5**, LocZ: **1**, RotX: **90**, RotY: **0**, and RotZ: **0** for the location and rotation of the plane, as shown in Figure 5.4.

Figure 5.4

Setting location and rotation for the plane

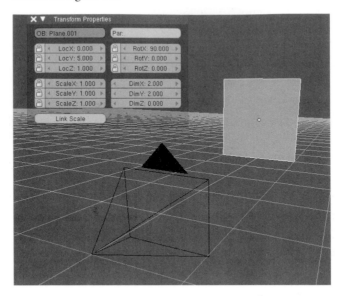

Figure 5.5

Subdividing

5. Tab into Edit mode. Make sure the mesh is entirely selected using the A key. Press the W key and select Subdivide from the menu, as shown in Figure 5.5. Scale the plane vertically down slightly by pressing the S key followed by the Z key (Figure 5.6).

Figure 5.6

Scaling vertically

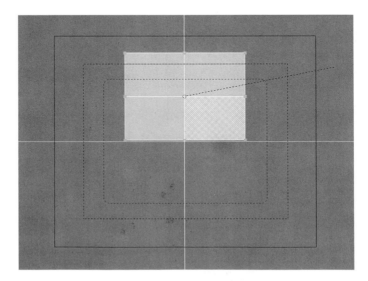

6. From the Mesh menu, execute the script for converting the quads to triangles: Mesh → Faces → Convert Quads To Triangles, as shown in Figure 5.7. The resulting

triangle mesh will look like they do in Figure 5.8, but this isn't quite what you want. The triangles in the upper-left and lower-right quad should be flipped. Select the lower-right quad and execute the flip triangle edges script by choosing Mesh → Faces → Flip Triangle Edges, as shown in Figure 5.9. Do the same with the upper-left quad to get the topology shown in Figure 5.10.

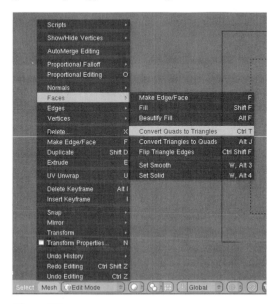

Figure 5.7
Converting quads to triangles

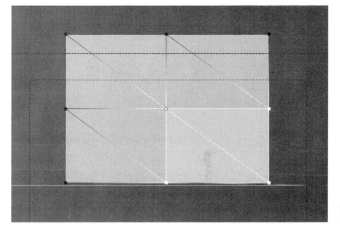

Figure 5.8
Resulting triangles

Figure 5.9
Flipping triangles

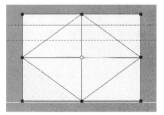

Figure 5.10
The finished triangle mesh

7. Tab into Object mode and duplicate the mesh by pressing Ctrl+D and then pressing Z to constrain the new object to move vertically. Move the second plane down below the first one, as shown in Figure 5.11.

8. Rename the new mesh object **Plane2**. Enter the new name in the OB field in the Link And Materials panel, as shown in Figure 5.12. This is important. By default, duplicated objects in Blender are given names ending with numbers, starting with .001. These numerical suffixes are used by SIO2 as the basis of *pseudo-instancing*, which you will read more about in Chapter 7. All you need to know now is that object names ending with such automatically generated suffixes will be basically ignored by SIO2 in the present example. So renaming this object is a requirement.

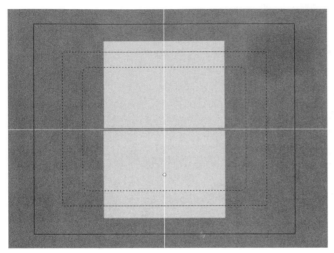

Figure 5.12
Renaming the object

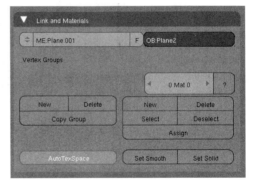

Figure 5.11
Duplicating the mesh

9. Now it's time to add some color to the scene. In this simple example, you won't need any materials or textures. Instead, you will use the simplest way to color a mesh that SIO2 can understand, namely vertex painting. Enter Vertex Paint mode with the header drop-down menu as shown in Figure 5.13. Adjust the vertex paint color and opacity using the panel shown in Figure 5.14. Paint each vertex of each plane a different color. Stick with primary colors like red (two RGB values set at 0 and one value set at 1) and secondary colors like yellow (two RGB values set at 1 and one value set at 0) as well as black (all three RGB values set at 0) and white (all three RGB values set at 1). You will be able to see the vertex colors in Textured display mode. The resulting scene, from the camera view, is shown in Figure 5.15 (unfortunately reprinted in grayscale, so you'll have to use your imagination with regard to the colors).

Figure 5.14

The Paint panel

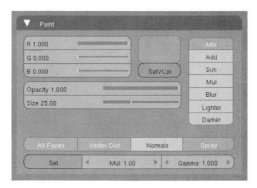

Figure 5.13

Entering Vertex Paint mode

Figure 5.15

The finished scene from the camera view, in Textured display mode

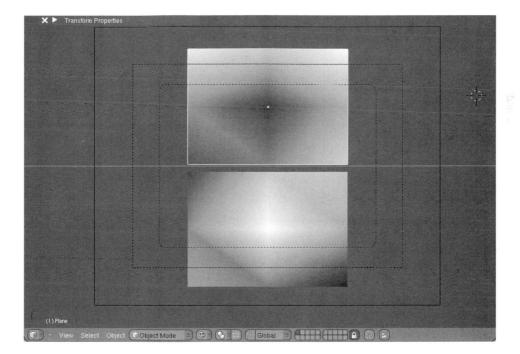

10. Change the scene name to **PickingScene** in the SCE field in the top header. Now open the SIO2 export script and run it exactly as you did in Chapter 3. You don't need to worry about exporting normals or triangulating the mesh. Simply make sure all objects are selected and export the contents of the file to an .sio2 file in the project directory.

Now you've got your 3D content and you're ready to do some experimenting with picking.

Implementing Color-Based Picking in SIO2

In your newly created project, open EAGLView.mm and change the render callback function initialization, just as you did in Chapter 4. Find the line

```
sio2->_SIO2window->_SIO2windowrender = templateRender
```

and change it to

```
sio2->_SIO2window->_SIO2windowrender = templateLoading;
```

Then add the declaration of templateLoading to template.h, among the other function declarations, as you also did in Chapter 4.

Drag and drop the file you just exported, PickingScene.sio2, from the Finder window into the Resources directory in the Xcode Groups & Files list.

Finally, modify template.mm as shown in the following code. In the explanations that follow, I'll be referring to specific lines of code, so make sure your line numbers correspond with what's printed here. This is the full code for template.mm:

```
10   #include "template.h"
11   #include "../src/sio2/sio2.h"
12
13   vec2 t;
14   unsigned char tap_select = 0;
15   SIO2object *selection = NULL;
16
17   void templateRender( void )
18   {
19       glMatrixMode( GL_MODELVIEW );
20       glLoadIdentity();
21
22       glClear( GL_DEPTH_BUFFER_BIT | GL_COLOR_BUFFER_BIT );
23
24       sio2->_SIO2camera = sio2ResourceGetCamera( sio2->_SIO2resource,
25                                           "camera/Camera");
26
27
28       if(sio2->_SIO2camera){
29           sio2Perspective( sio2->_SIO2camera->fov,
30                         sio2->_SIO2window->scl->x /
                                    sio2->_SIO2window->scl->y,
31                         sio2->_SIO2camera->cstart,
32                         sio2->_SIO2camera->cend );
33
34           sio2CameraRender( sio2->_SIO2camera );
35           sio2ResourceRender( sio2->_SIO2resource,
36                               sio2->_SIO2window,
37                               sio2->_SIO2camera,
38                               SIO2_RENDER_SOLID_OBJECT );
```

```
39
40          if(tap_select){
41              tap_select = 0;
42
43              printf("tx: %f ty: %f \n", t.x, t.y);
44
45              selection = sio2ResourceSelect3D( sio2->_SIO2resource,
46                                                sio2->_SIO2camera,
47                                                sio2->_SIO2window,
48                                                &t);
49
50              printf( "%s\n", selection->name );
51          }
52      }
53  }
54
55  void templateLoading( void )
56  {
57      unsigned int i = 0;
58
59      sio2ResourceCreateDictionary( sio2->_SIO2resource );
60
61      sio2ResourceOpen( sio2->_SIO2resource,
62                        "PickingScene.sio2", 1);
63
64      while( i != sio2->_SIO2resource->gi.number_entry )
65      {
66          sio2ResourceExtract( sio2->_SIO2resource, NULL );
67          ++i;
68      }
69      sio2ResourceClose( sio2->_SIO2resource );
70      sio2ResourceBindAllMatrix( sio2->_SIO2resource );
71      sio2ResourceGenId( sio2->_SIO2resource );
72      sio2ResetState();
73
74      sio2->_SIO2window->_SIO2windowrender = templateRender;
75  }
76
77  void templateScreenTap( void *_ptr, unsigned char _state )
78  {
79      if( _state == SIO2_WINDOW_TAP_DOWN ){
80          t.x = sio2->_SIO2window->touch[ 0 ]->x;
81          t.y = sio2->_SIO2window->scl->y -
82                    sio2->_SIO2window->touch[ 0 ]->y;
82          tap_select = 1;
83      }
84  }
```

```
85
86   void templateScreenTouchMove( void *_ptr )
87   {
88   }
89
90   void templateScreenAccelerometer( void *_ptr )
91   {
92   }
```

SIO2object **sio2ResourceSelect3D**(SIO2resource *resource*, SIO2camera *camera*, SIO2window *window*, vec2 *v*)

This function handles picking objects in a 3D space via screen touch. The function takes as arguments a resource manager *resource*, a camera object *camera*, a window object *window*, and a 2D vector *v* representing the point on the screen that was touched. It returns the selected SIO2object.

If you build and run this code as it is, you should see the two colorful planes on your simulator or device screen. They don't do much though. In order to see the functionality, you'll need to run the console. From the Xcode Run menu, choose Console. Now build and run your code again. You should now be able to pick the planes by clicking or tapping on them. The selected object's name will be printed to the console as shown in Figure 5.16. If you aren't able to get this working, go back and make sure you've got the code typed in correctly, or check the troubleshooting tips in Chapter 4.

Figure 5.16

Running your code in the iPhone simulator with the console

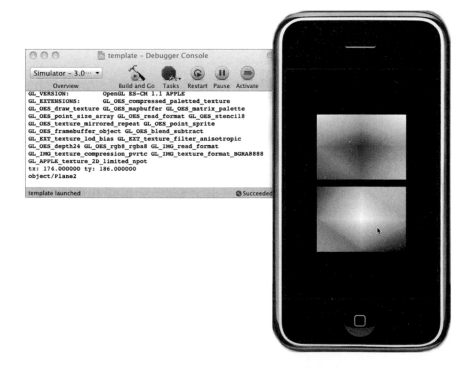

So how is this code working? Much of the code you typed in is the same as code you've seen in previous chapters. The resource loading code is pretty much identical to what you saw in Chapter 4. The new stuff here is related to the picking functionality. Lines 13 to 15 declare relevant variables. The first one, t of type vec2, should be somewhat familiar from Chapter 4. This is a two-dimensional vector that will hold the x- and y-coordinate values of the touch point. Note that the y-coordinate must be reversed by subtracting the touched coordinate from the total scale of the window along the y-axis. This is because the iPhone's touch screen y-coordinate is counted from the bottom corner up, whereas the OpenGL ES color buffer's y-coordinate is counted from the top corner down. The next variable, tap_select, will serve as a flag indicating whether a tap has landed. The selection variable holds a pointer to an SIO2object. As its name implies, this will be used to store a pointer to the 3D object that is selected (tapped) by the user.

The templateScreenTap function beginning at line 77 is where the tap is registered. Two things happen in this function: the x- and y-coordinate values of t are set according to the touch position, and tap_select is set to 1.

When tap_select is set to 1, the picking code in templateRender is executed according to the conditional statement on line 40. The first thing that happens is that tap_select is reset to 0 so that future taps can be registered separately. The printf statement on line 53 prints the x- and y-coordinates to the console.

Line 45 is where selection receives its value from the sio2ResourceSelect3D function. This is where the picking action happens. The function takes the resource manager, the camera, the window object, and the touch coordinate vector t and returns the selected object. Line 50 prints the name of the selected object to the console.

A Closer Look at the Picking Code

It's worthwhile to take a closer look at sio2ResourceSelect3D. The fact is, it's worthwhile to take a closer look at any function you use because understanding how a function does its job will give you insights into when it's appropriate and how to get the most out of using it. Understanding the workings of the built-in SIO2 functions will also be enormously valuable when debugging your own code. It's a good idea to be careful when looking at files in the src directory though. Any edits you make to these files will affect all of your projects because they all share a single src directory. In general, you won't want to modify these files, but you might occasionally want to print out some diagnostic messages as you explore the functionality. Just be sure to leave source files as you found them when you're done.

Xcode provides numerous tools for navigating and debugging code, and the more you can learn about these tools, the faster and more efficiently you'll be able to write code. In order to drill into the sio2ResourceSelect3D function definition itself, you'll use one of these tools now. Right-click over the function call in line 45. When you do, you'll see the name of the function highlighted in blue and a menu will appear. From the menu, select Jump To Definition as shown in Figure 5.17. Voilà! You are immediately taken directly to the function definition in sio2_resource.cc.

Figure 5.17

Jumping to a function definition

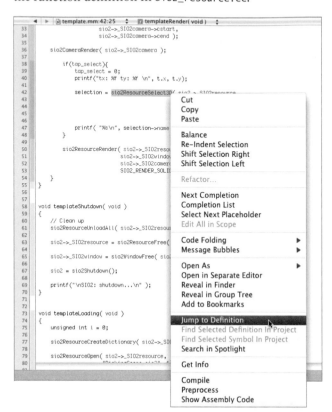

The code for the sio2ResourceSelect3D function looks like this:

```
2549   SIO2object *sio2ResourceSelect3D( SIO2resource *_SIO2resource,
2550                                     SIO2camera   *_SIO2camera,
2551                                     SIO2window   *_SIO2window,
2552                                     vec2         *_v )
2553   {
2554       unsigned int i = 0,
2555       selection = 0;
2556
2557       col4 col;
2558
2559       while( i != _SIO2resource->n_object )
2560       {
2561           SIO2object *_SIO2object =
2562                   ( SIO2object * )_SIO2resource->_SIO2object[ i ];
```

```
2563            sio2GenColorIndex( selection, _SIO2object->col );
2564
2565            if( sio2ObjectRender( _SIO2object,
2566                                  _SIO2window,
2567                                  _SIO2camera,
2568                                  0, 1 ) )
2569            { ++selection; }
2570            else
2571            { _SIO2object->col->a = 0; }
2572
2573            ++i;
2574        }
2575
2576        glReadPixels( ( int )_v->x,
2577                      ( int )_v->y,
2578                      1, 1,
2579                      GL_RGBA, GL_UNSIGNED_BYTE, &col );
2580
2581        if( !col.a )
2582        { return NULL; }
2583
2584        i = 0;
2585        while( i != _SIO2resource->n_object )
2586        {
2587            SIO2object *_SIO2object =
2588                    ( SIO2object * )_SIO2resource->_SIO2object[ i ];
2589            if( !memcmp( &col, _SIO2object->col, 4 ) )
2590            { return _SIO2object; }
2591
2592            ++i;
2593        }
2594
2595        return NULL;
2596  }
```

void **sio2GenColorIndex**(unsigned int *index*, col4 *col*)

This function generates an array of unique RGBA colors. The *index* value determines how many colors are generated, and the generated colors are stored in the color array col.

After declaring the necessary variables, the function begins looping through all of the objects in the scene on line 2559 using the SIO2resource->n_object value from the resource manager. This value holds the number of objects in the scene, so the i value in this loop will iterate through all the objects. The `sio2GenColorIndex` function assigns a unique color to each object, replacing the object's original color. You can dig into this function the same way you did before, but for the purpose of this description, it's enough to know generally what's being done. The first color has R, G, and B values of 0, and subsequent colors increment the B value by 1.

The `sio2ObjectRender` function on line 2565 renders the frame to the OpenGL color buffer. The conditional here is to ensure that objects intended to be invisible are given `_SIO2object->col->a` values of 0 so that they will not be selected later.

On line 2576, `glReadPixels` is called. This is an OpenGL ES function that takes the coordinate values of a location on the screen, in this case the touch point, and assigns the RGBA values of the point to a variable. In this case, the `col` variable receives the color information.

Finally, the loop beginning at 2587 iterates through the objects, comparing their temporary color with the color of the current pixel, as assigned by `glReadPixels`. This comparison happens on line 2589. The `memcmp` C function compares two chunks of memory and returns zero if they are identical. The result of doing this is to return the object whose temporary color is identical to the pixel being touched. In this way, picking is accomplished without the need for any fancy spatial calculations other than the ones that come for free with rendering.

To see the `glReadPixels` and color assignment more vividly, try reading the pixels and printing out their output *before* the generation of the color index on line 2563 by inserting the following code before that line:

```
glReadPixels( ( int )_v->x,
              ( int )_v->y,
              1, 1,
              GL_RGBA, GL_UNSIGNED_BYTE, &col );
printf("r:%u, g:%u, b%:u", col.r, col.g, col.b)
```

This will print the original vertex colors of the planes. You can repeat the `printf` line after `glReadPixels` is called the second time to see how the values change. Be sure to delete these additions to the source code when you've gotten the idea.

Adding Picking to Hello3DWorld

Now you'll return to the `Hello3DWorld` project from Chapter 4 and add picking functionality to that application. If you followed the previous section, then adding picking to `Hello3DWorld` will be pretty straightforward, but there are two main complications. These are lighting and materials. Both lighting and materials influence the color of individual pixels in a way that the generated color assignment does not control. The way this needs to be dealt with is by disabling lighting and materials just before entering the picking function. Another difference is that for this application, selection will be done with a double tap because spinning the globe involves a single tap already.

The double-tap functionality is written into templateScreenTap by taking advantage of the sio2->_SIO2window->n_tap value, which holds the number of times the screen has been touched in rapid succession. Modify your templateScreenTap from what you finished with in Chapter 4 as follows:

```
void templateScreenTap( void *_ptr, unsigned char _state )
{
    if( _state == SIO2_WINDOW_TAP_DOWN ){
        start.x = sio2->_SIO2window->touch[ 0 ]->x;
        start.y = sio2->_SIO2window->touch[ 0 ]->y;
        if( sio2->_SIO2window->n_tap == 2 )
        {
            tap_select = 1;
        }
    }
}
```

Note that there is a new variable here: *tap_select*. You will need to declare this variable at the beginning of template.mm, just as you did in the picking example program from the previous section, with the line unsigned char *tap_select* = 0;. While you're at it, declare another variable called *message* in exactly the same way, as an unsigned char initialized to 0. The variable *message* will be used to determine which message to print to the screen, depending on what object has been tapped. You'll also want to declare a two-dimensional vector *t* to hold the x and y touch coordinates that will be passed to the selection function. Do this in the line just before the templateRender function definition, with the line vec2 t;.

The code for the actual selection is as follows:

```
if(tap_select){
        tap_select = 0;
        sio2LampResetLight();
        sio2MaterialReset();

        t.x = sio2->_SIO2window->touch[ 0 ]->x;
        t.y = sio2->_SIO2window->scl->y -sio2->_SIO2window->touch[ 0 ]->y;

        selection = sio2ResourceSelect3D( sio2->_SIO2resource,
                                sio2->_SIO2camera,
                                sio2->_SIO2window,
                                &t);
    if(selection){
        if(strcmp( selection->name, "object/Sphere" ) == 0)
        {
            message = 2;
```

```
                            }else{
                                message = 1;
                            }
                        }else{
                            message = 1;
                        }
                    }
                //font rendering code goes here
```

Most of this will be familiar from the previous section, with the exception of the two commands near the beginning of the code block: the call to sio2LampResetLight and the call to sio2MaterialReset. These functions respectively reset (that is to say, disable) the current lighting conditions and material settings. As mentioned previously, this is necessary to ensure that the generated picking colors on the objects are solid and (in Blender terminology) shadeless.

```
void sio2LampResetLight(SIO2resource *resource)
void sio2MaterialReset(SIO2resource *resource)
```

These functions disable and reset the machine states for lights and materials, respectively.

The conditional used to set the *message* value has two levels. The first checks if there is a selected object at all. The reason for this is that the background plane does not in fact cover the entire background of the view. A strip of screen real estate at the top and bottom of the view is empty, although you can't tell because the background plane is also black. If there is a selected object, then the line if(strcmp(*selection->name*, "object/ Sphere") == 0) is used to compare the name of the selection with the string representing the name of the sphere object. The strcmp C function compares strings and returns 0 if strings are identical. If that's the case, *message* gets a 2 value. In any other case, the background has been selected, so *message* gets a 1 value. It's not necessary to explicitly compare any other strings since there are only two possibilities.

At the moment, you haven't yet programmed any kind of feedback, so if you build and run your application, nothing will actually happen when you double-tap the screen. To test the application so far, try using the printf command to print the value of *message* to the console. I'll leave that as an exercise. You might need to go online to refresh your memory about how to print unsigned char values with printf, but it's good practice to hunt down that kind of information on your own. In the next section, you'll learn how to use bitmap fonts to print feedback from your application directly to the iPhone screen. When you do finally render the fonts, the code for rendering will begin immediately after the selection code block you just wrote, so for the time being, add a comment to mark the place where the font render code will go.

Working with Text and Fonts

OpenGL|ES is a low-level graphics programming API. On one hand, this means that the programmer has absolute control over every graphical element that appears on the screen, down to the pixel. On the other hand, however, it means that some of the things that you might take for granted from high-level programming frameworks—such as buttons, widgets, and text—must often be created nearly from scratch. The SIO2 engine makes a lot of this easier, but in the case of fonts, there is still a fair amount of setup to be done.

Bitmap Fonts

OpenGL|ES uses *bitmap fonts*, which are fonts represented in a single bitmap image. If you have worked with text in the BGE as described in my book *Mastering Blender* (Sybex, 2009), you already have seen a use of bitmap fonts. In OpenGL|ES game creation, bitmap fonts are widely used.

Several bitmap font files are included with the SIO2 SDK in the SIO2_SDK directory under data/SDK_textures. In the example to follow, you'll be using the default16x16. tga file as the font file. Drag that file to the Resources directory under Groups & Files in Xcode to make it accessible to your application.

Fonts and Materials in SIO2

SIO2 helps you to manage fonts much like it helps you to manage 3D assets. The SIO0font data type is used to store information about a font. It stores the font's material, size, and transformation data, among other things. As with any other data type, in order to use a font object in your program, you must declare a variable of the appropriate data type. Declare a font variable called _SIO2font_default near the beginning of your program, where the other variables are declared, and set it to NULL like this:

```
SIO2font *_SIO2font_default = NULL;
```

Loading Fonts

Loading fonts works a little bit differently than loading 3D resources because the font is not supplied by the .sio2 file but rather by a bitmap font image file. In this section, you'll look at the code to load the font you will later use to write a message to the screen. The code in this section goes into the definition of templateLoading. Specifically, place all of this code between the line

```
sio2ResetState();
```

and the lines

```
sio2->_SIO2camera = sio2ResourceGetCamera( sio2->_SIO2resource,
                                           "camera/Camera");
```

Aside from the addition of this code, the templateLoading definition will remain the same.

The font loading code to add begins with the declaration of three variables for three different SIO2 data types: SIO2image, SIO2material, and SIO2stream. The SIO2image will hold the bitmap font image. The SIO2material will hold the font's material (this is how the font gets its color attributes). Finally, the SIO2stream provides a data stream to enable the image data to be loaded into SIO2:

```
SIO2image       *_SIO2image        = NULL;
SIO2material    *_SIO2material      = NULL;

SIO2stream      *_SIO2stream        = NULL;
```

The next line opens the data stream with the bitmap font image as an argument and passes the stream to the *_SIO2stream* variable:

```
_SIO2stream = sio2StreamOpen( "default16x16.tga", 1 );
```

SIO2stream sio2StreamOpen(char *fname, unsigned char rel)

This function opens a data stream from the file with the name *fname*. The second argument, rel, determines whether a relative or an absolute path name is used when opening the file.

If all has gone well with opening the data stream, it is then used to load the image data into video memory. First an SIO2image is initialized with the same name as the image file, then the image data is passed from the stream to the SIO2image object, and then the image and its associated textures are bound using the sio2ImageGenId function. Once these steps are completed, the data stream is closed and the memory it used is released:

```
if( _SIO2stream )
{
    _SIO2image = sio2ImageInit( "default16x16.tga" );
    sio2ImageLoad( _SIO2image, _SIO2stream );
    sio2ImageGenId( _SIO2image, NULL, 0.0f );
    _SIO2stream = sio2StreamClose( _SIO2stream );
```

SIO2image sio2ImageInit(const char *image_name)

This function initializes an SIO2image structure with the name *image_name*.

Next, initialize the material using the font name as the material name. Set the material object's blend value to SIO2_MATERIAL_COLOR. This determines how the material's texture channels will mix. (You'll learn more about material blending in Chapter 6.) Next, the image object is assigned to the first channel of the SIO2material object:

```
_SIO2material = sio2MaterialInit( "default16x16" );
_SIO2material->blend = SIO2_MATERIAL_COLOR;

_SIO2material->_SIO2image[ SIO2_MATERIAL_CHANNEL0 ] = _SIO2image;
```

Once the material has been set up, it is time to construct the font itself. This begins with a call to sioFontInit, the initialization function for fonts (the _SIO2font_default_ variable to store the font has already been declared). The font object then receives the material that you just set up:

```
_SIO2font_default = sio2FontInit( "default16x16" );
_SIO2font_default->_SIO2material   = _SIO2material;
```

SIO2font **sio2FontInit**(const char *font_name)

This function initializes an empty SIO2font object with the name *font_name*.

The next few lines tell SIO2 how to interpret the font image. The _SIO2font_default->n _char_ value holds the number of characters per row in the bitmap image. The _SIO2font _default->size_ value holds the height in pixels of each character, and the _SIO2font_default-> space_ value determines how many pixels will be placed between letters in words:

```
_SIO2font_default->n_char   = 16;
_SIO2font_default->size  = 16.0f;
SIO2font_default->space  = 8.0f;
```

Once the details of the font have been assigned, sio2FontBuild is called with the SIO2font object as the argument to build the font. Finally, the conditional code block that began with if(_SIO2stream_){ is closed:

```
sio2FontBuild( _SIO2font_default );
}
```

void **sio2FontBuild**(SIO2font *font)

This function builds the SIO2font *font* by applying the font texture to individual letters according to the parameters that have been set for the font.

Rendering Fonts

Now that the font has been built in templateLoading, you can render it to the screen. The code for this takes place in templateRender, as you might have guessed. Insert the code at the place where you previously left the comment //font rendering code goes here.

The first step is to enter orthogonal render mode. You can learn more about what this means in Appendix B, but for the time being the important thing is that it is the render mode to use for two-dimensional rendering. For this reason, the SIO2 function for entering the mode is sio2WindowEnter2D:

```
sio2WindowEnter2D( sio2->_SIO2window, 0.0f, 1.0f );
```

```
void sio2WindowEnter2D(SIO2window *window, "oat cstart, "oat cend)
```

This function puts the SIO2window *window* into orthogonal render mode. The parameters
cstart and cend determine the location of the front and back clipping panes, defining the
depth of the view volume.

The next step is to position the text in the screen. You'll give it an x-coordinate value
of 100 and a y-coordinate of 420. Remember, y is counted from the bottom of the screen.

```
{
    _SIO2font_default->_SIO2transform->loc->x = 100.0f;
    _SIO2font_default->_SIO2transform->loc->y = 420.0f;
```

The color of the font and the content of the message printed depend upon the value of
the *message* variable, which in turn depends upon which object is tapped. A good control
structure to use in C for multiple-case scenarios is the *switch conditional*. With the switch
conditional, the value of the argument to switch is read, and when it matches a case clause,
the code for the corresponding case is executed. In the following example, when *message* is
1 the font material color is set to white and the text "Hello 3D Space" is printed using the
sio2FontPrint function. If *message* is 2, the material color is set to green and the text "Hello
3D World!" is printed. Cases in a switch conditional should always end with break;.

```
switch( message )
{
    case 1:
    {
        _SIO2font_default->_SIO2material->diffuse->x = 1.0f;
        _SIO2font_default->_SIO2material->diffuse->y = 1.0f;
        _SIO2font_default->_SIO2material->diffuse->z = 1.0f;
        _SIO2font_default->_SIO2material->diffuse->w = 1.0f;

        sio2FontPrint( _SIO2font_default,
                       SIO2_TRANSFORM_MATRIX_APPLY,
                       "Hello 3D Space!" );
        break;
    }

    case 2:
    {
        _SIO2font_default->_SIO2material->diffuse->x = 0.5f;
        _SIO2font_default->_SIO2material->diffuse->y = 1.0f;
        _SIO2font_default->_SIO2material->diffuse->z = 0.0f;
        _SIO2font_default->_SIO2material->diffuse->w = 1.0f;

        sio2FontPrint( _SIO2font_default,
```

```
                              SIO2_TRANSFORM_MATRIX_APPLY,
                              "Hello 3D World!" );

                         break;
                    }
               }
```

unsigned char **sio2FontPrint**(SIO2font *font*, unsigned char *use_matrix*, const char *fmt*)

This function prints to the screen the string in *fmt* using the font font. The use_matrix flag
determines whether the transformation matrix is bound or applied. Both of these options
have the same effect, but the former is faster because it takes advantage of the SIO2 engine
calculating the transformation once and reusing the same transformation rather than using
the standard GL operations.

When the message has been printed, reset the material and font for next time:

```
                    sio2MaterialReset();
                    sio2FontReset();
```

void **sio2FontReset**(void)

This function clears the currently bound fonts.

At this point, it would be a good idea to add a comment to indicate where the multi-
touch text feedback code introduced in the next section will go:

```
                    //multi-touch text feedback code will go here
               }
```

When all of the 2D text rendering is done, leave the 2D render mode:

```
                    sio2WindowLeave2D();
```

If everything has been entered correctly up until this point, you should be able to run
the application on your simulator or device and have the appropriate message appear
when the globe and the background are tapped, as shown in Figure 5.18.

It's also possible to create your own bitmap fonts, using the font builder software
included with the SIO2 SDK. To do this, find the F2IBuilder.jar executable in the
SIO2_SDK/exporter directory. When you run this file you'll be able to create bitmap fonts
from whatever fonts you have installed on your system, as shown in Figure 5.19. You can
download fonts from resources such as www.dafont.com, install them on your system, and
then create bitmap fonts using the SIO2 Font Builder.

Figure 5.18

Messages depending on where the screen is double-clicked

Figure 5.19

The Font Builder utility

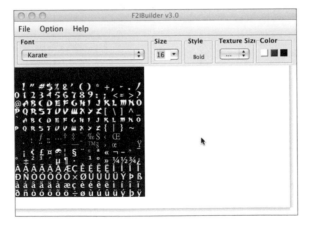

Using Multi-touch Functionality

One of the most exciting interface innovations of the iPhone and iPod Touch is the possibility to use multiple-touch input. You can easily access coordinates, tap, and move event data from multiple simultaneous touches. You have already worked with a single touch using *sio2->_SIO2window->touch*[0]. Multiple touches can be accessed simply by incrementing the index in the square brackets of the *touch[]* array as appropriate. The following code shows you how to do this. It should be inserted in the templateRender function at the place where you previously left the comment //multi-touch text feedback code will go here.

It begins by determining whether at least one touch has been registered. The *sio2->_SIO2window->n_touch* value holds the number of simultaneous touches that are presently registering:

```
if( sio2->_SIO2window->n_touch )

{
```

Next the location and color of the font are set:

```
_SIO2font_default->_SIO2transform->loc->y = 24.0f;
_SIO2font_default->_SIO2transform->loc->x = 80.0f;
_SIO2font_default->_SIO2material->diffuse->x = 1.0f;
_SIO2font_default->_SIO2material->diffuse->y = 0.2f;
_SIO2font_default->_SIO2material->diffuse->z = 0.0f;
_SIO2font_default->_SIO2material->diffuse->w = 1.0f;
```

Next, you'll iterate from zero to the value of *sio2->_SIO2window->n_touch* to produce the full range of indices for whatever number of touches are currently registered. For each index, you'll print out the "Touch #%d X:%.0f Y:%.0f" formatted message with the x-, y-, and z-coordinates. Then increment the *y* value of the font location by 20 pixels so that the next touch message is offset upward from the previous one. Finally, reset the material and then the font as shown:

```
unsigned int j = 0;
while( j != sio2->_SIO2window->n_touch )
{
        sio2FontPrint( _SIO2font_default,
        SIO2_TRANSFORM_MATRIX_APPLY,
        "Touch #%d X:%.0f Y:%.0f", j,
        sio2->_SIO2window->touch[ j ]->x,
        sio2->_SIO2window->touch[ j ]->y );

        _SIO2font_default->_SIO2transform->loc->y += 20.0f;
        ++j;
}
        sio2MaterialReset();
}
sio2FontReset();
```

Build and run your application now. You should be able to spin the globe, double-tap to pick the globe, and see printed feedback with the coordinates of multiple touches. If any details of the ordering or organization of the code presented here are unclear, refer to the full code of template.mm reprinted at the end of this chapter.

Packaging Your App

At this point, you've probably begun to wonder how to give your application its own unique name and icon to appear on the SpringBoard screen in the device. This is very simple to do. To change the name, open Edit Active Target from the Project menu. Find the Product Name field as shown in Figure 5.20 and edit it to contain the name you want to use for your app.

Figure 5.20

Giving the app a name

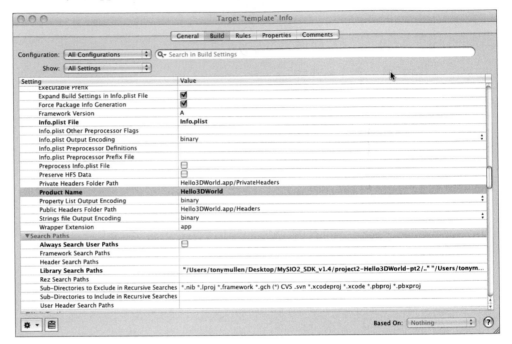

To create an icon, you can use any image you like. The only constraint is that the image must be exactly 57 pixels by 57 pixels in size. You can use image editing software such as GIMP to resize or crop any image. For the Hello3DWorld application, I simply rendered the scene in Blender and then cropped and resized the image to 57×57 as shown in Figure 5.21. I saved the file as helloworld.png. Like all other resources used by your app, this image must also be dragged and dropped into the Resources directory in the Groups & Files window in Xcode.

To get your application to use your icon file, open the application's Information Property List file by clicking Info.plist in the Resources directory of Groups & Files. This will bring the property list up in the Xcode property list editor. Enter your custom icon filename in the Icon File field as shown in Figure 5.22. Alternately, you can simply name your own icon Icon.png and name your app initialization screen default.png.

When you've done this, build and run your application again to see the new icon and application name on the SpringBoard screen.

Figure 5.21

An image to use for an icon

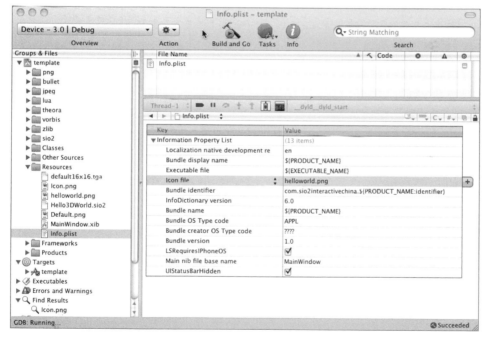

Figure 5.22

Assigning an icon file

You've covered a lot of ground in this chapter, and by now you should have a pretty good idea of how interactivity can be coded into your applications. In Chapter 6 you'll learn much more about creating an immersive 3D environment to explore.

The Complete Code

The full code for the Hello3DWorld `template.mm` file is reprinted here. Don't forget that in order for this to work properly, `EAGLview.mm` must be edited to set `templateLoading` as the initial rendering callback function, and `template.h` must have the declaration of `templateLoading` added, as described in this chapter and in Chapter 4.

```
/*
 *  template.mm
 *  template
 *
 *  Created by SIO2 Interactive on 8/22/08.
 *  Copyright 2008 SIO2 Interactive. All rights reserved.
 */

#include "template.h"

#include "../src/sio2/sio2.h"

float spin_factor = 0.0;
unsigned char message = 0;
unsigned char tap_select = 0;

SIO2font *_SIO2font_default = NULL;
SIO2object *selection = NULL;

vec2 t;
void templateRender( void )
{
    glMatrixMode( GL_MODELVIEW );
    glLoadIdentity();
    glClear( GL_DEPTH_BUFFER_BIT | GL_COLOR_BUFFER_BIT );

    static SIO2object *earth = sio2ResourceGetObject( sio2->_SIO2resource,
                                                "object/Sphere" );

    if( earth )
    {
        earth->_SIO2transform->rot->z += (spin_factor * 0.05f );
        sio2TransformBindMatrix( earth->_SIO2transform );
    }

    if( spin_factor > 0.0f )
    { spin_factor -= 1.0f; }

    else if(spin_factor < 0.0f )
    { spin_factor += 1.0f; }

    sio2LampEnableLight();
```

```
sio2CameraRender( sio2->_SIO2camera );
sio2ResourceRender( sio2->_SIO2resource,
                    sio2->_SIO2window,
                    sio2->_SIO2camera,
                    SIO2_RENDER_SOLID_OBJECT | SIO2_RENDER_LAMP);


if(tap_select){
    tap_select = 0;
    sio2LampResetLight();
    sio2MaterialReset();

    t.x = sio2->_SIO2window->touch[ 0 ]->x;
    t.y = sio2->_SIO2window->scl->y -
          sio2->_SIO2window->touch[ 0 ]->y;

    selection = sio2ResourceSelect3D( sio2->_SIO2resource,
                                      sio2->_SIO2camera,
                                      sio2->_SIO2window,
                                      &t);
    if(selection){
        if(strcmp( selection->name, "object/Sphere" ) == 0)
        {
            message = 2;
        }else{
            message = 1;
        }
    }else{
        message = 1;
    }
}

sio2WindowEnter2D( sio2->_SIO2window, 0.0f, 1.0f );
{
    _SIO2font_default->_SIO2transform->loc->x = 100.0f;
    _SIO2font_default->_SIO2transform->loc->y = 420.0f;
    switch( message )
    {
        case 1:
        {
            _SIO2font_default->_SIO2material->diffuse->x = 1.0f;
            _SIO2font_default->_SIO2material->diffuse->y = 1.0f;
            _SIO2font_default->_SIO2material->diffuse->z = 1.0f;
            _SIO2font_default->_SIO2material->diffuse->w = 1.0f;

            sio2FontPrint( _SIO2font_default,
                    SIO2_TRANSFORM_MATRIX_APPLY,
```

```
                                             "Hello 3D Space!" );
                    break;
                }

                case 2:
                {
                    _SIO2font_default->_SIO2material->diffuse->x = 0.5f;
                    _SIO2font_default->_SIO2material->diffuse->y = 1.0f;
                    _SIO2font_default->_SIO2material->diffuse->z = 0.0f;
                    _SIO2font_default->_SIO2material->diffuse->w = 1.0f;

                    sio2FontPrint( _SIO2font_default,
                                   SIO2_TRANSFORM_MATRIX_APPLY,
                                   "Hello 3D World!" );

                    break;
                }
            }
            sio2MaterialReset();
            sio2FontReset();
            if( sio2->_SIO2window->n_touch )
            {
                _SIO2font_default->_SIO2transform->loc->y = 24.0f;
                _SIO2font_default->_SIO2transform->loc->x = 80.0f;
                _SIO2font_default->_SIO2material->diffuse->x = 1.0f;
                _SIO2font_default->_SIO2material->diffuse->y = 0.2f;
                _SIO2font_default->_SIO2material->diffuse->z = 0.0f;
                _SIO2font_default->_SIO2material->diffuse->w = 1.0f;

                unsigned int j = 0;
                while( j != sio2->_SIO2window->n_touch )
                {
                    sio2FontPrint( _SIO2font_default,
                    SIO2_TRANSFORM_MATRIX_APPLY,
                    "Touch #%d X:%.0f Y:%.0f", j,
                    sio2->_SIO2window->touch[ j ]->x,
                    sio2->_SIO2window->touch[ j ]->y );

                    _SIO2font_default->_SIO2transform->loc->y += 20.0f;
                    ++j;
                }
                sio2MaterialReset();
            }
            sio2FontReset();
        }
        sio2WindowLeave2D();
    }

void templateShutdown( void )
```

```
{
    sio2ResourceUnloadAll( sio2->_SIO2resource );
    sio2->_SIO2resource = sio2ResourceFree( sio2->_SIO2resource );
    sio2->_SIO2window = sio2WindowFree( sio2->_SIO2window );
    sio2 = sio2Shutdown();
    printf("\nSIO2: shutdown...\n" );
}


void templateLoading ( void )
{
    unsigned int i = 0;
    sio2ResourceCreateDictionary( sio2->_SIO2resource );
    sio2ResourceOpen( sio2->_SIO2resource,
                     "Hello3DWorld.sio2", 1);

    while( i != sio2->_SIO2resource->gi.number_entry )
    {
        sio2ResourceExtract( sio2->_SIO2resource, NULL );
        ++i;
    }


    sio2ResourceClose( sio2->_SIO2resource );
    sio2ResourceBindAllImages( sio2->_SIO2resource );
    sio2ResourceBindAllMaterials( sio2->_SIO2resource );
    sio2ResourceBindAllMatrix( sio2->_SIO2resource );
    sio2ResourceGenId( sio2->_SIO2resource );
    sio2ResetState();

    SIO2image        *_SIO2image        = NULL;
    SIO2material     *_SIO2material      = NULL;
    SIO2stream       *_SIO2stream        = NULL;

    _SIO2stream = sio2StreamOpen( "default16x16.tga", 1 );

    if( _SIO2stream )
    {
        _SIO2image = sio2ImageInit( "default16x16.tga" );
        {
            sio2ImageLoad( _SIO2image, _SIO2stream );
            sio2ImageGenId( _SIO2image, NULL, 0.0f );
        }
        _SIO2stream = sio2StreamClose( _SIO2stream );

        _SIO2material = sio2MaterialInit( "default16x16" );
        {
            _SIO2material->blend = SIO2_MATERIAL_COLOR;
            _SIO2material->_SIO2image[ SIO2_MATERIAL_CHANNEL0 ] =
                           _SIO2image;
```

```
            }

            _SIO2font_default = sio2FontInit( "default16x16" );
            _SIO2font_default->_SIO2material   = _SIO2material;
            _SIO2font_default->n_char    = 16;
            _SIO2font_default->size  = 16.0f;
            _SIO2font_default->space  = 8.0f;
            sio2FontBuild( _SIO2font_default );
        }

        sio2->_SIO2camera = sio2ResourceGetCamera( sio2->_SIO2resource,
                                            "camera/Camera");

        sio2Perspective( sio2->_SIO2camera->fov,
                        sio2->_SIO2window->scl->x / sio2->_SIO2window->scl->y,
                        sio2->_SIO2camera->cstart,
                        sio2->_SIO2camera->cend );

        sio2->_SIO2window->_SIO2windowrender = templateRender;
}

vec2 start;
void templateScreenTap( void *_ptr, unsigned char _state )
{
    if( _state == SIO2_WINDOW_TAP_DOWN ){
        start.x = sio2->_SIO2window->touch[ 0 ]->x;
        start.y = sio2->_SIO2window->touch[ 0 ]->y;
        if( sio2->_SIO2window->n_tap == 2 )
        {
            tap_select = 1;
        }
    }
}

void templateScreenTouchMove( void *_ptr )
{
    if( sio2->_SIO2window->n_touch )
    {
        spin_factor = sio2->_SIO2window->touch[ 0 ]->x - start.x;
    }
}

void templateScreenAccelerometer( void *_ptr )
{
}
```

CHAPTER 6

Creating an Immersive Environment in SIO2

One of the most important and interesting aspects of 3D games and environments is how immersive the 3D world can become for the player or viewer. Whether it's a first-person adventure or an architectural walk-through, being able to explore and navigate a 3D virtual scene from within can be extremely engaging, even on a comparatively tiny handheld screen. In this chapter, you'll learn how to use Blender and the SIO2 engine to set up such an immersive environment and how to control the camera's movements to enable users to put themselves right in the middle of the scene.

- Modeling the ground and sky
- Creating an immersive environment in SIO2
- Exploring the environment with a moving camera
- The Complete Code

Modeling the Ground and the Sky

Before you can create an immersive interactive environment for your iPhone using SIO2, you need to create the 3D assets you need to build the environment. You'll begin by using Blender to create a simple grassy field and a realistic sky as a background. This will require minimal actual modeling, but it will make use of a few premade textures and will take advantage of Blender's excellent texture baking functionality.

All the textures you need can be found in the textures directory of the project directory for this chapter. The original grass texture is a free texture created by Bo Hammarberg and provided for unrestricted use on ShareCG at www.sharecg.com/pf/full_uploads.php?pf _user_name=hobobo&division_id=0. The sky map is from Blender user M@dcow's collection on the BlenderArtists online forum at http://blenderartists.org/forum/showthread .php?t=24038.

Once you've created the sky and ground and set up the camera, you'll turn to the SIO2 code to bring the scene into your iPhone and create a simple walk-through.

Creating a Ground Plane in Blender

You'll begin by creating a grassy field surrounded by rolling hills, with a deep hole near the middle of the field. To do this, fire up a new session of Blender and follow these steps:

1. Press the spacebar and choose Add → Mesh → Plane from the pop-up menu that appears, as shown in Figure 6.1. Depending on your default settings in Blender, the plane may be in Edit mode or in Object mode. If the plane is in Edit mode, tab into Object mode. Press Alt+G and Alt+R to clear the rotation and location so that the plane is situated as shown in Figure 6.2.

2. Tab into Edit mode and scale the mesh up as shown in Figure 6.3 by pressing the S key and then entering the number **32** to scale up by a factor of 32.

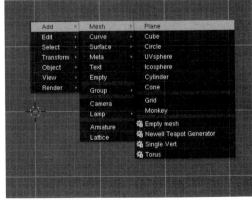

Figure 6.1
Adding a plane

3. Press the W key to bring up the special mesh editing menu, and then select Subdivide Multi as shown in Figure 6.4. Enter **18** in the dialog box for the number of cuts as shown in Figure 6.5, and then click OK.

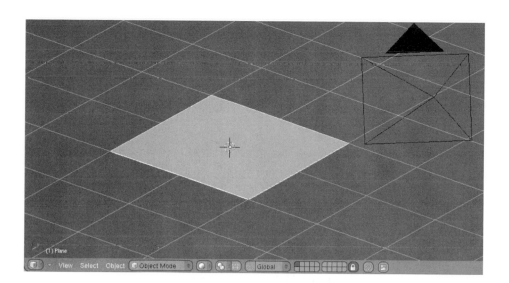

Figure 6.2

Clearing location and rotation

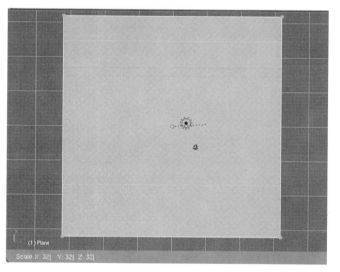

Figure 6.3

Scaling the plane up in Edit mode

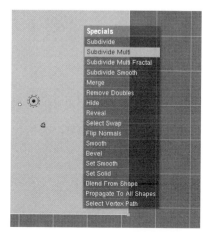

Figure 6.4

Selecting Subdivide Multi

Figure 6.5

Making 18 subdivision cuts

4. From the Mesh menu in the header of the 3D viewport, choose the menu entry Mesh → Faces→ Convert Quads To Triangles, as shown in Figure 6.6. The resulting triangulated mesh is shown in Figure 6.7.

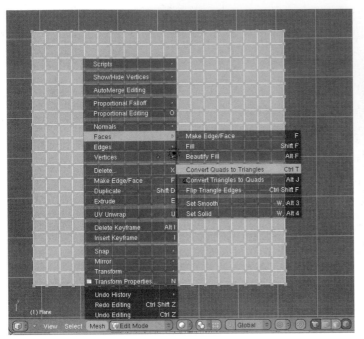

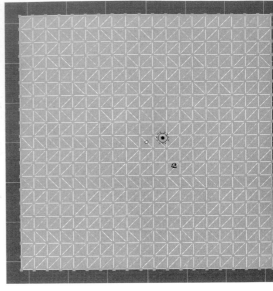

Figure 6.6
Converting quads to triangles

Figure 6.7
The triangulated mesh

5. To create the hills around the field, you'll use Blender's sculpt tool. Select Sculpt Mode from the Mode menu in the 3D viewport header as shown in Figure 6.8. Press the N key to bring up the Sculpt Properties floating window over the 3D viewport, and begin sculpting by using the mouse to draw the deformations onto the mesh, as shown in Figure 6.9. Continue sculpting until you've got a shape something like the

Figure 6.8
**Entering
Sculpt mode**

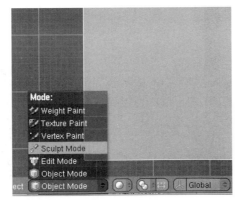

one shown in Figure 6.10. Click the Set Smooth button in the Links And Materials panel of the Edit buttons area as shown in Figure 6.11 to come up with a smoothly shaded shape like the one shown in Figure 6.12.

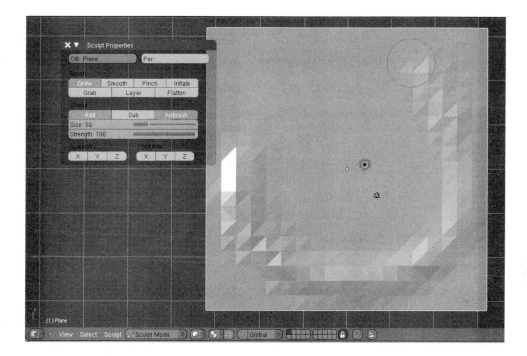

Figure 6.9

Sculpting a circular ridge

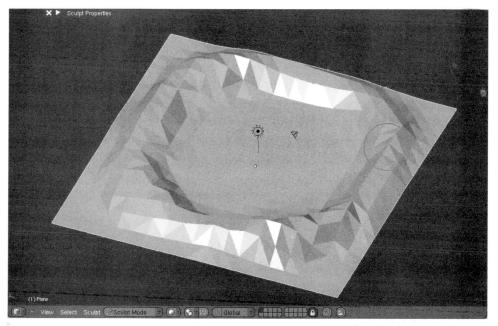

Figure 6.10

The sculpted mesh

Figure 6.11

The Set Smooth button

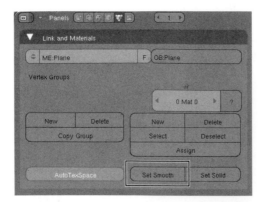

Figure 6.12

The sculpted mesh with smooth shading

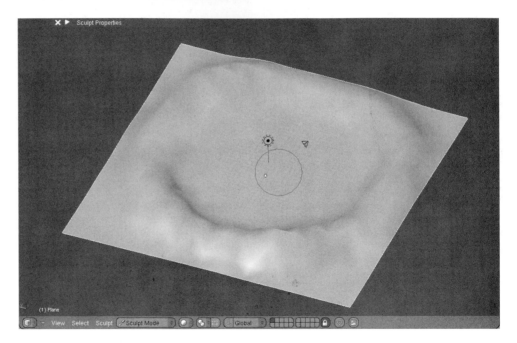

6. Press 7 on the number pad to view the object from above. Tab into Edit mode and press the B key to box-select an area of the mesh as shown in the first image in Figure 6.13, and then press the W key and choose Subdivide to subdivide the area as shown in the second image.

7. Activate proportional editing and select Smooth Falloff from the proportional editing menu shown in Figure 6.14. Select a single vertex in the middle of the area you just subdivided and translate the vertex directly downward as shown in Figure 6.15. You can adjust the size of the proportional editing tool's area of influence by using your mouse wheel or by using the + and - keys on your keyboard. The resulting mesh should look something like the one shown in Figure 6.16.

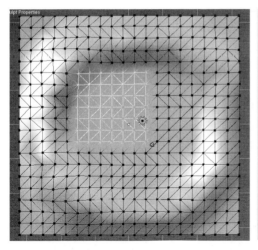

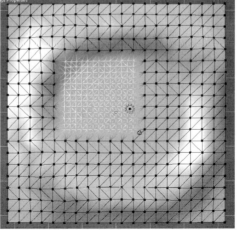

Figure 6.13

Subdividing a section of the mesh

Figure 6.14

The proportional editing tool with Smooth Falloff

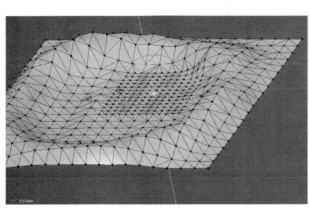

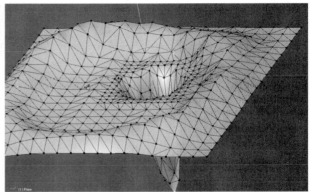

Figure 6.15

Modeling a hole by translating a vertex

Figure 6.16

The modeled mesh

8. Tab into Object mode and select the Lamp object by right-clicking on it. By default, this is an omnidirectional lamp. Change the lamp type to Sun in the Lamp buttons area. Sun lamps create uniform, parallel illumination for an entire scene. The location of the sun lamp does not matter, only its direction. Select Textured from the Draw Type menu on the 3D viewport header so that you can see the effect of the lighting on the scene; then rotate the sun so that it illuminates the scene as shown in Figure 6.17.

9. Add a material and a UV texture by clicking the New buttons in the appropriate places in the Link And Materials panel and the Mesh panel as shown in Figure 6.18.

Figure 6.17

Setting up the directional (sun) lamp

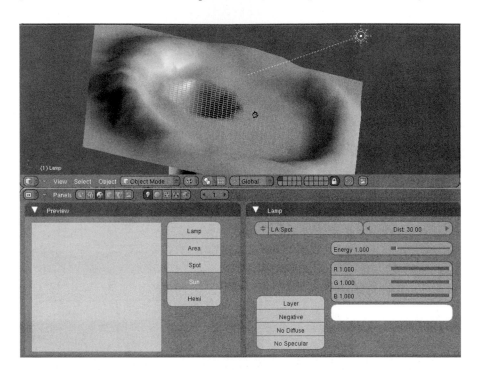

Figure 6.18

Adding a material and a UV texture

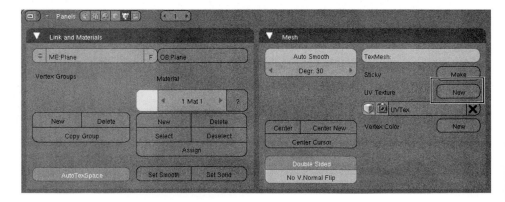

10. Open a UV/Image Editor window next to the 3D viewport, enter Edit mode, and select the entire mesh with the A key as shown in Figure 6.19. Put your mouse over the UV/Image Editor and press the E key to unwrap the mesh, as shown in Figure 6.20. The resulting unwrapped mesh is shown in Figure 6.21.

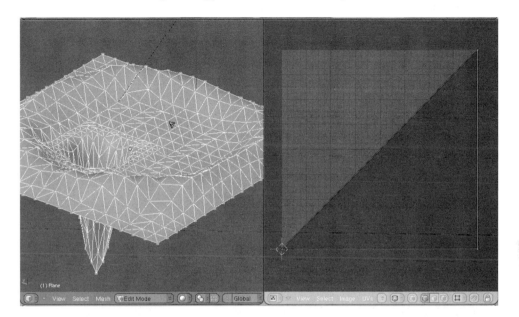

Figure 6.19

Preparing to unwrap the mesh

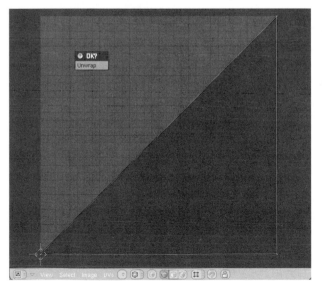

Figure 6.20

Unwrapping the mesh

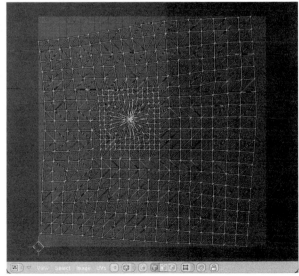

Figure 6.21

The unwrapped mesh

11. From the Image menu in the header of the UV/Image Editor, choose Image → Open as shown in Figure 6.22. Find the grass texture on your hard drive and open it, as shown in Figure 6.23.

Figure 6.22

Opening an image

Figure 6.23

Adding a grass texture

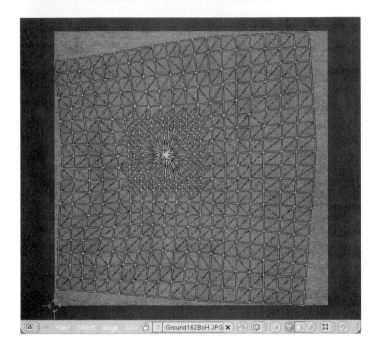

12. Add a texture to the Blender material on the ground object, as shown in Figure 6.24. On the Map Input tab, select UV for the mapping coordinates as shown in Figure 6.25. In the Texture buttons area, select Image from the Texture Type drop-down menu as shown in Figure 6.26. In the Image panel, select the grass texture image from the Load drop-down menu, as shown in Figure 6.27. In the Shaders tab of the Materials buttons area, set the specularity (Spec) value to about **0.048** and the hardness (Hard) to about **14** as shown in Figure 6.28.

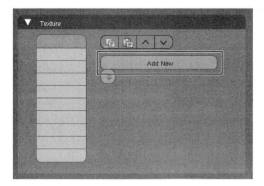

Figure 6.24

Adding a texture to the material

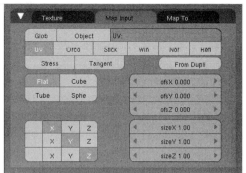

Figure 6.25

Selecting UV as the Map Input coordinates

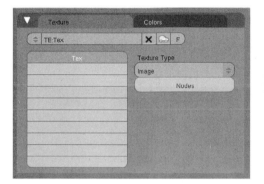

Figure 6.26

Selecting Image for the texture type

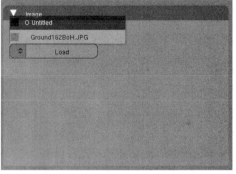

Figure 6.27

Selecting the grass texture

Figure 6.28

Setting specularity and hardness values

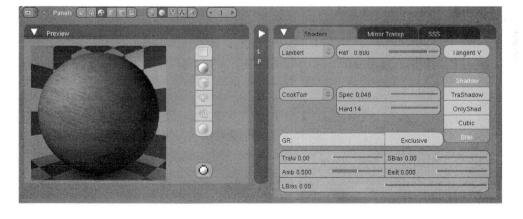

13. The material you've just created will be rendered. Now you will create another UV texture image to receive the baked texture that will result from the render. To do this, activate another UV texture by clicking the UV Texture New button on the

Mesh panel, as shown in Figure 6.29. Tab into Edit mode and choose Image → New from the Image menu in the header of the UV/Image Editor. In the New Image dialog box, enter **1024** for Width and Height and choose UV Test Grid as shown in Figure 6.30, and then click OK. The resulting UV test grid image will be mapped to the ground object as shown in Figure 6.31.

Figure 6.29

Adding a second UV texture

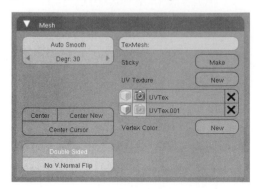

Figure 6.30

Creating a new test grid image in the UV Image Editor

Figure 6.31

The new image mapped onto the mesh

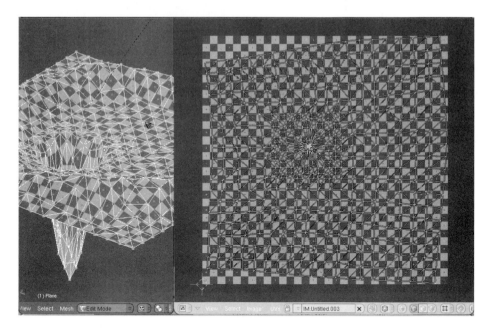

14. In the World buttons area, click the Ambient Occlusion button on the Amb Occ panel to activate ambient occlusion. Select the Both option as shown in Figure 6.32 to activate both additive and subtractive ambient occlusion. In the Render buttons area, click the BAKE button on the Bake tab to bake the full render as shown in Figure 6.33. When you do this, the full render, including lighting, will be baked to the active image texture, as shown in Figure 6.34. Be sure to save the image itself by

selecting Save from the Image menu of the UV/Image Editor. Call the saved image **baked-ground.jpg** and select JPEG from the file format menu in the header of the file browser.

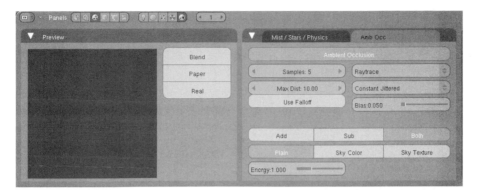

Figure 6.32

Turning on ambient occlusion

Figure 6.33

Baking the full render

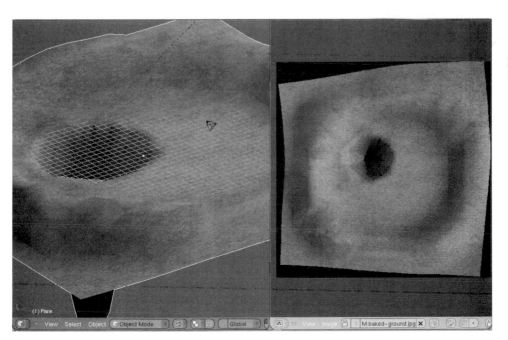

Figure 6.34

The baked texture

15. This newly created texture will be the one you will use in the SIO2 environment, so it must be associated with a material. In the Texture buttons subcontext of the Material buttons, replace the grass texture image with the baked_ground.jpg image by selecting the latter image from the Load drop-down menu as shown in Figure 6.35.

16. You're finished with the Lamp object. You can delete the lamp with the X key, or, if you'd prefer to keep it around just in case you want to tweak something later, you can simply put it on another layer by pressing the M key and selecting any layer besides Layer 1 to place it. As you've seen before, the SIO2 exporter ignores everything that's not on Layer 1, so this is a handy way to put unneeded objects out of the way.

Figure 6.35

Replacing the image on the material texture

Solid Ground for SIO2

You've now modeled and textured the ground. To get the effect you want in SIO2, you'll need to set the ground and the camera to be able to interact as physical objects. First, place the camera in the location and rotation you want it to be in when your walk-through begins. You can enter transformation values directly by pressing the N key to open up the Transform Properties floating panel, shown in Figure 6.36. The camera's transform values here are LocX: **10**, LocY: **–12**, LocZ: **1**, RotX: **90**, RotY:**0**, and RotZ: **0**.

Finally, set the Blender physics properties for the camera and the ground. Set these in the Logic buttons area (F4) as shown in Figure 6.37. The Camera object should have Bounds activated with Box selected, as shown on the left. The Plane object should have Static and Actor selected and its bounds should be Triangle Mesh, as shown on the right. You'll see more about how the physics simulation works when you look at the SIO2 code later in this chapter.

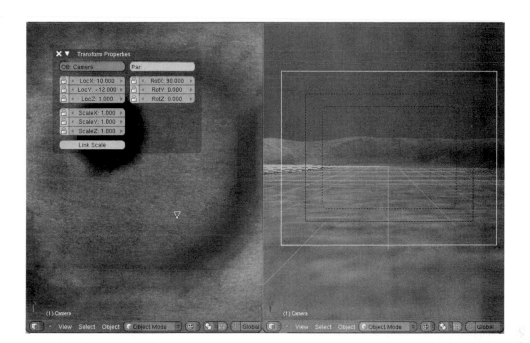

Figure 6.36

Location and rotation for the camera

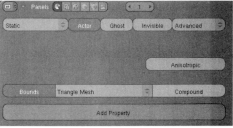

Figure 6.37

Physics properties for the camera and the ground

Creating a Convincing Sky Dome

You could start in right now with the SIO2 code, but if you did so, the background of the scene on your iPhone would be solid black. Since you're already working in Blender, you may as well go ahead and finish creating the background of the world. It also simplifies the discussion to get the modeling out of the way first and then turn to the coding.

Blender's world texture mapping system is able to handle several kinds of sky mapping, but most of these mappings cannot be translated directly into SIO2 (or for that matter, Blender's own game engine). When you create games either for the Blender Game Engine (BGE) or for SIO2, it is necessary to have your sky mapped onto a UV texture applied to a mesh. The method here for creating a sky dome is a simple but very effective way to convert an angular sky map into a UV map that can be used in this way. To do this, follow these steps:

1. Switch to an empty layer by clicking a layer button in the header of the 3D viewport. It doesn't matter which layer, but it should be one with nothing on it, as in Figure 6.38. You'll see shortly why you don't want other objects on this layer. Add a UV sphere by pressing the spacebar and selecting Add → Mesh → UVsphere as shown in Figure 6.39. Enter **8** for both Segments and Rings in the sphere parameters dialog box, as shown in Figure 6.40, and then click OK. Make sure you're in Object mode, and then enter Alt+G and Alt+R to clear location and rotation.

Figure 6.38

Switching to an empty layer

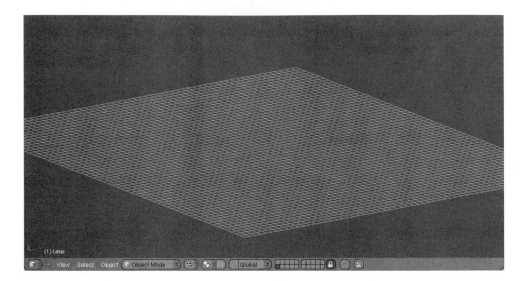

Figure 6.39

Adding a UV sphere

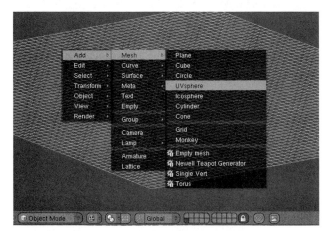

Figure 6.40

Parameters for the sphere

2. If you're in perspective view mode, toggle into orthogonal view by pressing 5 on the number pad, and then press 1 on the number pad to look down the y-axis at the sphere. Tab into Edit mode. Press B to activate the box-select tool and select the lowermost rings; then press the X key and choose Vertices from the delete menu to delete the vertices, as shown in Figure 6.41. Tab into Object mode and set smooth shading as shown in Figure 6.42.

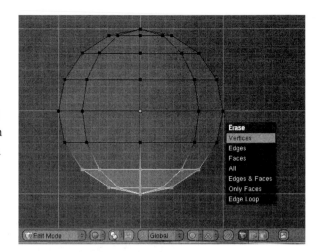

3. Add a new material by clicking New in the Material buttons area on the Link And Materials panel, shown in Figure 6.43. This new material needs two main properties. First, it needs to be shadeless. Set it as shadeless in the Material panel as shown in Figure 6.44. The second thing this material needs is ray mirroring. On the Mirror Transp tab, click Ray Mirror to activate ray-traced mirroring, and set the RayMir value to the maximum possible value of 1 as shown in Figure 6.45.

Figure 6.41

Deleting the lowermost rings

Figure 6.42

Setting smooth shading

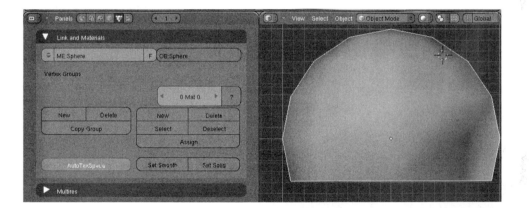

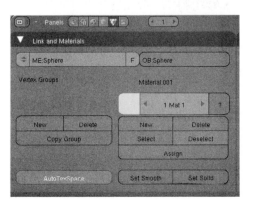

Figure 6.43

Adding a new material

Figure 6.44

Setting the material to shadeless

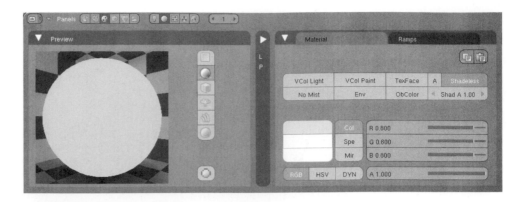

Figure 6.45

Setting ray mirroring to the maximum value

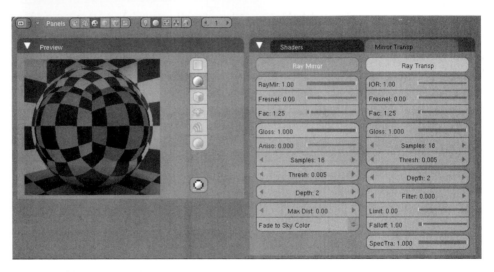

Figure 6.46

Adding a world texture

4. Now turn to the world buttons to add a sky texture. To do this, click the Add New button on the Texture And Input tab as shown in Figure 6.46. In the Texture buttons area, select Image as the texture type as shown in Figure 6.47 and load the angmap12.jpg image from your hard drive as shown in Figure 6.48. The complete settings for the world texture are shown in Figure 6.49. Note that the Real, Hori, and AngMap options are selected.

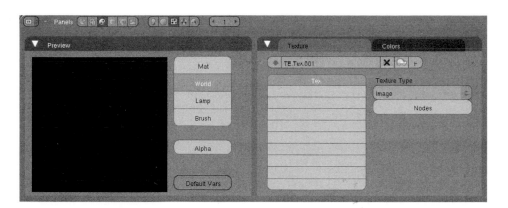

Figure 6.47

Selecting Image texture type

Figure 6.48

Loading the sky map

Figure 6.49

Settings for the world texture

5. Blender uses this angular sky map as its background when it renders. Because the sphere's surface is a perfect ray mirror, this sky map is reflected in the surface of the mirror, as you can see by doing a Shift+P render preview, shown in Figure 6.50. The trick is to bake this reflection onto a UV image texture. To do this, you must add a UV texture to the sphere object by clicking the New button at the UV Texture entry on the Mesh panel, shown in Figure 6.51. Unwrap the sphere as usual by pressing the A key to select all vertices in Edit mode and then pressing the E key in the UV/Image Editor. The resulting unwrapped sphere is shown in Figure 6.52.

6. In the UV/Image Editor header menu, choose Image → New, and create a 1024×1024-pixel UV test grid image. The result of this is shown in Figure 6.53.

Figure 6.50

The reflective material in render preview

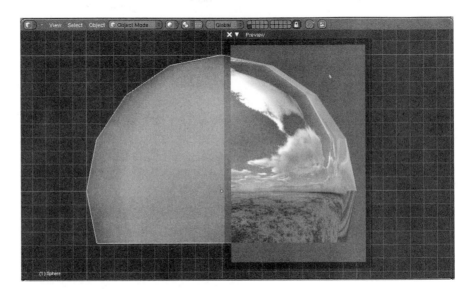

Figure 6.51

Adding a UV texture

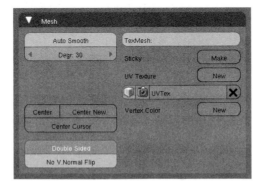

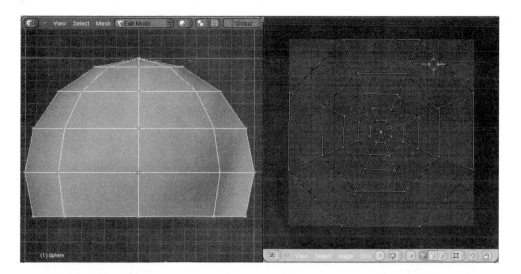

Figure 6.52

The unwrapped sphere

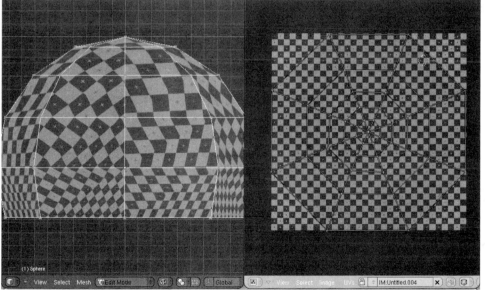

Figure 6.53

The sphere with a UV test grid mapped to it

Figure 6.54

Baking the full render

7. Go to the Bake panel in the Render buttons area. Ensure that Full Render is selected as shown in Figure 6.54 and click the BAKE button. After a few moments, the result of the bake will appear, as shown in Figure 6.55. Save this image as a JPEG file called baked-sky.jpg as shown in Figure 6.56, just as you saved the baked-ground.jpg file previously.

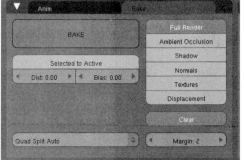

Figure 6.55
**The result of
the bake**

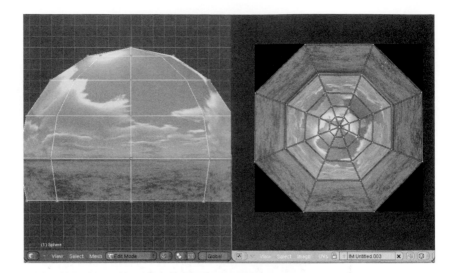

Figure 6.56
Saving the image

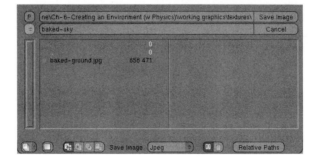

8. Flip the normals of the dome by selecting all with the A key while in Edit mode, then pressing the W key to bring up the mesh special editing menu and selecting Flip Normals, as shown in Figure 6.57. This will result in the texture being projected inward, as shown in Figure 6.58, which is appropriate for a sky dome.

Figure 6.57
**Flipping
the normals**

Figure 6.58
**The textured sphere
with inward-
pointing normals**

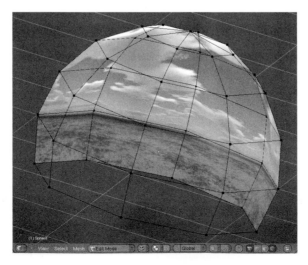

9. Tab into Object mode, press M, and then choose the Layer 1 button (the leftmost square button in the top row of the two layer buttons) from the layer selection dialog as shown in Figure 6.59. Click OK. Go to Layer 1 by clicking the corresponding square layer button in the header of the 3D viewport. In Layer 1 you will see both the ground and the sky objects together, with the sky disproportionately small in comparison, as shown in Figure 6.60. With the sky object selected, tab into Edit mode and scale the sky dome up as shown in Figure 6.61. The completed scene with both sky and ground should look something like the one shown in Figure 6.62.

Figure 6.59

Placing the sky dome on Layer 1

Figure 6.60

The sky dome out of proportion to the ground

Figure 6.61

Scaling the sky dome in Edit mode

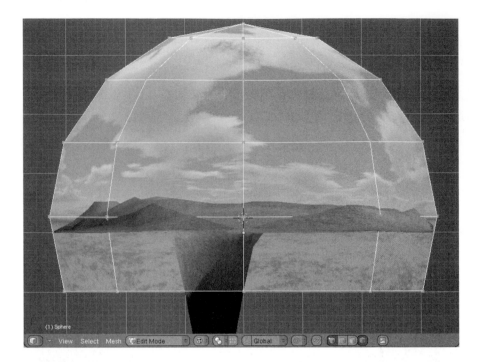

Figure 6.62

The completed scene

10. As you did previously with the ground, it's necessary to ensure that the texture is associated with the sky object's material and that the material settings are correct. First disable the ray mirroring on the material by clicking the Ray Mirror button, as shown in Figure 6.63. Then add a new texture to the material as shown in

Figure 6.64. In the Texture buttons area, make the texture an Image texture and load the baked sky image, as shown in Figure 6.65. Set the Map To coordinates to UV, as shown in Figure 6.66.

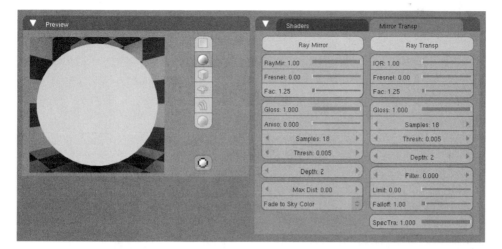

Figure 6.63
Disabling mirroring

Figure 6.64
Adding a material texture

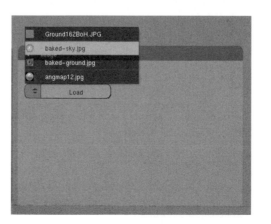

Figure 6.65
Selecting the baked sky image

Figure 6.66

**Setting map
input to UV**

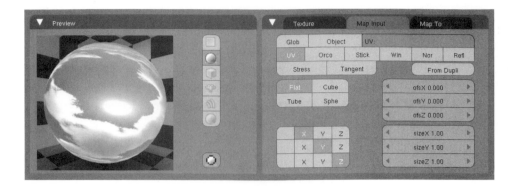

You're all finished with the sky dome now. If you press 0 on the number pad, you can enter the camera view. The scene should look something like the one shown in Figure 6.67 when you look at it from the camera's point of view.

Figure 6.67

**The scene from the
camera view**

Exporting the `.sio2` File

Before you can use this scene in the SIO2 engine, you need to export it to a `.sio2` file, just as you did previously with the scene for the Hello3DWorld app.

To specify the name of the `.sio2` file, change the value of the SCE: field in the User Preferences header at the top of the Blender screen, shown in Figure 6.68. By default, this value is Scene, so the exported file will be called `Scene.sio2` by default. Change this value to **ImmersiveScene** to make it clear which file you're dealing with.

Figure 6.68

The SCE: field

The process for exporting is identical to the process described in the last section of Chapter 3. Be sure that all and only the objects you want to export are located on Layer 1 and that they are all selected. You can select all objects by pressing the A key in Object mode. If you don't remember the details of running the exporter script, review the end of Chapter 3 for the details. You should wind up with a file called `ImmersiveScene.sio2` in your project directory as well as an uncompressed subdirectory called `ImmersiveScene`. You can browse this directory to make sure that all the objects, materials, and images have been correctly exported.

Creating an Immersive Environment in SIO2

In the following sections, you'll bring contents of `ImmersiveScene.sio2` into the SIO2 engine environment. The code in these sections is adapted from the official SIO2 Tutorial 6.1. After you've gone through this chapter and Chapter 7, you can study that tutorial and the following tutorial, number 6.2, to see some alternative approaches and to read further commentary on the code.

To bring the scene into SIO2, you first need to make the changes to `EAGLview.mm` and `template.h` that are necessary to add the `templateLoading` function to `template.mm`.

In `EAGLview.mm`, change the line

```
sio2->_SIO2window->_SIO2windowrender = templateRender;
```

to

```
sio2->_SIO2window->_SIO2windowrender = templateLoading;
```

In `template.h`, add the line

```
void templateLoading( void );
```

among the other function declarations.

You'll need to return to `EAGLview.mm` to make a few more changes to set up the physics simulation, but for now turn to `template.mm`.

Setting Up the Scene

You'll need to make changes to several functions in `template.mm`. As always, you'll find the complete code for the file at the end of the chapter.

The *templateLoading* Function

The first function to look at is `templateLoading`. This function begins in the usual way, by loading the resources from the appropriate `.sio2` file and binding them:

```
void templateLoading( void )
{
    unsigned int i = 0;

    sio2ResourceCreateDictionary( sio2->_SIO2resource );
```

```
sio2ResourceOpen( sio2->_SIO2resource,
                        "ImmersiveScene.sio2", 1 );

while( i != sio2->_SIO2resource->gi.number_entry )
{
    sio2ResourceExtract( sio2->_SIO2resource, NULL );
    ++i;
}

sio2ResourceClose( sio2->_SIO2resource );
sio2ResetState();

sio2ResourceBindAllImages( sio2->_SIO2resource );
sio2ResourceBindAllMaterials( sio2->_SIO2resource );
sio2ResourceBindAllMatrix( sio2->_SIO2resource );
```

This code should all look familiar because it's essentially identical to what you saw in
the `Hello3DWorld` application. Don't forget to place `ImmersiveScene.sio2` into the `Resources`
directory in the Groups & Files window of Xcode.

The next line introduces new material:

```
sio2ResourceBindAllPhysicObjects( sio2->_SIO2resource,
                                      sio2->_SIO2physic );
```

---

void **sio2ResourceBindAllPhysicObjects**(SIO2resource *resource*, SIO2physic *physics*)

This function binds all objects with collision and physical characteristics handled by the
resource manager *resource*. The behavior of the physical objects is determined by the properties of the physical world stored in the SIO2physic structure *physics*.

This line binds the objects with physics simulation properties associated with them.
In this case, both the ground and the camera have physical bounds associated with them.
The `sio2->_SIO2physic` object is an SIO2 physics structure. This must be initialized first,
which has not yet been discussed. Your application will crash if you try to run this without initializing this structure. Later in the chapter you will see how a physics structure is
initialized and assigned in the `EAGLview.mm` file. For now, it's enough to know that this is
the data structure that carries the physical properties of a specific environment.

The next few lines of `templateLoading` are also familiar:

```
sio2ResourceGenId( sio2->_SIO2resource );

sio2->_SIO2camera =
        ( SIO2camera * )sio2ResourceGet( sio2->_SIO2resource,
```

```
                        SIO2_CAMERA,
                        "camera/Camera" );


    sio2Perspective( sio2->_SIO2camera->fov,
                        sio2->_SIO2window->scl->x /
                            sio2->_SIO2window->scl->y,
                        sio2->_SIO2camera->cstart,
                        sio2->_SIO2camera->cend );
```

These lines set up the camera and the perspective view. They are also identical to corresponding lines in Hello3DWorld.

The next lines contain some more new material:

```
    sio2->_SIO2camera->rad = 1.0f;
    sio2->_SIO2camera->mass    = 75.0f;
    sio2->_SIO2camera->height = 1.84f;

    sio2PhysicAddCamera( sio2->_SIO2physic,
                            sio2->_SIO2camera );

    sio2->_SIO2camera->_btRigidBody->setFriction( (btScalar)0.50 );
    sio2->_SIO2camera >_btRigidBody->setRestitution( (btScalar)0.0 );
```

These lines begin to set physical properties for the camera. The first line exits the function if no camera has been set. The next lines set the radius, mass, and height physical properties for the camera. Radius and height values are measured in meters, and the mass value is measured in kilograms. These are the values that the Bullet physics simulation will use for calculations on the camera object. The next line adds the camera to the physics simulation. The last two lines set the friction and restitution values for the camera's rigid body simulation. Friction determines how easily the camera moves over physical surfaces. For example, a higher friction value would prevent the camera from sliding down a slope, while a lower friction value would allow the camera to slide easily. The restitution value determines how much energy is lost when the object impacts another object, affecting the first object's bounciness. A zero value for restitution will cause the object to stop dead on impact.

The next two lines are necessary to begin the physics simulation:

```
    sio2PhysicPlay( sio2->_SIO2physic );
    sio2->_SIO2window->fps = 30;
```

---

void **sio2PhysicPlay**(SIO2physic *physics*)

This function launches the SIO2physic structure *physics* and activates the physical simulation properties of the world.

The call to sio2PhysicPlay launches the physics simulator, and the following line initializes the first frames-per-second (fps) value to 30. Calculating the simulation step from the delta time value gives good results, but the method encounters a divide-by-zero error on the first frame if the fps is not set manually in advance, so this avoids the problem.

Finally, templateRender is assigned as the render callback function, just as in previous examples:

```
sio2->_SIO2window->_SIO2windowrender = templateRender;

}
```

The *templateRender* Function

The templateRender function without camera motion is very simple. However, there is one piece of functionality that you haven't seen before, and that is the ability to work with the orientation of the screen. In this application, you will be able to switch between portrait and landscape screen orientation by double-tapping the screen. To set that up, a global variable must be defined. Before you begin defining any related functions, declare the variable *screen_orientation* as an unsigned char initialized to 0 at the beginning of the file, where other global variables have been defined just after the introductory comments, like this:

```
unsigned char screen_orientation = 0;
```

You can now use that variable in your code. The templateRender code, without camera movement, looks like this:

```
void templateRender( void )
{
    glMatrixMode( GL_MODELVIEW );
    glLoadIdentity();

    glClear( GL_DEPTH_BUFFER_BIT );

    if( screen_orientation )
    { sio2WindowEnterLandscape3D(); }

//camera movement code goes here

    sio2CameraRender( sio2->_SIO2camera );
    sio2CameraUpdateFrustum( sio2->_SIO2camera );

    sio2ResourceCull( sio2->_SIO2resource,
                      sio2->_SIO2camera );

    sio2ResourceRender( sio2->_SIO2resource,
                        sio2->_SIO2window,
```

```
                    sio2->_SIO2camera,
                    SIO2_RENDER_SOLID_OBJECT);

        if( screen_orientation )
            { sio2WindowLeaveLandscape3D(); }
    }
```

Note how *screen_orientation* is used. If the value is 1, sio2WindowEnterLandscape3D is called, and the corresponding sio2WindowLeaveLandscape3D is called when rendering is finished. This function does exactly what it says: It causes the screen to be rendered in landscape format.

Another thing to note is the call to glClear. The GL_COLOR_BUFFER_BIT option is included in the default template code for this call. You may recall from the Hello3DWorld example why this option can be deleted in this case. In that example, a solid plane covered the rendered background. In this example, the rendered background will always be taken up by the sky dome texture and therefore will be redrawn for every frame. For this reason it is not necessary to clear the color buffer.

Finally, take note of the //camera movement code goes here comment. This is a placeholder for code that will be described later in the chapter for controlling the movement of the camera.

The *templateScreenTap* Function

The templateScreenTap function is as follows:

```
    void templateScreenTap( void *_ptr, unsigned char _state )
    {
        if( _state == SIO2_WINDOW_TAP_DOWN && sio2->_SIO2window->n_tap == 2 )
        {
            screen_orientation = !screen_orientation;
            if( screen_orientation )
            {
                [[UIApplication sharedApplication]
                setStatusBarOrientation:
                    UIInterfaceOrientationLandscapeRight
                animated: YES]; }
             else
            {
                [[UIApplication sharedApplication]
                setStatusBarOrientation: UIInterfaceOrientationPortrait
                animated: YES]; }
        }

        //camera movement code goes here

    }
```

The conditional begins by assessing whether a double-tap has occurred. It does this by checking whether the touch state is SIO2_WINDOW_TAP_DOWN and the tap count in sio2->_ SIO2window->n_tap is 2. If this is the case, the current value of the *screen_orientation* variable is negated, which results in toggling the value on and off. Depending on the resulting value, the screen is set to either landscape mode or portrait mode. You might notice that the code inside this last conditional looks different from most of the other code you've worked with so far. This is because those code blocks are some relatively rare examples of cases where Objective-C proper is used in template.mm. Whereas most of the code you have been working with in SIO2 has been based on C or in some cases C++, these code blocks call native iPhone functions and are therefore written in Objective-C. This serves as a reminder that C, C++, and Objective-C code is seamlessly integrated in .mm files. It's beyond the scope of this book to give a complete introduction to the syntax of Objective-C clauses, but in this case, it's enough to know that this code sets the application to landscape rendering in the first case and portrait in the second case.

Finally, as was done in templateRender, a comment is inserted as a placeholder where you'll later add the code dealing with camera movement.

The templateScreenTouchMove function is entirely concerned with camera movement, so for the moment you can leave the definition empty; you'll return to it shortly.

Setting Up Physics Simulation

There are a few more changes that need to be made to the EAGLview.mm file in order to activate physics simulation.

In the drawView function, the first block of code needs to have one new function call, to the sio2PhysicRender function. The resulting block of code is identical to the template code except for that function call, as shown here:3

```
if( sio2->_SIO2window->_SIO2windowrender )
{
    sio2PhysicRender( sio2->_SIO2physic,
                        1.0f / 60.0f, 1 );
    sio2->_SIO2window->_SIO2windowrender();
    sio2WindowSwapBuffers( sio2->_SIO2window );
}
```

void **sio2PhysicRender**(SIO2physic *physics*, "oat *timestep*, int *pass*)

This function advances the physical simulation according to the real-time interval represented by *timestep*. The *pass* value determines how fine-grained the simulation is temporally, that is, how many increments are calculated for each timestep. A high value for pass will yield a more precise and sensitive simulation. A low value, for example, may result in fast-moving objects passing right through collision objects.

The `sio2PhysicRender` function advances the physical simulation by one timestep. The number of timesteps advanced by this function call is determined by the third argument value, and the real-time duration of a single timestep (in seconds) is determined by the second argument to the function.

In the `createFrameBuffer` function, the code block beginning with `if( !sio2 )` needs to have some changes made.

At the beginning of the code block, a three-dimensional vector variable needs to be declared to represent the force of gravity, as follows:

```
vec3 gravity = { 0.0f, 0.0f, -9.8f };
```

The vector's x, y, and z values are set to mimic the natural force of gravity, which is approximately 9.8 (m/s²) along the negative z-axis (in other words, down).

The next few lines remain unchanged from the default template:

```
sio2Init( &tmp_argc, tmp_argv );
sio2InitGL();
sio2->_SIO2window = sio2WindowInit();
sio2WindowUpdateViewport( sio2->_SIO2window,
                          0, 0, backingWidth,
                          backingHeight );
sio2->_SIO2resource = sio2ResourceInit( "default" );
```

After these lines, the following two new lines must be added:

```
sio2->_SIO2physic = sio2PhysicInit( "earth" );
sio2PhysicSetGravity( sio2->_SIO2physic, &gravity );
```

SIO2physic **sio2PhysicInit**(char *name*)

This function initializes and returns a new SIO2physic structure with the name *name*. The SIO2physic structure holds the physical parameters of the virtual environment, such as the force and direction of gravity.

---

void **sio2PhysicSetGravity**(SIO2physic *physics*, vec3 *gravity*)

This function sets the gravity value of the SIO2physic structure *physics*. Gravity is represented by the three-dimensional vector gravity. The gravity force setting can be any strength in any direction, but natural Earth gravity is approximately –10 along the z-axis.

The first line initializes a physics system and assigns it to the `sio2->_SIO2physic` variable. You've already seen how this variable is accessed in `templateLoading`. The next line sets the gravity for the physics system.

Everything else in the function is the same as in the default template, except one last thing. This example will not be using the accelerometer in any way, so it is not necessary to assign the accelerometer callback function. You can simply comment out the line that does that, like this:

```
//              sio2->_SIO2window->_SIO2windowaccelerometer =
//                              templateScreenAccelerometer;
```

Note that the line of code I refer to is broken into two lines here in order to fit properly on the book's page. If this is how it appears in your code, you need to comment both lines as shown, but probably it will appear in your code as a single line to be commented out.

At last, you're at a point where you can build and run your application! When you do, you should see a scene something like the one shown in Figure 6.69. The ground and sky should look right, and double-tapping the screen should result in the orientation changing. However, that's all the interaction you'll have. You won't be able to move the camera around to explore the scene. To do that, you'll need to add a bit more code.

Figure 6.69

Running the app

Exploring the Environment with a Moving Camera

Moving the camera around will require modifying templateRender, templateScreenTap, and templateScreenTouchMove. Furthermore, several global variables need to be declared at the top of the template.mm file. Declare the following variables as shown:

```
char  MOV_DIR = 0;
float ROT_Z = 0.0f;
float speed = 0.0f;
```

These three variables will hold the direction the camera is moving, the degree of rotation around the z-axis, and the speed the camera is moving, respectively.

Movement in *templateRender*

In templateRender, insert the following code at the point where the //camera movement code goes here comment was left as a placeholder:

```
if( ROT_Z )
{
    sio2TransformRotateZ( sio2->_SIO2camera->_SIO2transform,
                          ROT_Z );
}
if( MOV_DIR  )
{
    sio2->_SIO2camera->_btRigidBody->setActivationState(
                                        ACTIVE_TAG
                                    );
    sio2->_SIO2camera->_btRigidBody->setLinearVelocity(
        btVector3(
            ( MOV_DIR * sio2->_SIO2camera->_SIO2transform->dir->x )
                                                                    *
speed,
            ( MOV_DIR * sio2->_SIO2camera->_SIO2transform->dir->y )
                                                                    *
speed,
                sio2->_SIO2camera->_btRigidBody->getLinearVelocity()[ 2 ]
                )); 
}
```

---

void **sio2TransformRotateZ**(SIO2transform *transform*, "oat *rotz*)

This function adds a rotation value of *rotz* around the z-axis to the SIO2transform structure *transform*. This results in the rotation of the object associated with the transform when the object is rendered.

The first conditional checks for a value for ROT_Z and then rotates the camera using sio2TransformRotate with the camera's transform object and the ROT_Z value as its arguments.

The second conditional first checks for the MOV_DIR value. If there is a non-zero value for MOV_DIR, rigid body physical simulation is activated for the camera. The next line sets the linear velocity for the rigid body camera. The MOV_DIR value will be either 1 or -1, so this value will determine whether the camera moves forward or backward. The argument to setLinearVelocity is a Bullet vector with the x and y values calculated based on the MOV_DIR and *speed* variable values. The third argument simply accesses the camera's own current linear velocity along z, so it does not change.

The actual values of MOV_DIR and *speed* will be set interactively using the touch functions.

Movement in *templateScreenTap*

Before defining the required functionality in templateScreenTap, declare a two-dimensional vector called *start*. This should be declared immediately before the templateScreenTap function definition so that it is easy to remember where it's being used. The declaration looks like this:

```
vec2 start;
```

In the templateScreenTap function definition, insert the following code in place of the //camera movement code goes here comment you left previously:

```
if( _state == SIO2_WINDOW_TAP_DOWN )
{
    start.x = sio2->_SIO2window->touch[ 0 ]->x;
    start.y = sio2->_SIO2window->touch[ 0 ]->y;
}
else if( _state == SIO2_WINDOW_TAP_UP )
{
    MOV_DIR = 0;
    ROT_Z = 0.0f;

}
```

This code simply assigns a value to the *start* vector's coordinates when the screen is first touched. When the user's finger is lifted from the screen, the function sets MOV_DIR to 0 and ROT_Z to 0.0f, effectively ceasing all camera movement when the touch ends.

The *templateScreenTouchMove* Function

The templateScreenTouchMove function is where most of the action happens in terms of camera movement:

```
void templateScreenTouchMove( void *_ptr )
{
    if( !sio2->_SIO2camera ){ return; }

    vec2 d;
```

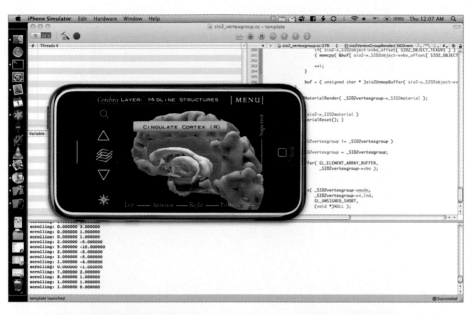

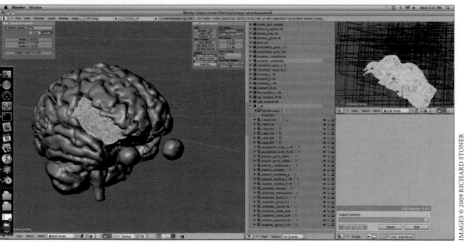

The extraordinary medical visualization app Celebrii-3D Brain Atlas for iPhone and iPod Touch is a great demonstration of how 3D graphics can be used for purposes other than gaming. Aimed at serious students of brain anatomy, Celebrii enables the user to get an in-depth look at the human brain and its associated anatomy. Here you can see the Celebrii project running in Xcode and the iPhone simulator (top) and the brain model in Blender (bottom). Learn more on the Celebrii website at http://cerebrii.com/.

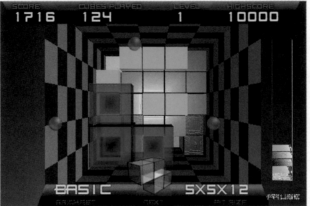

The iPhone and iPod touch provide a great platform for simple, clever, and engaging games such as Rarebyte's Black Sheep (www.rarebyte.com), Inovaworks' Dropoly (www .inovaworks.com/dropoly), and Naquatic's Touch Ski 3D (www.naquatic.com/games), the latter of which takes advantage of the revolutionary multi-touch interface to create a truly innovative skiing game interface.

The iPhone/iPod Touch's accelerometer feature enables highly intuitive interaction for gravity games like 4igames's Ivory Tower (www.4igames.com) and Rich Olson's Manic Marble (www.spambutcher.com/manicmarble/). Dumbgames.net's Guns of War (http://dumbgames.net/ Guns_of_War.html) uses the accelerometer feature to control the flight of a fighter plane.

The portability and intuitive interface of the iPhone/iPod Touch makes it perfect for amusements like iDev2's stress-relieving iPunch (`www.idev2.com/ipunch.mp4`) and challenge games like Rarebyte's iPentris (`http://ipentris.rarebyte.com`). Dumbgames.net's Guns of War splash screen shows the use of widgets similar to those described in Chapter 9.

Prophetic Sky's ambitious Townrs Defender (http://propheticsky.com/blog) is a fantasy role-playing game that packs a surprising amount of detail and game play into a single app. A variety of weapons, spells, maps, and characters keep things interesting. In addition to several screen shots, the main character rig is shown here in Blender (top).

Shootin' Annie is a fast-paced sharpshooting game featuring the cutest little gunslinger ever to grace the touch screen. Here you can see the character rig in Blender, with actions in the NLA Editor ready for export, as described in Chapter 8 of this book. The image on this page shows a work-in-progress simulator screen shot of the game. You can find out more at www.shootinannie.com.

SIO2 Interactive's own Meditation Garden is a terrific resource for learning advanced techniques in SIO2 programming. The whole package, including .blend files and texture images, and the full Xcode project is available for sale from the main SIO2 website (http://sio2interactive.com). The app features the use of Ipo curves, sound effects, custom options, solar flares, and a variety of other advanced tricks and techniques not described in this book. If you're looking to create a truly immersive environment in the iPhone, Meditation Garden is for you. Here you can see the garden in Blender and the app running in the simulator.

SIO2 Interactive's Hoops Frenzy is another educational package available for sale from the SIO2 website (`http://sio2interactive.com`). Hoops Frenzy is a physics-based, arcade-style, basketball hoop–shooting game that features a heavier emphasis on game-play-related features than Meditation Garden. If you want to build a snappy, fast-moving game, Hoops Frenzy has a lot of great ideas to draw from. Here you can see the full project in Xcode with the app running in the simulator.

First, SIO2 makes sure there's a camera and then declares a two-dimensional vector variable, *d*, to hold the change in x and y of the touch movement. The size and sign of the x and y-coordinates of d will be used to determine the values of *MOV_DIR* and *ROT_Z*. Figuring the correct values of *d* is slightly complicated by the fact that the view could be in either portrait or landscape render mode, which would lead to different results. This issue is handled by a conditional structure based on the value of *screen_orientation*:

```
if(!screen_orientation)
{
        d.y = sio2->_SIO2window->touch[ 0 ]->x - start.x;
        d.x = sio2->_SIO2window->touch[ 0 ]->y - start.y;
}else{
        d.y = sio2->_SIO2window->touch[ 0 ]->y - start.y;
        d.x = start.x - sio2->_SIO2window->touch[ 0 ]->x;

}
```

The next lines use the resulting value of *d.x* to determine values for *MOV_DIR* and *speed*. The change is registered only if a minimal threshold of difference is crossed, so merely tapping the screen will not move the camera. Once the threshold is passed, movement in the upward direction will move the camera forward and movement in the downward direction will move the camera backward. The distance of the touch movement from the original tap position will determine the speed of the movement:

```
if( d.x > 5.0f )
{
        MOV_DIR = -1;
        speed = ( d.x * 0.03f );
}

        else if( d.x < -5.0f )
{
        MOV_DIR = 1;
        speed = -( d.x * 0.03f );

}
```

The outermost conditional statements ensure that there is a minimum distance that the touch is moved in order for it to trigger a motion response so that this code is not executed every time the screen is tapped. The MOV_DIR value determines whether the movement is forward or backward.

Finally, the *d.y* value is used to determine the rotation. The further the touch moves from its initial position in a horizontal direction, the greater the rotation:

```
if( d.y > 2.0f || d.y < -2.0f )
{
        ROT_Z = -( d.y * 0.003f );
}

}
```

You can now build and run your code, and you'll find you can control the camera's movement by moving your finger or mouse around the screen. Experiment with adjusting the camera movement parameters to see how they affect the resulting movement.

The Complete Code

Several files have been changed for this application. The declaration of templateLoading was added to the template.h header file, two functions in EAGLview.mm were changed, and template.mm was edited. The following sections show you the complete code for these changes.

EAGLview.mm

The two functions that have been changed are included here in their entirety. Those functions are drawView and createFrameBuffer. The rest of the file should remain as it is in the default template.

The changed code for the drawView function in EAGLview.mm is as follows:

```
- (void)drawView {
    if( sio2->_SIO2window->_SIO2windowrender )
    {
        sio2PhysicRender( sio2->_SIO2physic,
                                1.0f / 60.0f, 1 );
        sio2->_SIO2window->_SIO2windowrender();
        sio2WindowSwapBuffers( sio2->_SIO2window );
    }
    glBindRenderbufferOES(GL_RENDERBUFFER_OES, viewRenderbuffer);
    [context presentRenderbuffer:GL_RENDERBUFFER_OES];

}
```

The complete code for the createFramebuffer function in EAGLview.mm is as follows:

```
- (BOOL)createFramebuffer {

    glGenFramebuffersOES(1, &viewFramebuffer);
    glGenRenderbuffersOES(1, &viewRenderbuffer);
    glBindFramebufferOES(GL_FRAMEBUFFER_OES, viewFramebuffer);
    glBindRenderbufferOES(GL_RENDERBUFFER_OES, viewRenderbuffer);
    [context renderbufferStorage:
        GL_RENDERBUFFER_OES fromDrawable:(CAEAGLLayer*)self.layer];
    glFramebufferRenderbufferOES(GL_FRAMEBUFFER_OES,
                                GL_COLOR_ATTACHMENT0_OES,
                                GL_RENDERBUFFER_OES, ↵
                                viewRenderbuffer);
```

```
    glGetRenderbufferParameterivOES(GL_RENDERBUFFER_OES,
                                    GL_RENDERBUFFER_WIDTH_OES,
                                    &backingWidth);
    glGetRenderbufferParameterivOES(GL_RENDERBUFFER_OES,
                                    GL_RENDERBUFFER_HEIGHT_OES,
                                    &backingHeight);
    glGenRenderbuffersOES(1, &depthRenderbuffer);
    glBindRenderbufferOES(GL_RENDERBUFFER_OES, depthRenderbuffer);
    glRenderbufferStorageOES(GL_RENDERBUFFER_OES,
                             GL_DEPTH_COMPONENT16_OES,
                             backingWidth, ↵
backingHeight);
    glFramebufferRenderbufferOES(GL_FRAMEBUFFER_OES,
                                 GL_DEPTH_ATTACHMENT_OES,
                                 GL_RENDERBUFFER_OES, ↵
depthRenderbuffer);

    if( !sio2 )
    {    vec3 gravity = { 0.0f, 0.0f, -9.8f };
        sio2Init( &tmp_argc, tmp_argv );
        sio2InitGL();
        sio2->_SIO2window = sio2WindowInit();
        sio2WindowUpdateViewport( sio2->_SIO2window,
                                  0, 0, backingWidth,
                                  backingHeight );
        sio2->_SIO2resource = sio2ResourceInit( "default" );
        sio2->_SIO2physic = sio2PhysicInit( "earth" );
        sio2PhysicSetGravity( sio2->_SIO2physic, &gravity );
        sio2WindowUpdateViewport( sio2->_SIO2window,
                                  0, 0, backingWidth,
                                  backingHeight );

        sio2->_SIO2window->_SIO2windowrender = templateLoading;
        sio2WindowShutdown( sio2->_SIO2window, templateShutdown );

        sio2->_SIO2window->_SIO2windowtap   =
            templateScreenTap;
        sio2->_SIO2window->_SIO2windowtouchmove   =
            templateScreenTouchMove;
//      sio2->_SIO2window->_SIO2windowaccelerometer =
//          templateScreenAccelerometer;
    }

    return YES;

}
```

EAGLview.mm

Here is the full code for template.mm:

```
#include "template.h"
#include "../src/sio2/sio2.h"

char  MOV_DIR = 0;
float ROT_Z = 0.0f;
unsigned char screen_orientation = 0;
float speed = 0.0f;


void templateRender( void )
{
    glMatrixMode( GL_MODELVIEW );
    glLoadIdentity();

    glClear( GL_DEPTH_BUFFER_BIT );

    if( screen_orientation )
    { sio2WindowEnterLandscape3D(); }

    if( ROT_Z )
    {
        sio2TransformRotateZ( sio2->_SIO2camera->_SIO2transform,
                                ROT_Z );
    }


    if( MOV_DIR  )
    {
        sio2->_SIO2camera->_btRigidBody->setActivationState(
                                                    ACTIVE_TAG
                                                        );
        sio2->_SIO2camera->_btRigidBody->setLinearVelocity(
            btVector3(
              ( MOV_DIR * sio2->_SIO2camera->_SIO2transform->dir->x )
                  * speed,
              ( MOV_DIR * sio2->_SIO2camera->_SIO2transform->dir->y )
                  * speed,
              sio2->_SIO2camera->_btRigidBody->getLinearVelocity()[ 2 ]
                  ) );
    }

    sio2CameraRender( sio2->_SIO2camera );
    sio2CameraUpdateFrustum( sio2->_SIO2camera );
```

```
        sio2ResourceCull( sio2->_SIO2resource,
                          sio2->_SIO2camera );


        sio2ResourceRender( sio2->_SIO2resource,
                            sio2->_SIO2window,
                            sio2->_SIO2camera,
                            SIO2_RENDER_SOLID_OBJECT);


        if( screen_orientation )
            { sio2WindowLeaveLandscape3D(); }
}


void templateLoading( void )
{
        unsigned int i = 0;
        sio2ResourceCreateDictionary( sio2->_SIO2resource );
        sio2ResourceOpen( sio2->_SIO2resource,
                          "ImmersiveScene.sio2", 1 );

        while( i != sio2->_SIO2resource->gi.number_entry )
        {
            sio2ResourceExtract( sio2->_SIO2resource, NULL );
            ++i;
        }


        sio2ResourceClose( sio2->_SIO2resource );
        sio2ResetState();

        sio2ResourceBindAllImages( sio2->_SIO2resource );
        sio2ResourceBindAllMaterials( sio2->_SIO2resource );
        sio2ResourceBindAllMatrix( sio2->_SIO2resource );

        sio2ResourceBindAllPhysicObjects( sio2->_SIO2resource,
                                          sio2->_SIO2physic );

        sio2ResourceGenId( sio2->_SIO2resource );

        sio2->_SIO2camera =
            ( SIO2camera * )sio2ResourceGet( sio2->_SIO2resource,
                                             SIO2_CAMERA,
                                             "camera/Camera" );

        sio2Perspective( sio2->_SIO2camera->fov,
                         sio2->_SIO2window->scl->x /
                             sio2->_SIO2window->scl->y,
```

```
                                     sio2->_SIO2camera->cstart,
                                     sio2->_SIO2camera->cend );

          sio2->_SIO2camera->rad = 1.0f;
          sio2->_SIO2camera->mass   = 75.0f;
          sio2->_SIO2camera->height = 1.84f;

          sio2PhysicAddCamera( sio2->_SIO2physic,
                                    sio2->_SIO2camera );

          sio2->_SIO2camera->_btRigidBody->setFriction( (btScalar)0.50 );
          sio2->_SIO2camera->_btRigidBody->setRestitution( (btScalar)0.0 );

          sio2PhysicPlay( sio2->_SIO2physic );
          sio2->_SIO2window->fps = 30;

          sio2->_SIO2window->_SIO2windowrender = templateRender;
}

void templateShutdown( void )
{
          // Clean up
          sio2ResourceUnloadAll( sio2->_SIO2resource );
          sio2->_SIO2resource = sio2ResourceFree( sio2->_SIO2resource );
          sio2->_SIO2window = sio2WindowFree( sio2->_SIO2window );
          sio2 = sio2Shutdown();
          printf("\nSIO2: shutdown...\n" );
}

vec2 start;
void templateScreenTap( void *_ptr, unsigned char _state )
{
          if( _state == SIO2_WINDOW_TAP_DOWN && sio2->_SIO2window->n_tap == 2 )
          {
              screen_orientation = !screen_orientation;

              if( screen_orientation )
              {
                  [[UIApplication sharedApplication]
                  setStatusBarOrientation:
                      UIInterfaceOrientationLandscapeRight
                  animated: YES]; }
               else
              {
```

```
                    [[UIApplication sharedApplication]
                    setStatusBarOrientation: UIInterfaceOrientationPortrait
                    animated: YES]; }
                }

        if( _state == SIO2_WINDOW_TAP_DOWN )
        {
            start.x = sio2->_SIO2window->touch[ 0 ]->x;
            start.y = sio2->_SIO2window->touch[ 0 ]->y;
        }
        else if( _state == SIO2_WINDOW_TAP_UP )
        {
            MOV_DIR = 0;
            ROT_Z = 0.0f;
        }
}


void templateScreenTouchMove( void *_ptr )
{
    if( !sio2->_SIO2camera ){ return; }

    vec2 d;

    if(!screen_orientation)
    {
        d.y = sio2->_SIO2window->touch[ 0 ]->x - start.x;
        d.x = sio2->_SIO2window->touch[ 0 ]->y - start.y;
    }else{
        d.y = sio2->_SIO2window->touch[ 0 ]->y - start.y;
        d.x = start.x - sio2->_SIO2window->touch[ 0 ]->x;
    }


    if( d.x > 5.0f )
    {
        MOV_DIR = -1;
        speed = ( d.x * 0.03f );
    }
        else if( d.x < -5.0f )
    {
        MOV_DIR = 1;
        speed = -( d.x * 0.03f );
    }
```

```
            if( d.y > 2.0f || d.y < -2.0f )
            {
                ROT_Z = -( d.y * 0.003f );
            }
    }


    void templateScreenAccelerometer( void *_ptr )
    {
    }
```

CHAPTER 7

Props and Physical Objects

In Chapter 6 you created an immersive environment in which you could navigate a camera around a scene with convincing ground and sky. In this chapter, you'll continue working on the same project, adding props and physical objects that can interact with the camera and with the world around them. You'll become more familiar with materials and some of the different options you have when working with them, and you'll discover ways to make your scene more realistic and engaging with complex-looking background objects that render quickly.

- ■ **Texture face objects and transparency**

- ■ **Fast foliage with billboards**

- ■ **Rigid body physics for interactive objects**

- ■ **Pseudo-instancing for efficient object handling**

- ■ **Working with low-poly collision maps**

- ■ **The Complete Code**

Texture Face Objects and Transparency

You now know how 3D objects and materials are brought into the SIO2 programming environment for use in your iPhone applications. In Chapter 4, you saw how real-time lighting can be used to illuminate moving objects, and in Chapter 6, you saw a much more efficient solution for getting convincing lighting on nonmoving surfaces using baking in Blender. So far, however, the materials and textures you've been using have all been solid and opaque. A lot of exciting visual possibilities open up when you incorporate alpha transparency in your materials.

Figure 7.1

An image with an alpha channel

In the following sections, you'll create a simple textured object to place in the 3D environment. In fact, you won't need to do any modeling at all because the object will be just a cube. The important things to learn here are how to set up the textures and materials in Blender and how to make SIO2 render the alpha transparency properly.

To make transparent materials, you'll need transparent textures. It's beyond the scope of this book to go into a lot of detail about the alpha channel in an image, but any good introduction to GIMP or Photoshop will give you all the details. For now, I'll stick to what you need to know to get a transparent texture to render in SIO2. You should, however, know that your image will need to be of a format that supports an alpha (A) channel. JPEG (.jpg) images have only R, G, and B channels, so they will not work for this purpose. Targa (.tga) and PNG (.png) files are the most commonly used files when an alpha channel is required.

You'll find a partially transparent image in the directory for this chapter, with the file name pyramid.tga. The image is shown in Figure 7.1. In the figure, the image itself is shown overlaid over Blender's default checkerboard test grid image so that you can see where pyramid.tga is transparent. The other important quality of this image is that it's 512×512 pixels in size, so it conforms to the power-of-two rule for OpenGL ES 1.1 images mentioned in Chapter 3. It is possible to work around this limitation since the addition of an extension in the 3.0 iPhone firmware update that supports arbitrarily sized textures. However, the OpenGL standard still requires power-of-two-sized images, and that's what I'm assuming in this book.

Alpha Texturing in Blender

To map this texture to a 3D object for use in SIO2, open your Blender scene from Chapter 6, `ImmersiveScene.blend`, and follow these steps:

1. With the 3D cursor placed in the middle of the scene, press the spacebar and add a cube object to the scene by choosing Add → Mesh→ Cube from the menu. In Object mode, place the cube somewhere on the grass surface in view of the camera, as shown in Figure 7.2.

2. Add a UV texture to the cube by clicking the New button that corresponds to UV Texture on the Mesh buttons panel shown in Figure 7.3.

Figure 7.2

Adding a cube to the scene

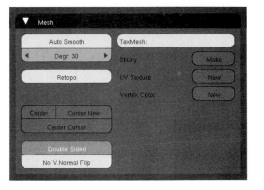

Figure 7.3

Adding a UV texture

3. Open a UV/Image Editor window. Tab into Edit mode in the 3D viewport and select the entire cube by pressing the A key. Load the texture pyramid.tga from your hard drive into the UV/Image Editor, as shown in Figure 7.4.

4. From the menu in the 3D Viewport header, select Mesh → Faces→ Convert Quads To Triangles to convert the faces of the object to triangles, as shown in Figure 7.5. The resulting cube will look like Figure 7.6; the texture mapping remains intact.

Figure 7.4

The textured cube

Figure 7.5

Converting quads to triangles

Figure 7.6

The triangulated mesh

5. With the cube still in Edit mode, bring up the Texture Face panel in the Edit buttons area. The settings for Texture Face are shown in Figure 7.7. In particular, select Alpha and Twoside. Alpha ensures that the image's alpha values are displayed as transparentness in the Blender viewport, but this has no effect in SIO2. Twoside does have an effect in SIO2. Without Twoside enabled, both SIO2 and Blender use backface culling, which makes faces invisible from the back side. In this case, you need to have the back sides visible so they show through the other transparent faces, so Twoside needs to be enabled.

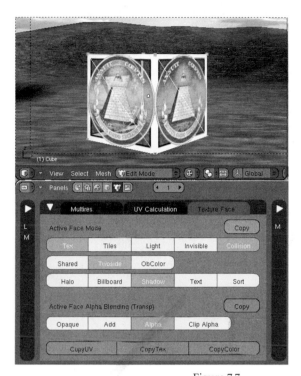

Note that Texture Face options apply only to the *active* face, not to all selected faces. Anytime you change the settings, you need to click the appropriate Copy button to copy the setting values from the active face to all selected faces. Also, be careful to use the correct Copy button. The Active Face Mode settings and the Active Face Alpha Blending (Transp) settings buttons have separate Copy buttons associated with them. In this case, click both the Copy buttons after you update the settings.

Figure 7.7

Texture Face settings

6. Textures in SIO2 are always associated with materials, so you need to add a material to this object, as you have done for all the other meshes you've worked with so far. Add pyramid.tga as an Image texture in the first texture channel of the material. The complete material settings and texture settings are shown in Figures 7.8 and 7.9, respectively. The Map Input value for the texture is Orco (although in this case, it amounts to the same as UV mapping because each quad is occupied by the full image). In the Map To panel, select Col and then select Color from the drop-down menu.

7. You're finished with the cube object in Blender for the time being. Export the scene to an .sio2 file. Remember, if you are reexporting, you should select the U (update) option on the exporter interface. If you are doing a fresh export, be sure that all the necessary objects are selected. If you do a fresh export and forget to select objects, you will get an error when you try to run your program and Xcode can't find the resources it needs. If you use the update option, renamed objects will be exported as new objects and the previous named object will not be deleted, so do a fresh export if you change any object names.

Figure 7.8

Material settings

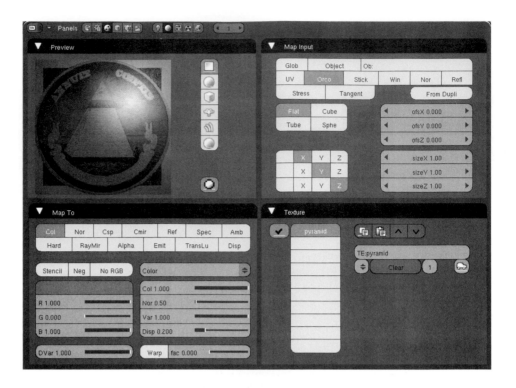

Figure 7.9

Texture settings

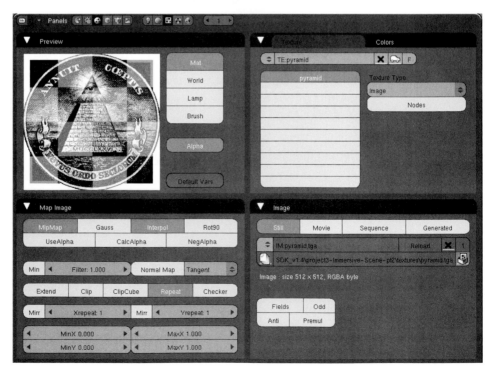

Rendering Alpha Transparency in SIO2

If you build and run now, you won't see your cube. This is because the cube uses alpha (depth) testing and transparency in its material and you haven't asked SIO2 to render those things. The function where you specify the kind of objects to be rendered is sio2ResourceRender, which is called in templateRender. Take a look at that function now. The call in your project so far looks like this:

```
sio2ResourceRender( sio2->_SIO2resource,
                    sio2->_SIO2window,
                    sio2->_SIO2camera,
                    SIO2_RENDER_SOLID_OBJECT );
```

Recall the description of sio2ResourceRender in Chapter 4. The last argument for this function is a bit mask argument representing the kinds of objects that should be rendered. You can include as many different types as you like, separated by disjunctions (the | symbol). You need to add the SIO2_RENDER_ALPHA_TESTED_OBJECT and SIO2_RENDER_TRANSPARENT_OBJECT options to get the cube to render correctly. To do that, edit the function call as follows:

```
sio2ResourceRender( sio2->_SIO2resource,
                    sio2->_SIO2window,
                    sio2->_SIO2camera,
                    SIO2_RENDER_SOLID_OBJECT |
                    SIO2_RENDER_ALPHA_TESTED_OBJECT |
                    SIO2_RENDER_TRANSPARENT_OBJECT);
```

You can now build and run your application, and the cube will appear! Like the image you used, the walls of the cube will be transparent, and the back walls will be visible through the cube.

> SIO2 enables you use to more material blending options than just alpha blending. Most of the blending options in the drop-down menu of the Map To panel in Blender behave similarly in SIO2 to how they behave in Blender.

Fast Foliage with Billboards

Although processing alpha transparency is more demanding on your device's resources than processing ordinary opaque surfaces, there are also cases where it can help you save a great deal of processing power by enabling you to substitute a 2D image on a plane for what would otherwise be a 3D object with heavy geometry. A classic example is to use simple rectangular planes with images of trees or foliage rather than actual models.

However, in a 3D game where the camera is free to move around other objects, simply setting up a plane with a picture of a tree is clearly no substitute for a 3D tree.

The solution to this is a technique known as *billboarding*. Billboards are 2D images that pivot to face directly toward the camera at all times. Because they pivot in this way, the player never sees the billboard from an oblique angle or from the side, so the 2D nature of the billboard is concealed. For objects that are not completely symmetrical around an axis, the effect of billboarding is not entirely accurate. For animals or people, billboards are not particularly effective because the appearance of an animal or person from the side is drastically different than the appearance from the front. For approximately symmetrical background objects such as trees, however, the inconsistencies are subtle enough that billboards are very effective in a game environment. In this section, you'll learn how to add billboard trees to your 3D environment.

The tree texture you'll use has already been created. The file is shown in Figure 7.10, over a backdrop of the Blender test grid pattern so that you can see the transparency of the alpha channel. You'll find it in the textures directory corresponding to this chapter in the archive that accompanies this book. The file is called tree_billboard.png.

Figure 7.10

A tree texture with a visibly transparent alpha channel

To create a billboard tree in your immersive scene, follow these steps:

1. In Object mode, add a plane to the scene by pressing the spacebar and choosing Add → Mesh → Plane from the menu. In Object mode, press Alt+G and Alt+R to center the object and clear its rotations. The plane should appear as shown in Figure 7.11. Tab into Edit mode and select all vertices with the A key. Press R and then X, and enter the numerical value **90** to rotate the plane's geometry.

2. With the plane selected, create a UV texture by clicking the appropriate New button on the Mesh buttons panel, as shown in Figure 7.12.

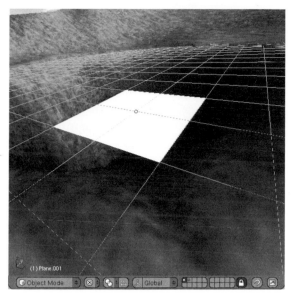

Figure 7.11

Adding a plane

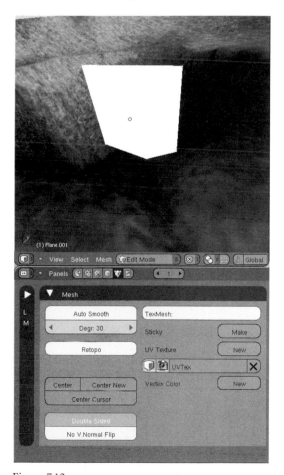

Figure 7.12

Creating a UV texture

3. Open a UV/Image Editor window. In the 3D viewport, make sure you're in Edit mode and press the A key to select all vertices. In the UV/Image Editor, open the tree texture image (shown in Figure 7.13) by choosing Image → Open from the header menu and then navigating to the tree_billboard.png file on your hard drive. If the mapping is upside down, you can rotate the selected vertices in the UV/Image Editor to correct it. Also, note that so the image would be square, the picture of the tree has been slightly squashed vertically. In Edit mode, with all the vertices selected, scale the mesh up slightly by pressing S followed by Z to constrain the scaling vertically and adjusting the height with the mouse. The resulting textured plane should look like Figure 7.14.

Figure 7.13

Adding a UV texture image

Figure 7.14

The correct UV mapping

4. With the plane selected and in Edit mode, bring up the Texture Face panel in the Edit buttons area and set the Texture Face settings as shown in Figure 7.15. Notably, make sure that Billboard is selected. This will tell SIO2 to treat the object as a billboard and keep it facing the camera.

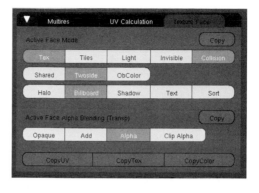

Figure 7.15

Texture Face settings

5. As with the cube object from the previous section, a textured material is necessary for the billboard object. Create a material for the plane and add an Image texture to the material's first texture channel. The pertinent material settings and texture settings are shown in Figure 7.16 and 7.17, respectively. There are no significant differences between these settings and the ones you used for the cube in the previous section.

Figure 7.16

Material settings

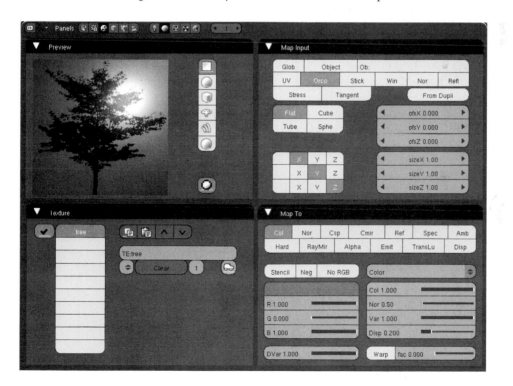

Figure 7.17

Texture settings

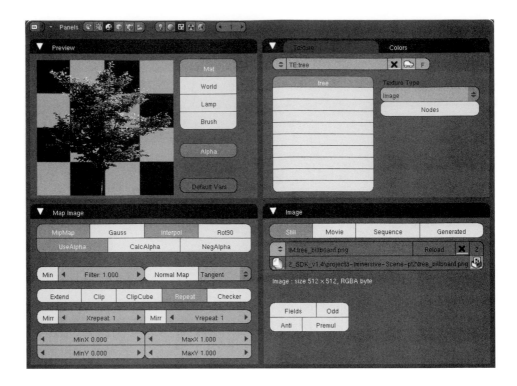

Figure 7.17

Texture settings

6. Reexport the scene, and then build and run your application. Drive the camera around the tree and look at it from various directions to see the billboarding effect in action. Wherever you go, the tree should look just as it does in Figure 7.18. If it doesn't, make sure that the rotation of the plane object is applied by pressing Ctrl+A.

Figure 7.18

The billboard tree in the iPhone simulator

The billboard examples in this chapter rotate cylindrically around their z-axis. Billboards can be set to rotate spherically by selecting the Halo option on the Texture Face panel. This is obviously not appropriate for trees, but it is useful for objects that float freely in space (for example, a planet in the background). Tutorial 4 from the official SIO2 package illustrates spherical billboards with patches of grass that rotate upward when the camera goes over them, giving the appearance of being crushed down underfoot.

You can set a threshold to clip alpha values below a certain value. You can raise this value to sharpen the outlines of alpha textures in cases where the edges would otherwise be fuzzy or have some residual noise. This is done by adjusting the Tralu (translucency) value for the material on the Shaders tab in the Materials buttons area.

Physics for Interactive Objects

An important aspect of an immersive environment is the simulation of physical interaction with the environment. You've already set up the basics of this by setting up physics and bounds for the ground and the camera. You can climb up and slide down the hills, for example, not to mention being able to stand on the ground without simply falling through it. These kinds of interactions enhance the reality of your surroundings.

There are other kinds of simulations that you can use as well to make objects you interact with even more responsive in their behavior. In the following sections, you'll see how to create objects that can be pushed and moved around.

Rigid Body Objects

For objects that need to move and roll, rigid body physics is appropriate. Objects with rigid body physics do not deform, but they are capable of having both linear and angular momentum, meaning that they can both move in space and turn in physically realistic ways. This enables them to tumble and roll convincingly.

To see this functionality in action, follow these steps to create a rigid body ball that you can push around in the game environment:

1. Add an Icosphere to the scene by pressing the spacebar and selecting Add → Mesh → Icosphere as shown in Figure 7.19. Place the object a little bit above the ground, preferably in view of the camera, as shown in Figure 7.20. In the figure, the sphere is shown in Edit mode so that you can see the geometry. Remember that to move an object from one place to another, you should always be in Object mode so that the object's center moves appropriately. Note that the center is where it belongs, in the middle of the sphere.

It's very important to be aware of where the center of your Blender object is and what transformations are affecting the object. Particularly when you deal with physics objects, having the center properly located in the middle of the mesh is important. Blender enables you to position the center in the mesh correctly by clicking the Center New button in the Mesh panel in the Edit buttons area while in Object mode. To clear transformations, press Alt+R to clear rotations, Alt+G to clear translations, and Alt+S to clear scaling. To apply rotations and scaling, press Ctrl+A. This will reset the scale and rotation values (to 1 and 0, respectively) while maintaining the current size and orientation of the object.

Figure 7.19

Adding an icosphere

Figure 7.20

The icosphere slightly above the ground

2. By default, the name of the icosphere object you just created is Sphere.001. Why is this? Recall that in Chapter 6 you used a UV sphere object to create the sky dome. That object was called Sphere. Blender automatically appends a three-digit suffix to the end of newly created objects that share a name with other already existing objects. Normally, this is no problem, but in SIO2, these suffixes have a special meaning, as you will see in the discussion of pseudo-instancing in the next section of this chapter. For this reason, you must change the name of Sphere.001 to something unique without the suffix. If you don't change the name, the new sphere will not be rendered. So change the object name to **Ball** in the OB field of the Link

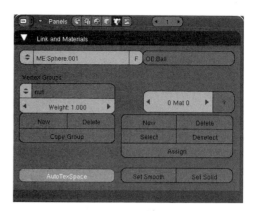

And Materials tab in the Edit buttons are, as shown in Figure 7.21. Note that I've left Sphere.001 in the ME field of the same panel. This is to underscore the point that the mesh datablock name (in the ME field) is not important. You can change this if you like for consistency, or you can simply ignore it.

3. With the Ball object selected in Object mode, set the physics settings in the Logic buttons area as shown in Figure 7.22. Set the ball to be an actor with the value Rigid Body selected from the drop-down menu in the upper-left portion of the panel. Set the Mass value to **20**. Mass units are kilograms in Bullet and, by extension, SIO2. Finally, click Bounds and select Sphere from the drop-down menu. This tells the physics simulation that the object's bounding shape is spherical.

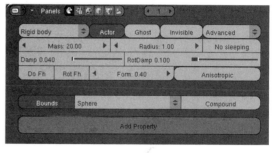

Figure 7.22

Rigid body physics for the ball

4. What you've done so far is all that's needed to get the rigid body simulation set up. However, because the ball has no material or texture, and because you're not using GL lighting in this exercise, the object will appear solid, in shadeless white, when you run your application. That's not very interesting to look at when you want to see rolling movement, so just for visibility purposes, use vertex paint to decorate the ball a little bit. Select Vertex Paint mode from the drop-down menu in the 3D viewport header and use the palette in the Paint panel of the Edit buttons area as shown in Figure 7.23. Use a couple of different colors so that it will be obvious when the ball rolls. Vertex colors are a great tool for visualizing and debugging your work. In general, you probably won't want to use vertex colors in a finished game project. You should texture your objects to make them look good.

Figure 7.23

**Vertex painting a
pattern on the ball**

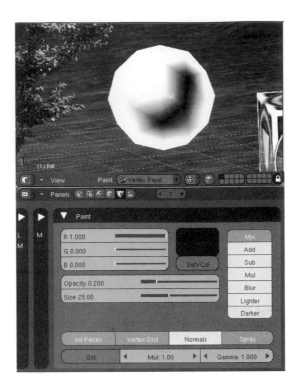

5. Reexport the scene, and then build and run your application. You should be able to navigate the area with your camera and bump the ball to make it roll. Try pushing the ball around the field and into the hole. You might notice that when you bump up against the ball, the camera seems to nose into the ball, poking through its surface. To fix this, select the camera, go to the Camera panel in the Edit buttons area, and find the Clipping Start/End values. Set the Start value to **0** to ensure that the beginning of the camera's viewable area is flush with the physical bounds of the camera object.

Static Physics for Obstacles

Your ball should be rolling nicely now. However, you may have noticed that there is some unconvincing behavior in the way it interacts with other props. In particular, the ball seems to be able to pass directly through the tree and the Plexiglas box! Obviously, that's not what you want.

If you've completed the exercises in this chapter and Chapter 6, then you probably already have a good idea of how to solve this. Both the cube and the tree plane need to be made into static physics objects, just as you did with the ground. The physics settings for the cube and the billboard tree are shown in Figure 7.24 and Figure 7.25, respectively. The only difference is in the bounding shapes of the two items. The cube has Box selected from the Bounds drop-down menu. Because the tree is just a single plane, you need to select the Triangle Mesh option of the drop-down menu. This is a more precise method of bounding in which the bounding shape is based on the actual geometry of the object.

Figure 7.24

Physics settings for the cube

Figure 7.25

Physics settings for the billboard tree

Pseudo-instancing for Efficient Object Handling

Every 3D object that you define requires memory to hold the details of its geometry. In a mobile platform like the iPhone, all resources are at a premium. You never want to use more memory than is necessary. For this reason, it is very useful to have some form of instancing, whereby you can store vertex data of multiple objects with the same geometry and other characteristics as a single vertex buffer object in the graphics processor and then instantiate the data as multiple 3D objects in the 3D space. SIO2 enables you to do something like this using its pseudo-instancing functionality.

SIO2 pseudo-instancing takes advantage of Blender's automatic three-digit suffix naming convention to recognize direct copies made of an object. Copies can be made of 3D objects in two main ways: by using Shift+D to do a standard duplication, in which the new object is composed of a duplicated data block, or by using Alt+D to do a linked duplication. In a linked duplication, a new object is created that shares the same geometry data with the original object. Figure 7.26 shows how two linked duplicate cubes change when the shape of one is edited. Any edit made to one mesh object will also be made to its linked duplicates.

Figure 7.26

Editing linked duplicates

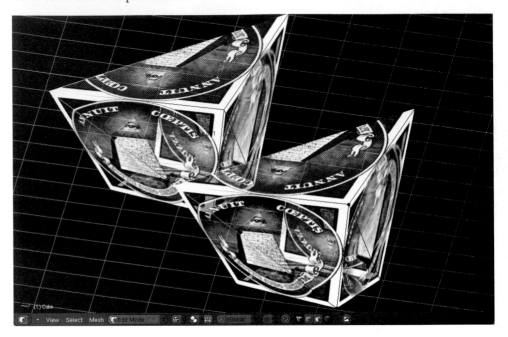

When copying objects for pseudo-instantiation in SIO2, you can use either method, but it's better to use Alt+D because this will better represent in Blender what will happen in SIO2 in either case. What SIO2 does is simply check the objects' names, and if the names end with a three-digit suffix, it treats them as instantiations of the original named object. Only object-level information like location, rotation, and scale is different.

In this example, you'll want multiple copies of the trees, boxes, and balls. Duplicate these objects one-by-one using Alt+D and place them wherever you want in your scene. The result should be similar to what's shown in Figure 7.27.

To make the instances render, it's necessary to bind them in the SIO2 code. Do this in templateLoading in the same place where you bind images, materials, matrices, and physics objects. Simply add the following line of code to bind instances along with the other similar function calls to bind the other assets:

```
sio2ResourceBindAllInstances( sio2->_SIO2resource );
```

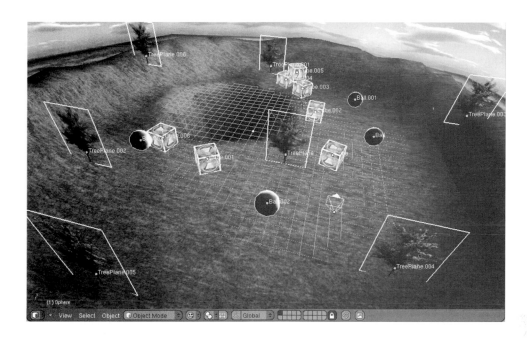

Figure 7.27

Copying balls and obstacles

```
void sio2ResourceBindAllInstances(SIO2resource *resource)
```

This function binds all objects created by pseudo-instancing. SIO2 identifies instances by name; any object whose name ends with the three-digit suffix assigned automatically by Blender to similarly named objects will be considered to be an instance in SIO2.

Once you've made this modification to the code, you can build and run your application to see it in action. All of the instantiated objects will be located in the appropriate places, as shown in Figure 7.28, and they should behave as you expect. Billboards pivot independently, and the movement and forces on each rigid body object are independent from those on the other rigid body objects.

Figure 7.28

Instances in the game environment

Working with Low-Poly Collision Maps

If you drive your camera up into the hills surrounding the little basin you've created, you'll find that your wanderings come to an unceremonious end when you drop off the edge of the world. This isn't usually a desirable state of affairs in a 3D game, but there is a simple way to prevent it in SIO2, by using invisible, low-polygon collision maps. These are basically invisible physical objects used to guide or control the player character's movement.

To set up a simple collision map that will prevent you from falling out of this scene, follow these steps:

1. Select the ground object and press Shift+S, and then choose Cursor To Selected from the menu to snap the 3D cursor to the object. This will ensure that a newly added object will be located at the center of the ground plane. Add a circle object in the usual way, as shown in Figure 7.29. Enter **8** to choose eight vertices in the Add Circle dialog box that appears. Enter Edit mode and scale the circle up so that it is as big as possible but still fits entirely within the ground plane, as shown in Figure 7.30. This is going to be the perimeter beyond which the camera is not allowed to move.

2. Tab into Edit mode and select all vertices with the A key. Press the E key to extrude the edges, and then press the Z key to constrain the extrusion vertically. Bring the extruded edges upward to form a wall like the one shown in Figure 7.31.

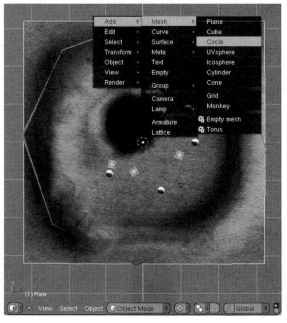

Figure 7.29

Adding a circle

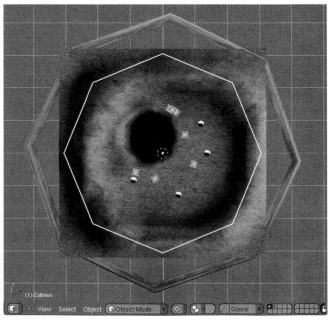

Figure 7.30

The circle scaled up

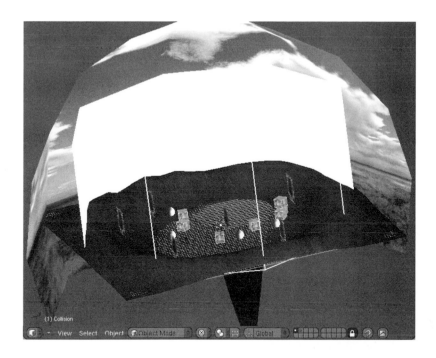

Figure 7.31

Creating a wall with the extruded circle

3. In the OB field on the Link And Materials panel, name the object **Collision**.

4. Set the Collision object's physics settings as shown in Figure 7.32, a static collision object with Triangle Mesh bounds.

Figure 7.32

Physics settings for the collision map

That's all you have to do to create the collision map object. You don't need textures or materials because the collision map is meant to be invisible anyway. In order to make this happen, you need to edit the code in template.mm. Add the following function call:

```
sio2EnableState( &sio2ResourceGetObject( sio2->_SIO2resource,
                        "object/Collision")->flags,
                        SIO2_OBJECT_INVISIBLE );
```

void **sio2EnableState**(unsigned int *var*, unsigned int *state*)

This is a general-purpose function that sets the value of a state for multistate structures. The *var* value generally represents the structure's state flags, and the *state* value is the state to be enabled on the structure.

Place this code as the second-to-last command in `templateLoading`, just before `sio2->_SIO2window->_SIO2windowrender = templateRender;`.

Once you've done that, reexport the scene, and then build and run your application. Try to climb out of the world with the camera. You will find that your movements around the edge of the scene are restricted by the collision map.

This chapter has covered a lot of material, but the additions to the `template.mm` code have been fairly minimal. This goes to show how much of SIO2's functionality is actually determined by what you do in Blender. This is one of the great strengths of the Blender/SIO2 workflow. In the next chapter, you'll learn even more about how sophisticated Blender content such as armature animation can be used in the SIO2 environment.

The Complete Code

To wrap up this chapter, here's the full `template.mm` code for the functionality described in this chapter (all other files are identical to those of Chapter 6):

```
#include "template.h"
#include "../src/sio2/sio2.h"

char  MOV_DIR = 0;
float ROT_Z = 0.0f;
unsigned char screen_orientation = 0;
float speed = 0.0f;

void templateRender( void )
{
    glMatrixMode( GL_MODELVIEW );
    glLoadIdentity();
    glClear( GL_DEPTH_BUFFER_BIT );

    if( screen_orientation )
    { sio2WindowEnterLandscape3D(); }

    if( ROT_Z )
    {
        sio2TransformRotateZ( sio2->_SIO2camera->_SIO2transform,
                              ROT_Z );
    }

    if( MOV_DIR )
    {
        sio2->_SIO2camera->_btRigidBody->setActivationState( ACTIVE_TAG );
        sio2->_SIO2camera->_btRigidBody->setLinearVelocity( btVector3(
                ( MOV_DIR * sio2->_SIO2camera->_SIO2transform->dir->x )

* speed,
```

```
                        ( MOV_DIR * sio2->_SIO2camera->_SIO2transform->dir->y )

* speed,
                        sio2->_SIO2camera->_btRigidBody->getLinearVelocity()[ 2
]
                        ) );
    }

    sio2CameraRender( sio2->_SIO2camera );
    sio2CameraUpdateFrustum( sio2->_SIO2camera );

    sio2ResourceCull( sio2->_SIO2resource,
                      sio2->_SIO2camera );

    sio2ResourceRender( sio2->_SIO2resource,
                        sio2->_SIO2window,
                        sio2->_SIO2camera,
                        SIO2_RENDER_SOLID_OBJECT |
                        SIO2_RENDER_ALPHA_TESTED_OBJECT |
                        SIO2_RENDER_TRANSPARENT_OBJECT);

    if( screen_orientation )
    { sio2WindowLeaveLandscape3D(); }
}

void templateLoading( void )
{
    unsigned int i = 0;
    if( !sio2->_SIO2resource->n_entry )
    { sio2ResourceCreateDictionary( sio2->_SIO2resource ); }

    sio2ResourceOpen( sio2->_SIO2resource,
                      "ImmersiveScene.sio2", 1 );

    while( i != sio2->_SIO2resource->gi.number_entry )
    {
        sio2ResourceExtract( sio2->_SIO2resource, NULL );
        ++i;
    }

    sio2ResourceClose( sio2->_SIO2resource );
    sio2ResetState();

    sio2ResourceBindAllImages( sio2->_SIO2resource );
    sio2ResourceBindAllMaterials( sio2->_SIO2resource );
    sio2ResourceBindAllMatrix( sio2->_SIO2resource );
```

```
            sio2ResourceBindAllInstances( sio2->_SIO2resource );
            sio2ResourceBindAllPhysicObjects( sio2->_SIO2resource,
                                              sio2->_SIO2physic );


            sio2ResourceGenId( sio2->_SIO2resource );


            sio2->_SIO2camera =
                ( SIO2camera * )sio2ResourceGet( sio2->_SIO2resource,
                                                 SIO2_CAMERA,
                                                 "camera/Camera"
    );

            sio2Perspective( sio2->_SIO2camera->fov,
            sio2->_SIO2window->scl->x / sio2->_SIO2window->scl->y,
                                   sio2->_SIO2camera->cstart,
                                   sio2->_SIO2camera->cend );


            if( !sio2->_SIO2camera ) { return; }


            sio2->_SIO2camera->rad = 1.0f;
            sio2->_SIO2camera->mass   = 75.0f;
            sio2->_SIO2camera->height = 1.5f;


            sio2PhysicAddCamera( sio2->_SIO2physic,
                                 sio2->_SIO2camera );


            sio2->_SIO2camera->_btRigidBody->setFriction( (btScalar)0.50 );
            sio2->_SIO2camera->_btRigidBody->setRestitution( (btScalar)0.0 );


            sio2PhysicPlay( sio2->_SIO2physic );
            sio2->_SIO2window->fps = 30;


            sio2EnableState( &sio2ResourceGetObject( sio2->_SIO2resource,
                                      "object/Collision")->flags,
                                      SIO2_OBJECT_INVISIBLE );


            sio2->_SIO2window->_SIO2windowrender = templateRender;
    }

void templateShutdown( void )
    {
        // Clean up
        sio2ResourceUnloadAll( sio2->_SIO2resource );
        sio2->_SIO2resource = sio2ResourceFree( sio2->_SIO2resource );
        sio2->_SIO2window = sio2WindowFree( sio2->_SIO2window );
        sio2 = sio2Shutdown();
```

```
        printf("\nSIO2: shutdown...\n" );
}


vec2 start;
void templateScreenTap( void *_ptr, unsigned char _state )
{
    if( _state == SIO2_WINDOW_TAP_DOWN && sio2->_SIO2window->n_tap == 2 )
    {
        screen_orientation = !screen_orientation;
          if( screen_orientation )
          { [[UIApplication sharedApplication] setStatusBarOrientation:
              UIInterfaceOrientationLandscapeRight animated: YES]; }
          else
          { [[UIApplication sharedApplication] setStatusBarOrientation:
              UIInterfaceOrientationPortrait animated: YES]; }
    }

    if( _state == SIO2_WINDOW_TAP_DOWN )
        {
            start.x = sio2->_SIO2window->touch[ 0 ]->x;
            start.y - sio2->_SIO2window->touch[ 0 ]->y;
        }
        else if( _state == SIO2_WINDOW_TAP_UP )
        {
            MOV_DIR = 0;
            ROT_Z = 0.0f;
        }
}


void templateScreenTouchMove( void *_ptr )
{
    if( !sio2->_SIO2camera )
    { return; }

    vec2 d;

    if(!screen_orientation){
        d.y = sio2->_SIO2window->touch[ 0 ]->x - start.x;
        d.x = sio2->_SIO2window->touch[ 0 ]->y - start.y;
    }else{
        d.y = sio2->_SIO2window->touch[ 0 ]->y - start.y;
        d.x = start.x - sio2->_SIO2window->touch[ 0 ]->x;
    }
    if( d.x > 5.0f )
    {
    MOV_DIR = -1;
```

```
                    speed = ( d.x * 0.03f );
                }
                else if( d.x < -5.0f )
                {
                    MOV_DIR = 1;
                    speed = -( d.x * 0.03f );
                }

                if( d.y > 2.0f || d.y < -2.0f )

                    ROT_Z = -( d.y * 0.003f );
                }
        }

        void templateScreenAccelerometer( void *_ptr )
        {
        }
```

CHAPTER 8

Animating a Character

So far, you've learned how to create interactive 3D worlds with props, physics, and lighting. There's much more you can do with Blender and SIO2, and in this chapter you'll be introduced to the powerful character animation capabilities of the SIO2 game engine. You'll learn how to create armature animation actions in Blender that can be exported to SIO2 just like other 3D content and how to incorporate the actions into your iPhone game play. You'll also learn more about how to control simple movements of objects in 3D space and see a simple method to obtain a real-time shadow effect using planar projection.

- ▪ **Animating a character in Blender**
- ▪ **Getting action in SIO2**
- ▪ **Taking a walk**
- ▪ **Quick and dirty real-time shadows**
- ▪ **The Complete Code**

Animating a Character in Blender

This chapter takes a slightly different approach from previous chapters in that it's not entirely self-contained from start to finish. Instead, working through the content of this chapter will require you to have access to the files in the archive that accompanies this book. The archive is freely available to download at www.sybex.com/go/iphoneblendersio2, so if you don't have it, please download it from that website.

Creating and animating a character from scratch in Blender is a significant undertaking, and the process is unfortunately beyond the scope of this book. If you are interested in doing a lot of character-oriented Blender work, I recommend my book *Introducing Character Animation with Blender* (Sybex, 2007), which gives a comprehensive introduction to all aspects of character creation and animation from mesh modeling to texturing to nonlinear animation.

This chapter will take the content of the file frankie_model.blend as its starting point. I recommend following the content using this rigged model. However, if you already have a fair idea of what you are doing with modeling and animation in Blender, you can follow the content with your own rigged character model as well.

The Frankie character is adapted from the character model created for the Blender Foundation's Apricot game project, which resulted in the open content game *Yo, Frankie!*. The game character in turn was based upon the Frankie character from the Blender Foundation's open movie *Big Buck Bunny.* All of the content from both of these projects is open and available to download freely. The characters and rigs from *Big Buck Bunny* are much too complex and detailed to be useful for iPhone game programming, but the game assets for *Yo, Frankie!* provide a great starting point to adapt a character. You can download the original *Yo, Frankie!* assets at www.yofrankie.org/download/.

Even though the *Yo, Frankie!* model was built for games, it's still on the heavy side for the iPhone, and the armature is more complex than necessary for the purpose of this tutorial, so I made some changes. I used the Poly Reducer script in the Mesh menu of the 3D header to reduce the number of triangles from 1,861 to a much lighter 990 triangles, as shown in Figure 8.1. The reduction impacted the look of the character, but given the small size of the iPhone screen, the quality is still acceptable. Reducing any further would have ruined the shape of the model or overly distorted the texture mapping.

I discarded both normal and specular textures. I resized the color texture in GIMP from 1024×1024 to 512×512 pixels, as shown in Figure 8.2. Again, the quality remains good enough for use on a small screen.

Figure 8.1
The Frankie mesh

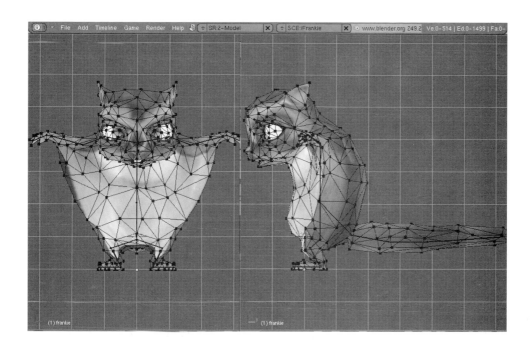

Figure 8.2
The resized texture

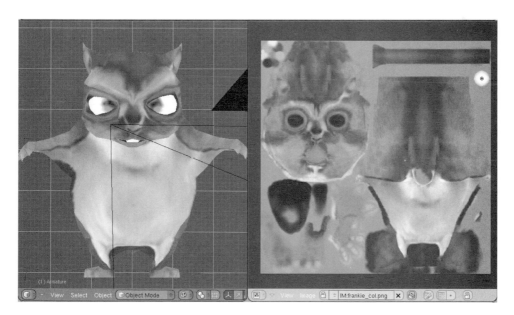

I deleted and re-created the armature. Appendix A covers the basics of how to create an armature and rig a mesh with it, so if you would like to use your own original or adapted model and you aren't sure how to do this, please check that appendix. The new armature is shown in Figure 8.3.

Figure 8.3

The armature

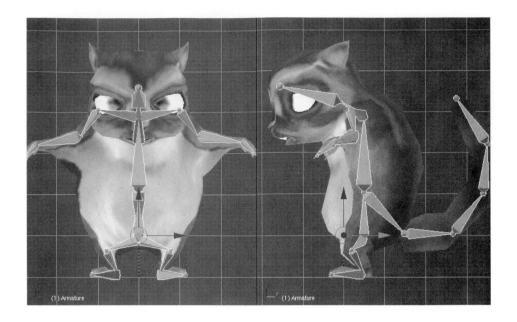

In Figure 8.4, you can see the bones labeled with their bone names. The bones are as follows:

Head	U_Leg.R(L)
Neck	L_Leg.R(L)
Shoulder.R(L)	Foot.R(L)
U_Arm.R(L)	Tail1
L_Arm.R(L)	Tail2
Hand.R(L)	Tail3
Back	Tail4
Pelvis	Tail5

This armature is on the high side in terms of the number of bones you should use. Try to use as few bones as possible. Also, this armature does not include features such as inverse kinematic (IK) constraints. However, this is not a limitation of SIO2. In fact, SIO2 does not use an armature animation system as such internally but rather exports mesh deformations for actions directly. In some respects, this makes the system less flexible than a full armature animation system would be, but it results in much better performance with the limited processing power of the iPhone platform. It also means that any mesh deformations can be incorporated into actions, including deformations resulting from IK or other constraints or even lattices. Furthermore, actions can be shared among multiple instances of an animated mesh without having to duplicate the animation sequence in memory. You can find out more about using those kinds of techniques in *Introducing Character Animation with Blender* (Sybex, 2007), but for this example, they will not be used.

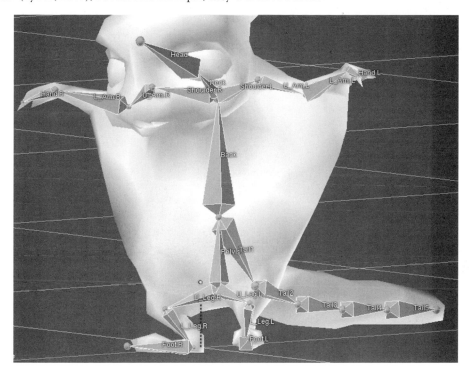

Figure 8.4

The armature with bone name labels visible

Creating a Simple Walk Cycle

The goal of this chapter's example is to make the Frankie character walk around the 3D scene, controlled by the movement of your finger on the screen. When the character is moving in space, he should obviously be moving his feet as well. When he's stopped, he should be standing with his feet planted. To accomplish this, you'll use two actions. First, create the walk cycle action by following these steps:

1. Set up your animation environment in a way that you can easily control what the character is doing and still see the Action Editor window. For animation, I prefer to set the armature visualization mode to stick visualization as shown in Figure 8.5. This helps to keep the position of the mesh easy to see. I also like to have two 3D windows open, one in orthogonal front view and one in side view, in addition to the Action Editor, as shown in Figure 8.6. Press 1 on the number pad to enter front view and 3 on the number pad to enter side view. Toggle into orthogonal view with the 5 key on the number pad.

Figure 8.5

Setting the armature to stick visualization

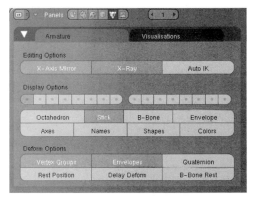

Figure 8.6

Splitting the window and opening the Action Editor

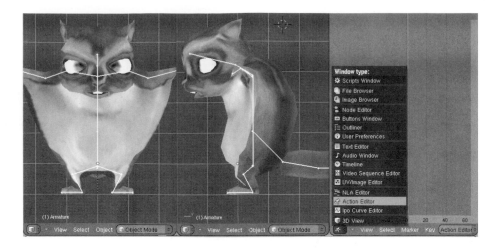

2. Be sure you are on frame 1 to pose the legs for the first frame of the animation. It's best to cycle on extreme poses, so the first and last frame will be identical extreme poses with the left foot forward. Select the U_Leg.L bone and rotate it clockwise forward as shown in Figure 8.7. When you've done this, select the right leg, U_Leg.R, and rotate that counterclockwise toward the rear (Figure 8.8).

3. Pose the arms as shown in Figure 8.9. The arms' pose should be the reverse of the legs, with the left arm rotated back and the right arm rotated forward.

4. Natural walking involves some up and down movement of the head and back. To animate this, slightly rotate the pelvis and back bones on the down step extremes, as shown in Figure 8.10 for the pelvis and 8.11 for the back. Finally, curl the bones of the tail by rotating each tail bone slightly counterclockwise, as shown in Figure 8.12.

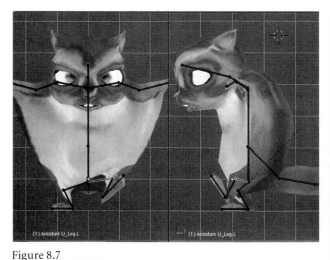

Figure 8.7

Rotating the left leg forward

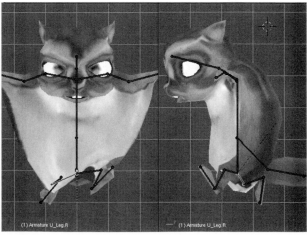

Figure 8.8

Rotating the right leg to the rear

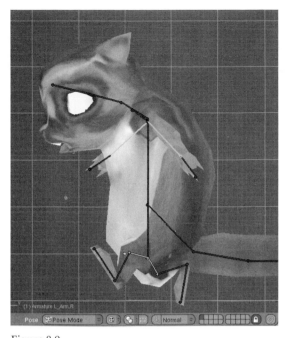

Figure 8.9

Posing the arms

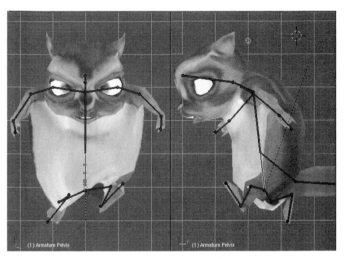

Figure 8.10

Rotating at the pelvis

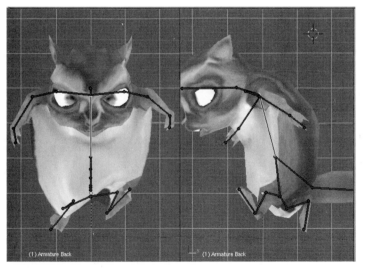

Figure 8.11

Rotating the back

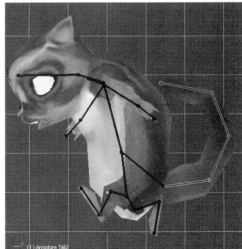

Figure 8.12

Curling the tail

5. By holding the Shift key as you right-click, select all of the bones you just posed, including the leg, arm, back, pelvis, and tail bones. Key them by pressing the I key with your mouse over the 3D viewport and selecting the LocRot option, as shown in

Figure 8.13. When you do this, a column of key frames will appear at frame 1 in the Action Editor, as shown in Figure 8.14. That's all there is to it for the first frame of this animation.

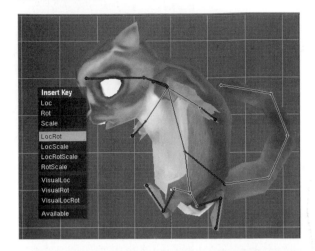

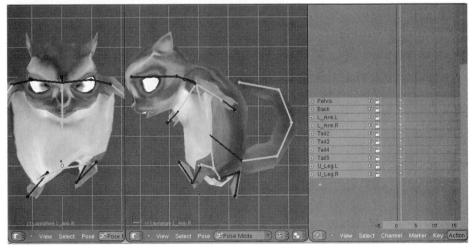

6. The next pose you're going to key is the reverse pose, where the forward and back legs and arms are flipped. Flipping poses in this way is often necessary, so Blender has an easy mechanism for doing it quickly. You'll use the pose clipboard, which enables you to copy and paste poses from one frame of an animation to another frame, with the option of pasting a pose in reverse. First, copy the pose by selecting all affected bones and clicking the Copy To Clipboard button on the 3D viewport header, highlighted in Figure 8.15. Next, advance five frames by pressing the right arrow button on the keyboard five times. Finally, paste the reversed pose by clicking the button highlighted in Figure 8.16. Note that both the copy and paste button icons may be

different in your own version of Blender. There are several icon options available to use in Blender, so the icons you're using depend on your own preference. The position of the buttons is the same, though, and it should be clear which buttons correspond to the ones in the figure.

7. The new pose must be keyframed or it will be lost when the frame is changed. So keyframe the pose by pressing the I key and selecting LocRot as shown in Figure 8.17, just as you did for the first pose. The new column of keyframes is shown in Figure 8.18.

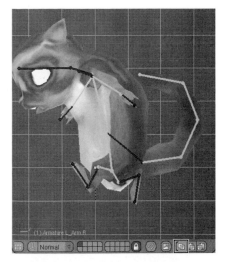

Figure 8.15

Copying the pose to the clipboard

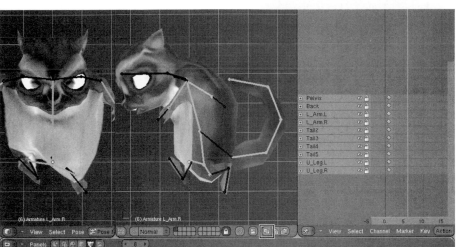

Figure 8.16

Advancing five frames and pasting the pose in reverse

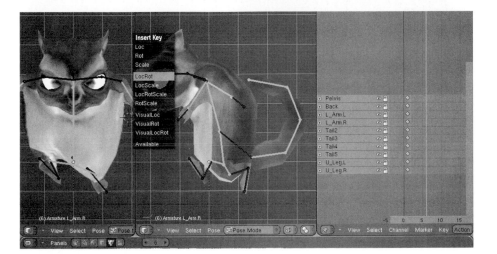

Figure 8.17

Keyframing the reversed pose

Figure 8.18

The second column of keyframes

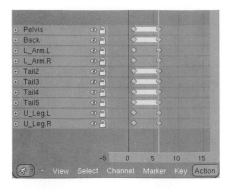

8. For the last frame of the action, which will be on frame 11, you want to have exactly the same pose as the one you keyframed on frame 1 so that the motion cycles smoothly. You can do this entirely in the Action Editor by copying the keyframes. Press the A key to toggle all keyframes unselected, and then press B and use the rectangle select tool to select the first column of keyframes, as highlighted in Figure 8.19. Press Shift+D to duplicate the keyframes, and then move them to the right (forward) 10 frames, from frame 1 to frame 11. While you're moving them, hold down the Ctrl key to snap them to whole frames, as shown in Figure 8.20.

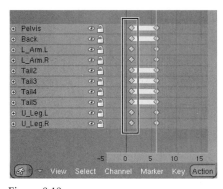

Figure 8.19

Selecting the first column of keyframes

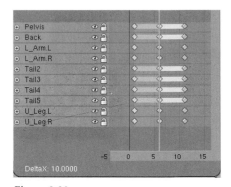

Figure 8.20

Moving the copied keyframes 10 frames forward

9. Previously, the pelvis and back bones were rotated slightly to create a hunched pose. When the walk peaks, the character's back should straighten. This occurs at frames 4 and 9. Move to frame 4 first, rotate both bones slightly clockwise, and key the pose as shown in Figure 8.21. Then copy the pose, advance to frame 9, and paste and key the pose as shown in Figure 8.22.

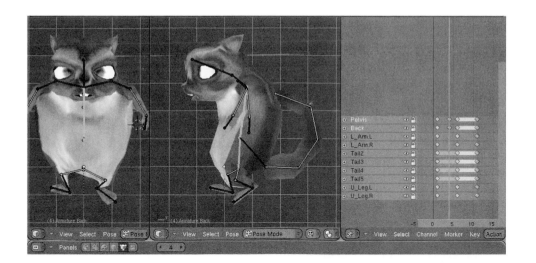

Figure 8.21

Keying an upright pose at frame 4

10. You can now look at your walk cycle by setting the start frame to 1 and the end frame to 10 in the Timeline as shown in Figure 8.23. Press Play to see the walk cycle repeat. Before you continue, rename the walking action you just created to **Walk** in the field in the Action Editor header shown in Figure 8.24.

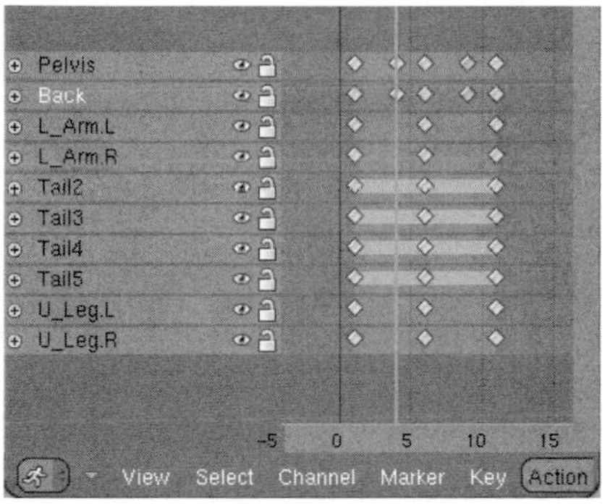

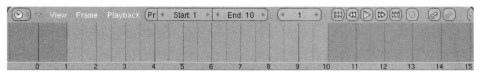

Figure 8.22

Copying the upright pose to frame 9

If you like, you can add a back-and-forth motion to the tail on your own. Just be sure that the keys on frame 1 are copied directly to frame 11 and that the overall animation remains simple.

Figure 8.23

Setting a 10-frame cycle in the Timeline

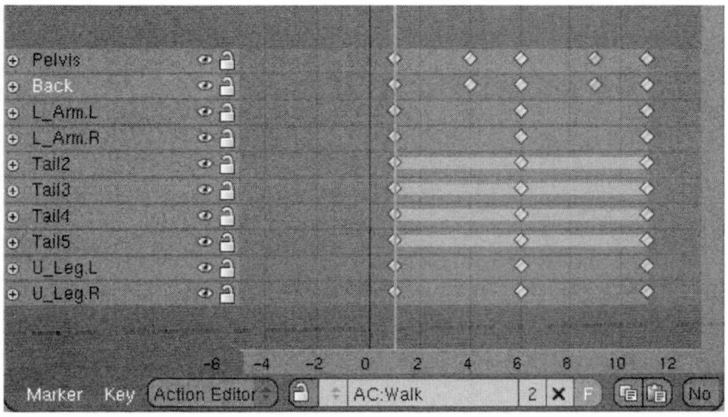

Figure 8.24

Naming the Walk action

Creating the Default Motion and NLA Strips

You've got your Walk action complete. You now need to create a second action that will be the default movement for Frankie when he's not walking around, and you need to use the Nonlinear Animation (NLA) Editor to convert the actions to NLA strips in order for them to be exported using the SIO2 exporter. Do these things by following these steps:

1. Add a new action by selecting ADD NEW in the drop-down menu of the Action Editor header as shown in Figure 8.25. This will create a new action that will be an exact copy of Walk. Select all keyframes with the A key and press the X key to delete them (Figure 8.26). Set the character to a rest pose by selecting all the bones in the 3D window with the A key and then pressing Alt+R to clear all rotations.

Figure 8.25

Adding a new action

Figure 8.26

Deleting all keyframes

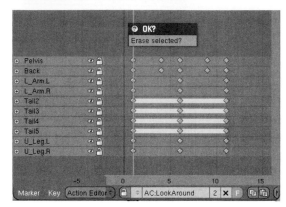

2. Create an action with the name **LookAround** as the default action for Frankie. You'll follow analogous steps to create this action as you did to create the Walk action. Figure 8.27 shows the poses at each key point in the action.

Figure 8.27

Poses at each point in the LookAround action

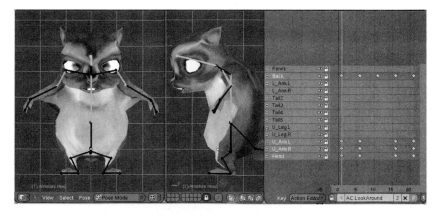

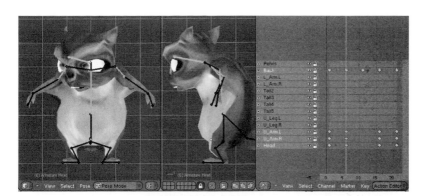

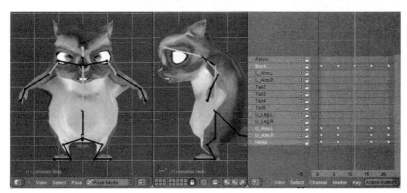

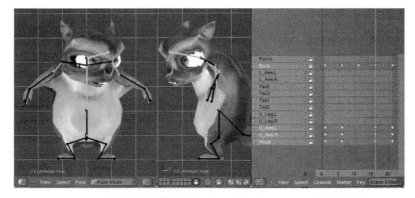

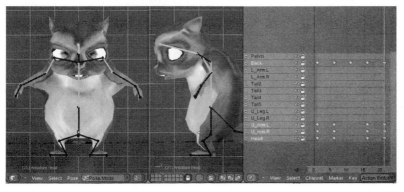

Figure 8.27

continued

Figure 8.28

Selecting an NLA Editor window type

3. Split your Action Editor horizontally and open an NLA Editor in the top window by selecting the entry from the Window Type drop-down menu shown in Figure 8.28. The resulting pair of windows, the Action Editor and NLA Editor together, should look something like Figure 8.29.

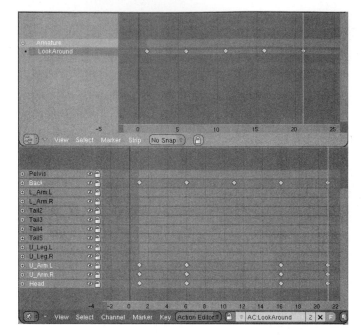

Figure 8.29

The NLA Editor and Action Editor with the LookAround action selected

4. Create an NLA strip to correspond with the LookAround action by pressing the C key over the NLA Editor, as shown in Figure 8.30. The resulting NLA strip is shown in Figure 8.31.

5. Select the Walk action from the drop-down menu in the Action Editor header, as shown in Figure 8.32. Doing this makes the Walk action the active action in the NLA Editor and makes it available to convert into an NLA strip. Again, convert the action to an NLA strip by pressing the C key. The resulting collection of NLA strips is shown in Figure 8.33.

Figure 8.30

Converting the LookAround action into an NLA strip

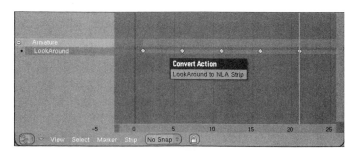

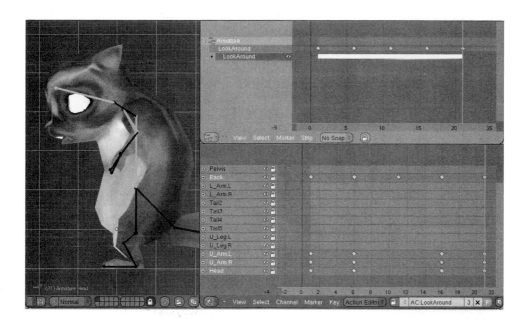

Figure 8.31

LookAround displayed as an NLA strip

Figure 8.32

Selecting Walk from the Action Editor header drop-down menu

Figure 8.33

Both actions converted to NLA strips

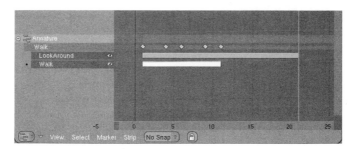

6. For the actions to be exported with the SIO2 exporter script, the NLA strips for the visions you want to extend must be set to be visible. In Figure 8.34, you can see the difference between visible settings and invisible settings. Toggling this value has basically the same function as selecting or deselecting 3D objects. In any case, be sure that all of the actions that you want to export to SIO2 are set to be visible. Also, please note that these settings can sometimes change after the SIO2 exporter has been called, causing other hard-to-detect problems in the software. So always be careful to ensure that the objects and actions that need to be visible are.

Figure 8.34
The visibility toggle
for NLA strips

To try to make the 3D environment a little more comfortable for Frankie the squirrel, I've added a textured plane for a floor, positioned just under his feet, as shown in Figure 8.35. You can experiment with this. Also, be sure to place the camera so that the character is in clear view. When you have a scene set up to your own satisfaction, export the objects to the .sio2 file format just as you have done in previous chapters.

There are no other special steps involved in exporting this content, aside from ensuring that all the actions are converted to strips and set as visible. Name the scene **iFrankie** and export it using the SIO2 exporter script. Once you've exported, you can close down Blender and turn to the code in Xcode.

Figure 8.35

The complete scene
with floor and
camera

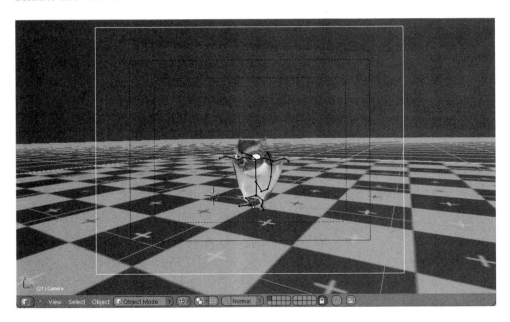

Getting Action in SIO2

Make a copy of the Template project, and fire up Xcode. Make sure you've dragged and dropped iFrankie.sio2 into the Groups & Files area of Xcode. Declare the templateLoading function in template.h and set it as the render callback function in EAGLview.mm, just as you have done for all the other examples in this book. As usual, the focus here is going to be on the changes you need to make to the default template.mm file.

Turning to `template.mm`, the first thing you need to do is declare some necessary variables at the top of the file, after the header includes:

```
SIO2object *frankie = NULL;
float FPS = 10.0f;
```

The *frankie* variable will hold the animated character mesh object, once it is loaded. The *FPS* variable will hold a frames-per-second value that will be necessary to play the actions later.

Now turn to the `templateLoading` function definition. A lot of what happens in this function should be standard by now (it's been shown several times throughout this book). You need to load the resources from the `iFrankie.sio2` file and bind them, just as in the previous examples. I'm going to skip the specific code for that here because it's identical to code from the previous chapters, but if you have any trouble recalling exactly how it should look in context, you can refer to the complete code at the end of this chapter. After loading and binding the resources and calling `sio2ResetState();`, add the following code:

```
frankie = sio2ResourceGetObject( sio2->_SIO2resource,
                              "object/frankie" );
```

This first line simply assigns the mesh object by the name of `frankie` (this name is determined by the Blender object name of the mesh) to the `frankie` SIO2object variable you just declared at the beginning of this section.

```
sio2ObjectInitAnimationAttributes( frankie );
```

Next is a call to the `sio2ObjectInitAnimationAttributes` function on the `frankie` object. This initializes the attributes necessary for setting and playing action animations on a mesh.

---

void **sio2ObjectInitAnimationAttributes**(SIO2object *object*)

This function creates a SIO2objectanimation structure and assigns it to the SIO2object *object*. The SIO2objectanimation structure holds the information necessary for an object to play action animations.

The next block of code calls the `sio2ObjectSetAction` function in order to set a current action for the object:

```
sio2ObjectSetAction( frankie,
          get_action( sio2->_SIO2resource,
              "iFrankie.sio2",
              "action/LookAround" ),
        0.01f,
        FPS );
```

The first argument tells which object will take the action—in this case, it's the frankie object. This object must have its animation attributes initialized, as was done in the previous line. The second argument is an action. In this case, you use a function called get_action to retrieve the LookAround action from the iFrankie.sio2 file. The get_action function is not a built-in function. You have to define it yourself, which you will see how to do later in this section. The next argument here represents the interval between repetitions of this action when it is looped. The higher this number is, the longer the pause will be between individual repetitions. A 0 (zero) value will result in an unsightly blink at each repetition, so for a smoothly repeating cycle, simply set a low value like **0.01f**. The last argument is the frame rate at which the animation should be played. This particular action looks best at a frame rate of 10 frames per second. If you want to run the animation at a higher frame rate, you would create the original action in Blender with more frames. For a very crude animation like the one you're working with here, you gain very little in quality by having a higher frame rate.

---

unsigned char **sio2ObjectSetAction**(SIO2object *object*, SIO2action *action*, "oat *interp*, "oat *fps*)

This function sets the current action for the *object*'s SIO2objectanimation structure to *action*. The *interp* value determines the amount of time between cycles of the animation, and the *fps* value determines the frame rate at which the action will be played.

Finally, the sio2ObjectPlay function is called on the frankie object. The second argument toggles cycling, with a 1 value indicating that the action should cycle and a 0 value indicating it should play just once and stop.

```
sio2ObjectPlay( frankie, 1 );
```

---

void **sio2ObjectPlay**(SIO2object *object*, unsigned char *loop*)

This function puts the object's SIO2animation structure into the SIO2_PLAY state, causing the current action to be rendered. The loop value determines whether the action is played as a repeating cycle (1) or is played just once (0).

Turn now to the templateRender function. A lot of what you see here is identical to code you've been introduced to in previous chapters, with a few small additions.

```
void templateRender( void )
{
    static float m[ 16 ] = { 0.0f };
    glClearColor( 0.8f, 0.9f, 1.0f, 1.0f );
```

The declaration of m[16] is a little premature because you won't be using it until later in the chapter when you create planar shadows. But for now, declare the variable to save the trouble of having to come back and do so later. The variable holds a 16-element array that will be used to represent a 4×4 matrix. You'll see what this has to do with shadows later.

The next line sets the color value that the color buffer is set to when it's cleared. The values I've put in here will yield a light sky blue, but any values will do.

```
glMatrixMode( GL_MODELVIEW );
glLoadIdentity();

glClear( GL_DEPTH_BUFFER_BIT | GL_COLOR_BUFFER_BIT );

if( !sio2->_SIO2camera )
{
    SIO2camera *_SIO2camera =
        ( SIO2camera * )sio2ResourceGet(
                                        sio2->_SIO2resource,
                                        SIO2_CAMERA,
                                        "camera/Camera" );

    if( !_SIO2camera )
    { return; }

    sio2->_SIO2camera = _SIO2camera;
    sio2Perspective( _SIO2camera->fov,
            sio2->_SIO2window->scl->x / sio2->_SIO2window->scl->y,
            _SIO2camera->cstart,
            _SIO2camera->cend );
}
```

The preceding code should all be immediately familiar. It has all been explained previously in the book, so if there are places that aren't clear, you should reread the earlier chapters where they are dealt with. Most of the next code block should also be familiar:

```
sio2WindowEnterLandscape3D();
{
    sio2CameraRender( sio2->_SIO2camera );

            //walking around code goes here

    //planar shadow code goes here

    sio2ResourceRender( sio2->_SIO2resource,
            sio2->_SIO2window,
            sio2->_SIO2camera,
            SIO2_RENDER_SOLID_OBJECT );
}
sio2WindowLeaveLandscape3D();

}
```

Only the two commented lines are really notable. The first says //walking around code goes here and the second says //planar shadow code goes here. As you have no doubt already surmised, you're going to be returning to those points in the function to add code later in this chapter.

Turn your attention to the templateScreenTap function. For the time being, all that is going to happen is that the character will enter a walk cycle when the screen is touched and return to looking around when the screen is not touched. Later you'll add touch movement code to make the character move around in space. For now, define templateScreenTap as follows:

```
void templateScreenTap( void *_ptr, unsigned char _state )
{
    if( _state == SIO2_WINDOW_TAP_DOWN )
    {
        sio2ObjectNextAction( frankie,
                              get_action( sio2->_SIO2resource,
                                          "iFrankie.sio2",
                                          "action/Walk" ),
                              0.01f,
                              FPS );
    }
    if( _state == SIO2_WINDOW_TAP_UP )
    {

        sio2ObjectNextAction( frankie,
                              get_action( sio2->_SIO2resource,
                                          "iFrankie.sio2",
                                          "action/LookAround" ),
                              0.01f,
                              FPS );
    }
    sio2ObjectPlay( frankie, 1 );

}
```

As you can see, depending on whether the event is a tap down (finger touching the screen) or a tap up (finger leaving the screen) event, the newly set action is either Walk or LookAround. The function that sets the new action is sio2ObjectNextAction, and the arguments are identical in meaning to those for sio2ObjectSetAction, explained previously. Finally, sio2ObjectPlay(frankie, 1) is called to set the mesh in motion with the new action. For now, that's all there is to this function.

unsigned char **sio2ObjectNextAction**(SIO2object *object*, SIO2action *action, "oat *interp*,
"oat *fps*)

This function sets the next action on a SIO2objectanimation structure that already has a
current action set. Its objects are identical in meaning to those of sio2ObjectSetAction.

You still can't build and run the program though. The get_action function has not yet
been defined. Define the function in template.mm above the other function definitions.
The code for the function is as follows:

```
SIO2action *get_action( SIO2resource *_SIO2resource,
                char   *_filename,
                char   *_name )
{
    SIO2action *_SIO2action =
        sio2ResourceGetAction( _SIO2resource, _name );

    if( !_SIO2action )
    {
        SIO2stream *_SIO2stream = sio2StreamInit("");
        sio2ResourceOpen( _SIO2resource, _filename, 1 );
        sio2->_SIO2resource = _SIO2resource;
        sio2ResourceExtractFile( _SIO2resource,
                                    _SIO2stream,
                                    _name, NULL );
        sio2ResourceClose( _SIO2resource );
        sio2StreamParse( _SIO2stream,
                    _SIO2resource->n_entry,
                    _SIO2resource->_SIO2entry );
            _SIO2stream = sio2StreamClose( _SIO2stream );
    }
    else
    { return _SIO2action; }
    return sio2->_SIO2action;

}
```

The basic idea behind this function is to access the actions when you need them rather
than loading them all at once with the other assets. Although the context of the code here
may be unfamiliar, the individual lines of the code are things that you've seen elsewhere,
namely in loading other assets from the .sio2 file.

Once this function has been defined, you can build and run your code. You should
see Frankie standing in the middle of the floor when the screen is not being touched and
walking in place when the screen is touched, as shown in Figure 8.36. If you release the
touch, he'll go back looking around while standing still.

Figure 8.36

Frankie looking around and walking in place

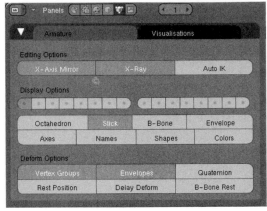

Taking a Walk

Obviously, a walk cycle isn't a lot of use if the character can't be made to actually go somewhere. In this section, you'll add the necessary functionality to make Frankie walk around (and out of) the scene.

The controls for the character's movement will be analogous to those of a radio-controlled car. Moving your finger upward on the screen (in landscape position) will move Frankie forward. Moving your finger downward moves him backward. Moving your finger to the left makes him turn to his own left, and moving your finger to the right makes him turn right. The distance your finger moves from the point where you first touch the screen will determine the speed with which Frankie moves or turns. Of course, this is not the only possible way you could implement character movement controls, but it's easy to understand and simple to implement, so for the present purposes, it's very suitable.

In order to do some simple calculations for the direction of the movement, you'll need to be able to return sine and cosine values for angles. This requires the C math library. Add this to the header includes:

```
#include <math.h>
```

You'll also need to declare some more variables. Declare the following variables with the others below the header includes:

```
float ROT_FACTOR;
float ROT_Z = 0.0f;
float DIST_FACTOR;
vec2 start;

vec2 d;
```

The first, second, and third variables will be used to control the character's rotation speed, the amount of rotation caused by a touch movement, and speed of translation movement. The last two variables are two-dimensional vectors representing, respectively, the starting point of a touch event and the distance of the touch movement.

Now turn your attention again to templateRender. Return to the point where you left the comment //walking around code goes here and replace that code with the following code block:

```
ROT_Z =+ ROT_FACTOR;

frankie->_SIO2transform->rot->z += ROT_Z;
```

The first line sets the increase of the z rotation of the object based on the ROT_FACTOR value. The ROT_FACTOR value is determined by the touch movement, so that will be set elsewhere in the code. The next line adds the increase value to the *frankie* object's absolute z rotation value. This rotates the object. Moving the object is somewhat more complicated. This is done with the following block of code:

```
frankie->_SIO2transform->loc->x +=
    DIST_FACTOR*
    sinf(frankie->_SIO2transform->rot->z*
    SIO2_DEG_TO_RAD);
frankie->_SIO2transform->loc->y -=
    DIST_FACTOR*
    cosf(frankie->_SIO2transform->rot->z/
    SIO2_DEG_TO_RAD);
```

If you are accustomed to working with Blender, your instinct may be to think in terms of a local coordinate system. Unfortunately, no such construct exists in SIO2, so translation must be done in terms of the object's "global" x- and y-coordinates. Fortunately, with a little bit of simple trigonometry, calculating the direction along the x- and y-axis is pretty simple. The direction on the x-axis turns out to be the sine of the angle of the z rotation, and the direction along the y-axis is the negative cosine of the angle of the z rotation. If you're not sure why this is, a quick review of sines and cosines in any basic math resource should make it completely clear. The sine and cosine of the angle are calculated using the math.h functions sinf and cosf, which take as their argument an angle expressed in radians. The _SIO2transform->rot->z value is stored in degrees, so the value must be converted by multiplying it by $\pi/180$. You can use the built-in constant

SIO2_DEG_TO_RAD to derive this value. Finally, the distance the object is translated is expressed by multiplying the cosine and sine values by the DIST_FACTOR value.

Once the appropriate location and rotation transforms have been calculated, it's necessary to call sio2TransformBindMatrix to apply the transformations to the object in the 3D space, as follows:

```
sio2TransformBindMatrix( frankie->_SIO2transform );
```

---

void **sio2TransformBindMatrix**(SIO2transform *transform*)

This function calls the required GL functions to apply the SIO2transform *transform* to the object in the 3D space for rendering. Until this function is called, the SIO2transform structure stores transformations but does not apply them to the object.

Now turn your attention again to templateScreenTap. It's necessary here to assign some values to variables to make it possible to calculate the screen touch movement. First, in the _state == SIO2_WINDOW_TAP_DOWN block, add the following code:

```
start.x = sio2->_SIO2window->touch[ 0 ]->x;

start.y = sio2->_SIO2window->touch[ 0 ]->y;
```

This simply sets the value of the x and y components of the *start* variable, recording the coordinates where the finger initially touches the screen.

Next, in the _state == SIO2_WINDOW_TAP_UP block, add the following lines:

```
d.x = 0.0f;
d.y = 0.0f;
ROT_FACTOR = 0.0f;
DIST_FACTOR = 0.0f;
```

These lines simply set the appropriate values to 0 (zero), stopping all translation and rotation movement when the finger has left the screen.

Finally, write the definition of templateScreenTouchMove as follows:

```
void templateScreenTouchMove( void *_ptr )
{
    if (!frankie){
        return;
    }
    if( sio2->_SIO2window->n_touch )
    {
        d.x = (sio2->_SIO2window->touch[ 0 ]->y - start.y)*0.05f;
        d.y = (sio2->_SIO2window->touch[ 0 ]->x - start.x)*0.05f;

        ROT_FACTOR = -d.x*0.5f ;
        DIST_FACTOR = d.y*0.005f ;


    }
}
```

I hope that most of what is happening here is fairly clear. The values of *d.x* and *d.y* are determined by the difference between the current touch value and the corresponding coordinate from the *start* vector. Dividing these values by 20 is arbitrary; 20 was simply a value arrived at by trial and error. Likewise, the coefficients used to obtain ROT_FACTOR and DIST_FACTOR are based on trial and error to attain the most responsive feel for the interface. Different values here would make the movement and rotation of the character more quick or sluggish.

Try building and running the application now. You should be able to control Frankie's walk around the 3D space just as you would control a radio-controlled car. With a little practice, you'll get the hang of it!

Quick and Dirty Real-Time Shadows

In the official SIO2 Tutorial 4 that came with your SIO2 SDK download, there's an interesting approach used to create real-time, responsive shadows that can be rendered very quickly. The downside of the approach is that the shadows must be opaque and they will work only when cast onto a completely flat plane. Since Frankie is walking around on just such a plane in this example, the approach will work nicely to add a level of realism to the scene.

The way these real-time shadows work is simple in principle. A transformation matrix is created that basically flattens a mesh. Shadow-casting objects in the scene are identified and operated on by the matrix to make them completely flat along the z-axis. This new mesh is colored black and placed just above the surface of the ground plane.

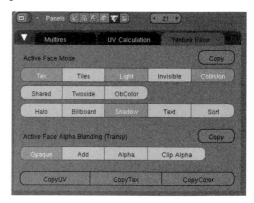

Figure 8.37

Setting an object to cast shadows

It's desirable to set this shadow-casting functionality to work only on specific, predetermined objects. The way to set a shadow-casting object is to select the Shadow option in the Texture Face panel for the object as shown in Figure 8.37 for the frankie mesh object. To obtain the shadow effect described in this section, be sure you set the Shadow value for the object and then update the export of your scene.

To implement planar shadows, it's first necessary to define another function. This time, define the function shadowmatrix. Define it above the other function definitions in your program, below the variable declarations, like this:

```
void shadowmatrix( float *_m, vec4 *_n, vec4 *_lpos )
{
    float dp = ( _n->x * _lpos->x ) +
    ( _n->y * _lpos->y ) +
    ( _n->z * _lpos->z ) +
    ( _n->w * _lpos->w );
```

```
    _m[ 0  ] = dp   - ( _lpos->x * _n->x );
    _m[ 4  ] = 0.0f - ( _lpos->x * _n->y );
    _m[ 8  ] = 0.0f - ( _lpos->x * _n->z );
    _m[ 12 ] = 0.0f - ( _lpos->x * _n->w );

    _m[ 1  ] = 0.0f - ( _lpos->y * _n->x );
    _m[ 5  ] = dp   - ( _lpos->y * _n->y );
    _m[ 9  ] = 0.0f - ( _lpos->y * _n->z );
    _m[ 13 ] = 0.0f - ( _lpos->y * _n->w );

    _m[ 2  ] = 0.0f - ( _lpos->z * _n->x );
    _m[ 6  ] = 0.0f - ( _lpos->z * _n->y );
    _m[ 10 ] = dp   - ( _lpos->z * _n->z );
    _m[ 14 ] = 0.0f - ( _lpos->z * _n->w );

    _m[ 3  ] = 0.0f - ( _lpos->w * _n->x );
    _m[ 7  ] = 0.0f - ( _lpos->w * _n->y );
    _m[ 11 ] = 0.0f - ( _lpos->w * _n->z );
    _m[ 15 ] = dp   - ( _lpos->w * _n->w );
}
```

This function takes the normal vector of the planar surface and a vector representing the position of the light in the sky and creates a 4×4 transformation vector to flatten a mesh according to these values. Each of the four blocks of code in the function represents a row of the matrix. It's beyond the scope of this book to go into detail about how transformation matrices work or how they are represented in C, so for a big-picture description of how this function works, this will have to suffice.

In template render, recall that you already declared a variable representing the 4×4 matrix as follows:

```
static float m[ 16 ] = { 0.0f };
```

You'll now use this variable when you calling the shadowmatrix function. The following code should be inserted at the spot where the //planar shadow code goes here comment was written:

```
if( !m[ 0 ] )
{
    vec4 n, lpos;
    n.x = n.y = n.w = 0.0f;
    n.z = 1.0f;
    lpos.x =   10.0f;
    lpos.y =   -5.0f;
    lpos.z =   20.0f;
    lpos.w =   0.0f;
    shadowmatrix( m, &n, &lpos );
}
```

This first code block sets the values for the normal vector and the light position vector and then creates a shadow matrix out of *m*.

The next code block begins with `glPushMatrix` so that the current matrix can be quickly accessed again by popping the matrix after the shadow transforms have been completed:

```
glPushMatrix();
{
        unsigned int i = 0;

        glMultMatrixf( &m[ 0 ] );
```

Here the *m* matrix is multiplied by the model/view matrix so that subsequent objects will be rendered flat along a plane.

The next block of code sets black as the drawing color:

```
        {
                vec4 shadow = { 0.0f, 0.0f, 0.0f, 1.0f };
                sio2StateSetColor( sio2->_SIO2state, &shadow );

        }
```

The remainder of this code runs through the objects registered in the Resource Manager. Shadow casting objects are selected, and those objects are enabled as shadow objects and rendered in the current rendering context, namely as flat black objects.

```
        glEnable( GL_POLYGON_OFFSET_FILL );
        glPolygonOffset( -10.0f, -10.0f );
        while( i != sio2->_SIO2resource->n_object )
        {
          SIO2object *_SIO2object =
            ( SIO2object * )sio2->_SIO2resource->_SIO2object[i];

          if( sio2IsStateEnabled( _SIO2object->flags,
                                  SIO2_OBJECT_SHADOW ) )
          {
                if( _SIO2object->dst < 0.0f )
                    { _SIO2object->dst = 1.0f; }

                sio2ObjectRender( _SIO2object,
                        sio2->_SIO2window,
                        sio2->_SIO2camera,
                        0, SIO2_TRANSFORM_MATRIX_BIND );
          }
          ++i;
        }
        sio2ObjectReset();
        glDisable( GL_POLYGON_OFFSET_FILL );
}
glPopMatrix();
```

```
void sio2StateSetColor(SIO2state *state, vec4 color)
```

This function sets the color value of the SIO2state structure *state* to the four-dimensional vector *color*.

```
static inline unsigned char sio2IsStateEnabled(unsigned int var,
    unsigned int state)
```

This is a general-purpose function for determining whether any given state *state* is enabled.

At the end of the code block, the matrix stack is popped and the model/view matrix returns to the state it was in prior to rendering the shadow.

You should now be able to build and run your application to see Frankie walking around with a shadow cast on the floor, as shown in Figure 8.38. In the next chapter, you'll look at how to augment the game environment with useful goodies such as splash screens and interactive buttons.

Figure 8.38

Frankie sees his shadow.

If your objects are not casting shadows, it's likely that you forgot to set them as shadow-casting objects in Blender before reexporting as shown in Figure 8.37. This is easy to over-look, so be sure not to forget it!

The Complete Code

Here's the complete template.mm code for the iFrankie application so far:

```
#include "template.h"
#include "../src/sio2/sio2.h"
#include <math.h>
```

```
SIO2object *frankie = NULL;

float ROT_FACTOR;
float ROT_Z = 0.0f;
float DIST_FACTOR;
//float FPS = 15.0f * (30 * sio2->_SIO2window->d_time);
float FPS = 10.0f;
vec2 start;
vec2 d;

void shadowmatrix( float *_m, vec4 *_n, vec4 *_lpos )
{
    float dp = ( _n->x * _lpos->x ) +
    ( _n->y * _lpos->y ) +
    ( _n->z * _lpos->z ) +
    ( _n->w * _lpos->w );

    _m[ 0  ] = dp    - ( _lpos->x * _n->x );
    _m[ 4  ] = 0.0f - ( _lpos->x * _n->y );
    _m[ 8  ] = 0.0f - ( _lpos->x * _n->z );
    _m[ 12 ] = 0.0f - ( _lpos->x * _n->w );

    _m[ 1  ] = 0.0f - ( _lpos->y * _n->x );
    _m[ 5  ] = dp    - ( _lpos->y * _n->y );
    _m[ 9  ] = 0.0f - ( _lpos->y * _n->z );
    _m[ 13 ] = 0.0f - ( _lpos->y * _n->w );

    _m[ 2  ] = 0.0f - ( _lpos->z * _n->x );
    _m[ 6  ] = 0.0f - ( _lpos->z * _n->y );
    _m[ 10 ] = dp    - ( _lpos->z * _n->z );
    _m[ 14 ] = 0.0f - ( _lpos->z * _n->w );

    _m[ 3  ] = 0.0f - ( _lpos->w * _n->x );
    _m[ 7  ] = 0.0f - ( _lpos->w * _n->y );
    _m[ 11 ] = 0.0f - ( _lpos->w * _n->z );
    _m[ 15 ] = dp    - ( _lpos->w * _n->w );
}


SIO2action *get_action( SIO2resource *_SIO2resource,
               char  *_filename,
               char  *_name )
{
    SIO2action *_SIO2action =
        sio2ResourceGetAction( _SIO2resource, _name );

    if( !_SIO2action )
    {
```

```
            SIO2stream *_SIO2stream = sio2StreamInit("");
            sio2ResourceOpen( _SIO2resource, _filename, 1 );
            sio2->_SIO2resource = _SIO2resource;
            sio2ResourceExtractFile( _SIO2resource,
                                     _SIO2stream,
                                     _name, NULL );
            sio2ResourceClose( _SIO2resource );
            sio2StreamParse( _SIO2stream,
                    _SIO2resource->n_entry,
                    _SIO2resource->_SIO2entry );
              _SIO2stream = sio2StreamClose( _SIO2stream );
        }
        else
        { return _SIO2action; }
        return sio2->_SIO2action;
    }


void templateRender( void )
{
    static float m[ 16 ] = { 0.0f };
    glClearColor( 0.8f, 0.9f, 1.0f, 1.0f );

    glMatrixMode( GL_MODELVIEW );
    glLoadIdentity();

    glClear( GL_DEPTH_BUFFER_BIT | GL_COLOR_BUFFER_BIT );

    if( !sio2->_SIO2camera )
    {
        SIO2camera *_SIO2camera =
            ( SIO2camera * )sio2ResourceGet(
                                sio2->_SIO2resource,
                                SIO2_CAMERA,
                                "camera/Camera" );

        if( !_SIO2camera )
        { return; }

        sio2->_SIO2camera = _SIO2camera;
        sio2Perspective( _SIO2camera->fov,
                sio2->_SIO2window->scl->x / sio2->_SIO2window->scl->y,
                _SIO2camera->cstart,
                _SIO2camera->cend );
    }

    sio2WindowEnterLandscape3D();
    {
```

```
sio2CameraRender( sio2->_SIO2camera );
ROT_Z =+ ROT_FACTOR;

frankie->_SIO2transform->rot->z += ROT_Z;
frankie->_SIO2transform->loc->x +=
    DIST_FACTOR*
    sinf(frankie->_SIO2transform->rot->z*
    SIO2_DEG_TO_RAD);
frankie->_SIO2transform->loc->y -=
    DIST_FACTOR*
    cosf(frankie->_SIO2transform->rot->z*
    SIO2_DEG_TO_RAD);

sio2TransformBindMatrix( frankie->_SIO2transform );

if( !m[ 0 ] )
{
    vec4 n, lpos;
    n.x = n.y = n.w = 0.0f;
    n.z = 1.0f;
    lpos.x =  10.0f;
    lpos.y =  -5.0f;
    lpos.z =  20.0f;
    lpos.w =   0.0f;
    shadowmatrix( m, &n, &lpos );
}

glPushMatrix();
{
    unsigned int i = 0;
    glMultMatrixf( &m[ 0 ] );
    {
        vec4 shadow = { 0.0f, 0.0f, 0.0f, 1.0f };
        sio2StateSetColor( sio2->_SIO2state, &shadow );
    }
    glEnable( GL_POLYGON_OFFSET_FILL );
    glPolygonOffset( -10.0f, -10.0f );
    while( i != sio2->_SIO2resource->n_object )
    {
      SIO2object *_SIO2object =
        ( SIO2object * )sio2->_SIO2resource->_SIO2object[i];

        if( sio2IsStateEnabled(
                    _SIO2object->flags,
                    SIO2_OBJECT_SHADOW ) )
        {
```

```
                                    if( _SIO2object->dst < 0.0f )
                                        { _SIO2object->dst = 1.0f; }

                                sio2ObjectRender( _SIO2object,
                                            sio2->_SIO2window,
                                            sio2->_SIO2camera,
                                            0, SIO2_TRANSFORM_MATRIX_BIND );
                        }
                        ++i;
                }
                sio2ObjectReset();
                glDisable( GL_POLYGON_OFFSET_FILL );
        }
        glPopMatrix();

        sio2ResourceRender( sio2->_SIO2resource,
                        sio2->_SIO2window,
                        sio2->_SIO2camera,
                        SIO2_RENDER_SOLID_OBJECT );
    }
    sio2WindowLeaveLandscape3D();
}


void templateShutdown( void )
{
    sio2ResourceUnloadAll( sio2->_SIO2resource );
    sio2->_SIO2resource = sio2ResourceFree( sio2->_SIO2resource );
    sio2->_SIO2window = sio2WindowFree( sio2->_SIO2window );
    sio2 = sio2Shutdown();
    printf("\nSIO2: shutdown...\n" );
}


void templateLoading(void){
    unsigned int i = 0;
    sio2ResourceCreateDictionary( sio2->_SIO2resource );

    sio2ResourceOpen( sio2->_SIO2resource,
                "iFrankie.sio2", 1 );

    while( i != sio2->_SIO2resource->gi.number_entry )
    {
        sio2ResourceExtract( sio2->_SIO2resource, NULL );
        ++i;
    }

    sio2ResourceClose( sio2->_SIO2resource );
```

```
        sio2ResourceBindAllImages( sio2->_SIO2resource );
        sio2ResourceBindAllMaterials( sio2->_SIO2resource );
        sio2ResourceBindAllMatrix( sio2->_SIO2resource );
        sio2ResourceGenId( sio2->_SIO2resource );
        sio2ResetState();

        frankie =
            sio2ResourceGetObject( sio2->_SIO2resource,
                                   "object/frankie" );
        sio2ObjectInitAnimationAttributes( frankie );
        sio2ObjectSetAction( frankie,
                    get_action( sio2->_SIO2resource,
                    "iFrankie.sio2",
                    "action/LookAround" ),
                    0.01f,
                    FPS );
        sio2ObjectPlay( frankie, 1 );
        sio2->_SIO2window->_SIO2windowrender = templateRender;
}


void templateScreenTap( void *_ptr, unsigned char _state )
{
        float fps = 15.0f * (30 * sio2->_SIO2window->d_time);
        if( _state == SIO2_WINDOW_TAP_DOWN )
        {
            sio2ObjectNextAction( frankie,
            get_action( sio2->_SIO2resource,
            "iFrankie.sio2",
            "action/Walk" ),
            0.01f,
            FPS );
            start.x = sio2->_SIO2window->touch[ 0 ]->x;
            start.y = sio2->_SIO2window->touch[ 0 ]->y;
        }
        if( _state == SIO2_WINDOW_TAP_UP )
        {
            d.x = 0.0f;
            d.y = 0.0f;
            ROT_FACTOR = 0.0f;
            DIST_FACTOR = 0.0f;

            sio2ObjectNextAction( frankie,
            get_action( sio2->_SIO2resource,
                    "iFrankie.sio2",
                    "action/LookAround" ),
```

```
                        0.01f,
                        FPS );
            }
        sio2ObjectPlay( frankie, 1 );
    }


void templateScreenTouchMove( void *_ptr )
{
    if (!frankie){
        return;
    }
    if( sio2->_SIO2window->n_touch )
    {
        d.x = (sio2->_SIO2window->touch[ 0 ]->y - start.y)*0.05f;
        d.y = (sio2->_SIO2window->touch[ 0 ]->x - start.x)*0.05f;

        ROT_FACTOR = -d.x*0.5f ;
        DIST_FACTOR = d.y*0.005f ;


    }
}


void templateScreenAccelerometer( void *_ptr )
{
}
    start.y = sio2->_SIO2window->touch[ 0 ]->y;
        }
        if( _state == SIO2_WINDOW_TAP_UP )
        {
            d.x = 0.0f;
            d.y = 0.0f;
            ROT_FACTOR = 0.0f;
            DIST_FACTOR = 0.0f;

            sio2ObjectNextAction( frankie,
            get_action( sio2->_SIO2resource,
                "iFrankie.sio2",
                "action/LookAround" ),
                0.01f,
                FPS );
        }
        sio2ObjectPlay( frankie, 1 );
    }

void templateScreenTouchMove( void *_ptr )
{
```

```
    if (!frankie){
        return;
    }
    if( sio2->_SIO2window->n_touch )
    {
        d.x = (sio2->_SIO2window->touch[ 0 ]->y - start.y)*0.05f;
        d.y = (sio2->_SIO2window->touch[ 0 ]->x - start.x)*0.05f;

        ROT_FACTOR = -d.x*0.5f ;
        DIST_FACTOR = d.y*0.005f ;

    }
}

void templateScreenAccelerometer( void *_ptr )
{
}
```

CHAPTER 9

Working with Widgets

In this chapter, you'll learn how to work with SIO2 widgets. Widgets provide an important general-purpose graphical resource and enable a much richer user interface for your application. They are used to create splash screens, buttons, icons, menus, and other two-dimensional visual elements. Getting comfortable with using widgets is a big step toward creating the kind of fully fleshed-out application experience that you can make available to others on the iTunes App Store.

- Making a splash with a simple widget
- Creating a responsive widget button with a local callback function
- The Complete Code

Making a Splash with Widgets

So far you've learned about how to create 3D assets for iPhone apps with Blender and how to bring them into an interactive environment with the SIO2 game engine. Most applications and games also rely on numerous graphical elements that are not based on 3D assets but rather use 2D graphics to convey information, to enhance the user interface, or simply to entertain. These graphical elements are known as *widgets*. Most iPhone apps use widgets in some way. Widgets may be used to create splash screens, loading screens, or menus. They are used to create interface elements such as buttons or icons that can be superimposed directly over the game view if necessary. Using widgets can greatly enhance the look and usability of your application.

In this chapter, you'll learn how to work with widgets. Specifically, you'll create a start screen for the `iFrankie` app from Chapter 8. From that screen, you'll use a button to launch the 3D part of the application. Both the start screen itself and the button will be widgets.

It's possible to make video widgets in SIO2. You'll find what you need to learn to create video images in the code sample tutorials that accompany the official SIO2 distribution. You'll find a guide to these tutorials in Appendix C of this book. For the purpose of this chapter, however, the widgets you'll use will all be still images.

The images for widgets can be created with any 2D graphics software. I use GIMP for raster graphics and Inkscape for vector graphics, both of which are open source and available for all major platforms. Adobe Photoshop and Adobe Illustrator are also excellent alternatives. The only real requirements are that you must be able to scale and crop your images and that you can handle JPEG and PNG graphics.

Choosing Image Formats

As you've seen when working with textures, you have a number of choices when it comes to which kinds of 2D graphics to use. The same is true when working with widgets. Raster graphics formats differ in terms of the amount and type of information they hold and the type of compression they use. To conserve memory and processing resources, you should always use the most compact format you can.

One of the basic determiners about which kind of graphics format you should use is whether you need alpha transparency or not. The JPEG format does not encode an alpha channel—JPEGs cannot be transparent or partially transparent. Obviously, this makes JPEGs inadequate for situations where the image needs to be transparent. However, a JPEG's lack of alpha information translates into a more compact file, so if your graphic does not need to be transparent (as is usually the case with splash screens and the like), JPEG is a good option. JPEG also uses a lossy compression algorithm that can result in very compact files if you are willing to give up some image quality. The level of compression you can get away with depends on the image.

For other kinds of widgets, such as buttons or oddly shaped icons, transparency is a must. The most commonly used graphics formats with gradated alpha transparency are PNG and Targa (TGA) files. TGA files are widely used in the game industry and have a number of advantages. They are extremely fast to load because they do not require the decompression step that PNG files require. For this reason, I recommend using TGA files for transparent graphics that are locally stored. Furthermore, there are a few things to be careful of when using PNGs as widgets. If you do opt to use PNGs, see the note about the importance of disabling PNG compression in Xcode.

> I recommend using TGA files for widgets, but if for some reason you prefer to use PNGs, you must realize that by default, Xcode compresses PNG files internally. This can present big problems when the PNGs are used as widget graphics and need to be drawn directly to the screen of your iPhone or iPod Touch device! If you are using PNG widgets and find that your application works fine in the simulator but crashes mysteriously when you build to the device, the chances are good that this Xcode PNG compression is the culprit. If you use PNGs for your widgets, you must disable PNG compression. Do this by going to Edit Project Settings in the Project menu of Xcode, selecting the Build option at the top of the Project Info window, and scrolling down until you find a check box corresponding to the Compress PNG Files entry under the Packaging header. Deselect the check box to disable PNG compression.

Widget Graphics for iFrankie

There's nothing particularly special about creating graphics for use as SIO2 widgets. As with all graphics you use in SIO2, you need to ensure that the dimensions in pixels are powers of two. When creating a splash screen, it's best to create the image to the size of the iPhone screen to minimize any kind or image quality loss that might result from having to scale the widget to fit the screen. The iPhone screen is 480×320 pixels, so you should first create your splash graphic at this size and then resize the canvas of your image to 512×512, as shown in Figure 9.1. You can find this image, `splash.jpg`, in the directory for the project associated with this chapter. I added a gray background to the unused portion of this image so that the complete image would stand out in against the white page, but this isn't necessary. The unused part of the graphic will be clipped and discarded when the widget is displayed on the 480×320 iPhone screen.

The button graphic is a PNG with alpha transparency so that it can appear as a circle, with a slight shadow behind it, as shown in Figure 9.2. Any of the graphics applications I mentioned previously will enable you to export graphics with transparent backgrounds. This graphic should be cropped to a size of 128×128 pixels.

Figure 9.1

The splash JPEG for iFrankie

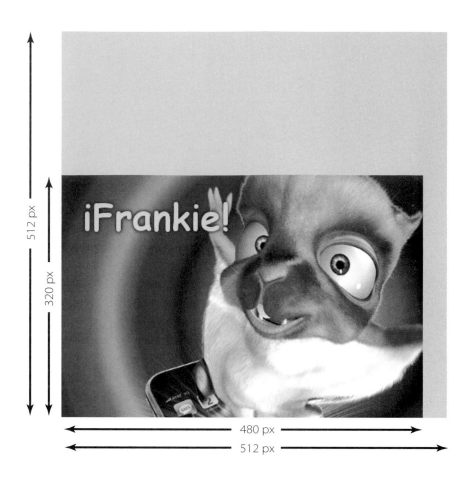

You can use these graphics, which are provided in the project directory, or you can create your own. If you create your own, give them the names `splash.jpg` and `button.tga`. Once you've got the graphics, drag and drop them into the `Resources` directory in the Groups & Files area of Xcode. Now you're ready to get your hands dirty with some SIO2 code.

Figure 9.2

The button TGA

Creating Active Widgets in SIO2

In the following sections, you'll make additions and changes to the `template.mm` file from Chapter 8, so go ahead and open that project up. Assuming that your `iFrankie` project is implemented as described in Chapter 8 and is running properly, there's only one more small change to a file other than `template.mm` that you must make. That change is in `EAGLView.mm`, where you need to initialize the widget handling functionality so that you can use widgets in your app. The command to do that is `sio2InitWidget();`, which you can call in the line directly after sio2InitGL(); in the if(!sio2) conditional block. Once you've added this line to EAGLView.mm, turn your attention to the template.mm file.

---

void **sio2InitWidget**(void)

This function sets aside memory in the main sio2 structure to store widget data. This general initialization function must be called before any individual widgets can be initialized.

Declaring Variables for Widgets

You'll be working with two widgets in this project: one for the splash screen and one for the button. Each widget will be associated with a specific image, as discussed in the first section of this chapter. In SIO2, images are associated with objects (and widgets) by means of materials, so this means that each of your widgets will need a material. Each of these various assets needs a corresponding variable to store it in, so the first thing you need to do is to declare the variables at the beginning of the template.mm file where your other global variables are declared (the actual order of the variables' declaration doesn't matter). Declare those variables like this:

```
SIO2widget    *splash_widget  = NULL;
SIO2material *splash_mat      = NULL;
SIO2image     *splash_im      = NULL;

SIO2widget    *button_widget  = NULL;
SIO2material *button_mat      = NULL;
SIO2image     *button_im      = NULL;
```

The first three lines declare variables for the widget, material, and image for the splash screen, and the next three lines declare corresponding variables for the button. The types of the variables are the SIO2 data types SIO2widget, SIO2material, and SIO2image. These variables can all be initialized to NULL. They'll get proper values at loading time.

While you're declaring variables, go ahead and declare a toggle for playing the start screen, as follows:

```
unsigned char startscreen = 1;
```

When the value is 1, the start screen will be shown. When the value switches to 0, the start screen will end and the 3D game play state will begin.

Loading Widgets and Assets

Logically, the next step is to load the widgets into the app. This occurs in the templateLoading function, so turn your attention to that function now. When you finished with Chapter 8, templateLoading contained the code to load the Blender 3D assets from the .sio2 file you exported. These assets must still be loaded, but before they are, you'll load the splash screen and button assets. The overall structure of templateLoading will be like this:

```
void templateLoading( void )
{
        SIO2stream *_SIO2stream = NULL;
        // Load the splash screen
        {
                //splash screen loading code goes here
        }

        // Load the button
        {
                //button loading code goes here
        }
// Load Blender 3D assets
        {
                //3D assets loading code from Chapter 8
        }
        sio2->_SIO2window->_SIO2windowrender = templateRender;
}
```

The first line inside the function creates a null SIO2stream object that will be used later to load the images. After that, there are three main blocks of code within the function. The first block loads the splash screen. The comment //splash screen loading code goes here holds the place where the splash screen loading code will go. Likewise for the button, the comment //button loading code goes here holds the place for the button loading code. The third placeholder, the comment //3D assets loading code from Chapter 8, shows you where the loading code from Chapter 8 will fit into this new templateLoading function.

As always, the last line of templateLoad assigns the templateRender callback as the render function.

The code for loading the splash screen template follows. This code should go in place of the //splash screen loading code goes here comment:

```
_SIO2stream = sio2StreamOpen( "splash.jpg", 1 );

splash_widget    = sio2WidgetInit  ( "splash" );
splash_mat       = sio2MaterialInit( "splash" );
splash_im        = sio2ImageInit   ( "splash" );
```

The loading code begins by using the previously declared SIO2stream variable and opening a data stream consisting of the splash.jpg image. As you've seen already in this book, streams are the way that data is passed into a program from an outside source. In this case, the source is the JPEG image that you placed in the Resources directory. The second argument to sio2StreamOpen tells SIO2 that the path to the file is relative to the present working directory. The next three lines initialize and give a name to the widget, material, and image structures that you declared at the top of the file. The variables are no longer NULL but now represent populated data structures.

```
SIO2widget *sio2WidgetInit( char *name )
SIO2material *sio2MaterialInit( char *name )
SIO2image *sio2ImageInit( char *name )
```

These functions initialize and return individual SIO2widget, SIO2material, and SIO2image structures. Any widget, material, or image must be initialized in this way, although this initialization happens behind the scenes when assets are loaded from an .sio2 file.

The code continues with the following lines:

```
sio2ImageLoad( splash_im , _SIO2stream );
sio2ImageGenId( splash_im , 0, 0.0f );
```

These lines associate the contents of the JPEG image file (which was brought into the program with the _SIO2stream data stream) with the SIO2image data structure splash_im and handle the necessary OpenGL texture processing for the SIO2image structure.

```
void sio2ImageLoad(SIO2image *image, SIO2stream *stream)
```

This function passes the image data from an incoming SIO2stream *stream* to the SIO2image structure *image*. The stream represents data read from an external image file such as a JPEG, PNG, or Targa file.

```
vo sio2ImageGenId(SIO2image *image, unsigned int "ags, "oat "1ter)
```

This function calls OpenGL texture functions and sets OpenGL texture parameters that correspond to SIO2 image values. The values passed in *flags* and *filter* represent SIO2image structure flags and filters to be converted to OpenGL flags and filter values.

The next lines associate the widget, material, and image with each other:

```
splash_widget->_SIO2material = splash_mat;
splash_mat->_SIO2image[ SIO2_MATERIAL_CHANNEL0 ] = splash_im ;
splash_mat->blend = SIO2_MATERIAL_COLOR;
```

The first line assigns splash_mat to the widget. The next line assigns splash_im to the first channel of the material. The last line sets the blending method to be

SIO2_MATERIAL_COLOR. In previous examples in this book, these steps were done as part of the process of populating objects and materials from Blender assets represented by .sio2 files. However, here the material and image have been constructed by hand, so the image must be assigned explicitly in the code.

The next two lines set the widget's size:

```
splash_widget->_SIO2transform->scl->x = splash_im->width;

splash_widget->_SIO2transform->scl->y = splash_im->height;
```

The size of the widget is set by simply assigning the width and height of the image to the x and y scale values on the widget's SIO2transform structure.

This is all you need to do to load the splash widget. The last line in this code block simply closes the stream so that it can be reused later:

```
_SIO2stream = sio2StreamClose( _SIO2stream );
```

Now turn your attention to the next block of code, where the button widget is to be loaded. The //button loading code goes here comment needs to be replaced by the following code:

```
SIO2stream *_SIO2stream = sio2StreamOpen( "button.tga", 1 );

button_widget    = sio2WidgetInit( "button" );
button_mat       = sio2MaterialInit( "button" );
button_im        = sio2ImageInit( "button" );

sio2ImageLoad( button_im, _SIO2stream );
sio2ImageGenId( button_im, 0, 0.0f );

button_widget->_SIO2material = button_mat;
button_mat->_SIO2image[ SIO2_MATERIAL_CHANNEL0 ] = button_im;
button_mat->blend = SIO2_MATERIAL_COLOR;

button_widget->_SIO2transform->scl->x = button_im->width;
button_widget->_SIO2transform->scl->y = button_im->height;
```

Up to this point, the button widget loading code is pretty much identical to the splash screen widget loading code (aside from the variable names). After this, however, things begin to change. The next two lines deal with the widget's placement:

```
button_widget->_SIO2transform->loc->x = 25.0f;
button_widget->_SIO2transform->loc->y = 50.0f;
```

This places the widget 25 pixels in along the x-axis and 50 pixels in along the y-axis. This step was not necessary in the case of the splash screen widget because the widget was placed at the origin (0 point) along both axes.

Aside from size and placement, the main difference between the splash widget and the button widget is that the button widget needs to be able to respond to touches. The next several lines deal specifically with the touch functionality of the button:

```
button_widget->area->x = button_im->width-20;
button_widget->area->y = button_im->height-20;
```

For touch-enabled widgets, it is necessary to set the area of the widget, which in this case refers to the touch-responsive area corresponding to the widget. This may be bigger or smaller than the viewable widget. In this case, the dimensions of the button's touchable area are set to be 20 pixels smaller than the dimensions of the button image.

The next line of code sets the callback function for the button widget:

```
button_widget->_SIO2widgettapdown = buttonPress;
```

This sets `buttonPress` as the function that will be called when the button widget receives a tap-down event. Of course, you have not yet defined this function, so if you attempt to build and run the application before doing so, you'll get an error and the project won't compile.

The next two lines activate the touch functionality:

```
sio2EnableState( &button_widget->flags, SIO2_WIDGET_ENABLED );
sio2WidgetUpdateBoundary(button_widget, sio2->_SIO2window );
```

In order for a widget to receive touch events, the boundary of the widget must be updated once after the widget is initialized and then again anytime the widget is moved or scaled. This is what is being done with the call to the `sio2WidgetUpdateBoundary` function. However, to update the boundary, you must enable the widget. For this reason, the call to `sio2EnableState` in the previous line must precede the boundary update.

---

unsigned char **sio2WidgetUpdateBoundary**(SIO2widget *widget*, SIO2window *window*)

This function sets the boundary of the SIO2widget structure *widget* with respect to the SIO2window structure *window*. The widget's area and location are used to determine the absolute location of its boundaries. The widget must be enabled for this function to work.

To update the boundary to receive touch events, you must enable a widget. Typically, this is done when the widget is loaded. If you want to load a widget and have it disabled, you should first enable it, then update its boundary, and then disable it with the `sio2Disable State` function (the arguments to this function are exactly the same as for `sio2EnableState`). After initially enabling and updating the boundary, you can disable and enable the state as many times as you like.

Finally, as in the case of the splash screen widget, you close the stream with the following code:

```
_SIO2stream = sio2StreamClose( _SIO2stream );
```

The third and final code block in the `templateLoading` function loads the 3D assets created in Blender from the `.sio2` file. In place of the comment `//3D assets loading code from Chapter 8`, you should paste the corresponding code from Chapter 8. Specifically, the code from Chapter 8 extends (inclusively) from the line

```
unsigned int i = 0;
```

to the line

```
sio2ObjectPlay( frankie, 1 );
```

After that, the render callback is set to `templateRender` and the `templateLoading` function is complete.

The Button Callback Function

In the loading code for the button widget, you saw that the touch event for the button would call a function called `buttonPress`. Now you need to define that function, near the beginning of the `template.mm` file, after the variables have been declared and before the other function definitions. The function definition should look like this:

```
void buttonPress(  void *_ptr, void *, vec2 *  )
{
    startscreen = 0;
}
```

All this function does is to flip the *startscreen* toggle. This is a very simplistic approach to game state management and will probably not scale well. But for the purpose of showing the basics of widget behavior, it is sufficient.

The Template Render Function

As in the other examples in this book, the `templateRender` function contains the code executed during the main render loop after loading has completed. The function's first few lines are the same as they are in Chapter 8 and in other examples in this book:

```
void templateRender( void )
{
    glMatrixMode( GL_MODELVIEW );
    glLoadIdentity();

    glClear( GL_DEPTH_BUFFER_BIT | GL_COLOR_BUFFER_BIT );
```

After this point, you will move the code from Chapter 8's `templateRender` function to a different function called `gameRender`, as discussed shortly. In the meantime, `templateRender` needs to be changed to accommodate the *startscreen* toggle behavior. This is done with a conditional code block as follows:

```
if( startscreen )
{
    sio2WindowEnter2D( sio2->_SIO2window, 0.0f, 100.0f );
    {
        sio2WindowEnterLandscape2D( sio2->_SIO2window );
        {
            sio2WidgetRender( splash_widget,
                                sio2->_SIO2window,
                                SIO2_TRANSFORM_MATRIX_APPLY );

            sio2WidgetRender( button_widget,
                                sio2->_SIO2window,
                                SIO2_TRANSFORM_MATRIX_APPLY );

            sio2MaterialReset();
        }
        sio2WindowLeaveLandscape2D( sio2->_SIO2window );
    }
    sio2WindowLeave2D();
}
```

If *startscreen* is 1, this code will be executed. The first thing that will happen is that SIO2 will enter 2D render mode. Obviously, for rendering 2D graphics there's no need for perspective calculations. The next thing that happens is that the window enters 2D landscape mode, which is the orientation of the widget you want to display. Then `sio2WidgetRender` is called for both widgets and the widgets are drawn. Note that widgets are drawn in the order that the render command is given, so the button will be drawn over the splash.

`unsigned char` **`sio2WidgetRender`**`(SIO2widget *widget, SIO2window *window, unsigned char *usematrix)`

This function draws the SIO2widget structure *widget* to the screen. The current SIO2window structure *window* must be passed as the second argument, and the third argument determines whether the transform matrix used is the SIO2 bound matrix or whether the transforms are calculated by OpenGL and applied. The flags for these two options are SIO2_TRANSFORM_MATRIX_BIND and SIO2_TRANSFORM_MATRIX_APPLY, respectively.

The case where startscreen is 0, which indicates that the button has been tapped, is handled by the following code:

```
else
{
        gameRender();
        if( splash_widget )
        {
                splash_widget   = sio2WidgetFree   ( splash_widget );
                splash_mat      = sio2MaterialFree( splash_mat );
                splash_im       = sio2ImageFree    ( splash_im );
                sio2MaterialReset();
                sio2WidgetReset();
        }
    }
}
```

This calls gameRender and frees the resources from the now unused widgets.

SIO2widget **sio2WidgetFree**(SIO2widget *widget*)

This function frees the resources that had been used for the SIO2widget structure *widget*.

Game Render Function

The gameRender function contains the functionality to render the game environment, which was handled by templateRender in Chapter 8. The beginning and end of the function definition look like this:

```
void gameRender( void )
{
    static float m[ 16 ] = { 0.0f };
    //Code in the place of this comment is
     //identical to Chapter 8's templateRender code
    sio2WindowLeaveLandscape3D();
}
```

The redacted content is identical to the corresponding content from Chapter 8's templateRender function.

Once you've gotten this code moved to its new home in gameRender, you can build and run the app. You'll be welcomed by the splash screen shown in Figure 9.3. Once you tap the Go! button, you'll be taken to the interactive 3D environment from Chapter 8.

You've now learned the basics of creating interactive 3D content and constructing a simple interface for your game. As you can surely imagine, this is just the beginning. To begin taking the next step in your learning, you should refer to Appendix C for an overview of the official SIO2 tutorials and a guide to some of the other advanced learning resources available.

Developing for the iPhone is a lot of fun, and the possibility of creating a top-notch 3D game and making it available to the world through the iTunes App Store is a thrill. I hope I have helped to encourage you to do just that, and I look forward to seeing some exciting new 3D offerings for the iPhone from readers of this book!

Figure 9.3

The splash screen and button running in the simulator

The Complete Code

Here's a complete overview of the code for `template.mm`. To save space, functions and large code blocks that are identical to those printed at the end of Chapter 8 are redacted and a note has been inserted at those points to let you know.

As always, it's necessary to edit `EAGLView.mm` so that `templateLoading` is assigned as the initial render callback and to include the function prototype in `template.h`. If you're continuing from Chapter 8, then you've already done these things.

A new change that needs to be made is to initialize widgets. Do this by adding the call `sio2InitWidget();` after `sio2InitGL();` in `EAGLView.mm`.

```
#include "template.h"
#include "../src/sio2/sio2.h"

SIO2widget    *splash_widget  = NULL;
SIO2material *splash_mat      = NULL;
SIO2image     *splash_im      = NULL;

SIO2widget    *button_widget  = NULL;
SIO2material *button_mat      = NULL;
SIO2image     *button_im      = NULL;

SIO2object *frankie = NULL;

float ROT_FACTOR;
```

```
float ROT_Z = 0.0f;
float DIST_FACTOR;
float FPS = 10.0f;
vec2 start;
vec2 d;

unsigned char startscreen = 1;

void shadowmatrix( float *_m, vec4 *_n, vec4 *_lpos )
{
    The code for this function is identical to Chapter 8.
}

void buttonPress(  void *_ptr, void *, vec2 *  )
{
    printf("Button pressed!\n");
    startscreen = 0;
}

SIO2action *get_action( SIO2resource *_SIO2resource,
                                     char      *_filename,
                                     char      *_name )
{
    The code for this function is identical to Chapter 8.
}

void gameRender( void )
{
    static float m[ 16 ] = { 0.0f };
    glClearColor(0.7f, 0.8f, 1.0f, 1.0f);
    if( !sio2->_SIO2camera )
    {
      SIO2camera *_SIO2camera
            = ( SIO2camera * )sio2ResourceGet(
                                  sio2->_SIO2resource,
                               SIO2_CAMERA,

"camera/Camera" );
            if( !_SIO2camera )
            { return; }

            sio2->_SIO2camera = _SIO2camera;

            sio2Perspective( _SIO2camera->fov,
                            sio2->_SIO2window->scl->x /
                               sio2->_SIO2window->scl->y,
                            _SIO2camera->cstart,
```

```
                              _SIO2camera->cend );
    }

    sio2WindowEnterLandscape3D();
    {
        sio2CameraRender( sio2->_SIO2camera );
        ROT_Z =+ ROT_FACTOR;

        frankie->_SIO2transform->rot->z += ROT_Z;
        frankie->_SIO2transform->loc->x +=
                        DIST_FACTOR*
                        (float)sin(frankie->_SIO2transform->rot->z/
                        (180/3.14159265));
        frankie->_SIO2transform->loc->y -=
                        DIST_FACTOR*
                        (float)cos(frankie->_SIO2transform->rot->z/
                        (180/3.14159265));
        sio2TransformBindMatrix( frankie->_SIO2transform );

        if( !m[ 0 ] )
        {
            vec4 n, lpos;
            n.x = n.y = n.w = 0.0f;
            n.z = 1.0f;
            lpos.x =  10.0f;
            lpos.y =  -5.0f;
            lpos.z =  20.0f;
            lpos.w =   0.0f;
            shadowmatrix( m, &n, &lpos );
        }

        glPushMatrix();
        {
        The code between these brackets is identical to Chapter 8.
        }
        glPopMatrix();

        sio2ResourceRender( sio2->_SIO2resource,
                            sio2->_SIO2window,
                            sio2->_SIO2camera,
                            SIO2_RENDER_SOLID_OBJECT );
    }
    sio2WindowLeaveLandscape3D();
}

void templateRender( void )
{
    glMatrixMode( GL_MODELVIEW );
```

```
            glLoadIdentity();

            glClear( GL_DEPTH_BUFFER_BIT | GL_COLOR_BUFFER_BIT );

            if( startscreen )
            {
                sio2WindowEnter2D( sio2->_SIO2window, 0.0f, 100.0f );
                {
                    sio2WindowEnterLandscape2D( sio2->_SIO2window );
                    {
                        sio2WidgetRender( splash_widget,
                                          sio2->_SIO2window,
                                          SIO2_TRANSFORM_MATRIX_APPLY );
                        sio2WidgetRender( button_widget,
                                          sio2->_SIO2window,
                                          SIO2_TRANSFORM_MATRIX_APPLY );
                        sio2MaterialReset();
                    }
                    sio2WindowLeaveLandscape2D( sio2->_SIO2window );
                }
                sio2WindowLeave2D();
            }
            else
            {
                gameRender();
                if( splash_widget )
                {
                    splash_widget  = sio2WidgetFree  ( splash_widget );
                    splash_mat = sio2MaterialFree( splash_mat   );
                    splash_im    = sio2ImageFree   ( splash_im       );
                    sio2MaterialReset();
                    sio2WidgetReset();
                }
            }
        }


        void templateLoading( void )
        {
            // Load the splash screen
            {
                SIO2stream *_SIO2stream = sio2StreamOpen( "splash.jpg", 1 );

                splash_widget  = sio2WidgetInit  ( "splash" );
                splash_mat = sio2MaterialInit( "splash" );
                splash_im    = sio2ImageInit   ( "splash" );

                sio2ImageLoad( splash_im , _SIO2stream );
                sio2ImageGenId( splash_im , 0, 0.0f );
```

```
        splash_widget->_SIO2material = splash_mat;
        splash_mat->_SIO2image[  SIO2 MATERIAL_CHANNEL0 ] = splash_im ;
        splash_mat->blend = SIO2_MATERIAL_COLOR;

        splash_widget->_SIO2transform->scl->x = splash_im->width;
        splash_widget->_SIO2transform->scl->y = splash_im->height;

        _SIO2stream = sio2StreamClose( _SIO2stream );
    }


    // Load the button
    {
        SIO2stream *_SIO2stream = sio2StreamOpen( "button.tga", 1 );

        button_widget   = sio2WidgetInit  ( "button" );
        button_mat = sio2MaterialInit( "button" );
        button_im   = sio2ImageInit   ( "button" );

        sio2ImageLoad( button_im, _SIO2stream );
        sio2ImageGenId( button_im, 0, 0.0f );

        button_widget->_SIO2material = button_mat;
        button_mat->_SIO2image[  SIO2_MATERIAL_CHANNEL0 ] = button_im;
        button_mat->blend = SIO2_MATERIAL_COLOR;

        button_widget->_SIO2transform->scl >x = button_im->width;
        button_widget->_SIO2transform->scl->y = button_im->height;
        button_widget->_SIO2transform->loc->x = 25.0f;
        button_widget->_SIO2transform->loc->y = 50.0f;
        button_widget->area->x = button_im->width-20;
        button_widget->area->y = button_im->height-20;
        button_widget->_SIO2widgettapdown = buttonPress;

        sio2EnableState( &button_widget->flags, SIO2_WIDGET_ENABLED );
        sio2WidgetUpdateBoundary(button_widget, sio2->_SIO2window );
        _SIO2stream = sio2StreamClose( _SIO2stream );
    }


    // Load Blender 3D assets
    {
        unsigned int i = 0;
        sio2ResourceCreateDictionary( sio2->_SIO2resource );
        sio2ResourceOpen( sio2->_SIO2resource,
                          "iFrankie.sio2", 1 );

        while( i != sio2->_SIO2resource->gi.number_entry )
        {
```

```
                                    sio2ResourceExtract( sio2->_SIO2resource, NULL );
                                    ++i;
                            }
                            sio2ResourceClose( sio2->_SIO2resource );
                            sio2ResourceBindAllImages( sio2->_SIO2resource );
                            sio2ResourceBindAllMaterials( sio2->_SIO2resource );
                            sio2ResourceBindAllMatrix( sio2->_SIO2resource );
                            sio2ResourceGenId( sio2->_SIO2resource );

                            sio2ResetState();
                            frankie =
                                    sio2ResourceGetObject( sio2->_SIO2resource,
                                                           "object/frankie" );
                            sio2ObjectInitAnimationAttributes( frankie );
                            sio2ObjectSetAction( frankie,
                                                 get_action( sio2->_SIO2resource,
                                                             "iFrankie.sio2",
                                                             "action/LookAround" ),
                                                 0.01f,
                                                 FPS );
                            sio2ObjectPlay( frankie, 1 );
                    }
                    sio2->_SIO2window->_SIO2windowrender = templateRender;
            }


            void templateShutdown( void )
            {
                    The code for this function is identical to Chapter 8.
            }


            void templateScreenTap( void *_ptr, unsigned char _state )
            {
                    The code for this function is identical to Chapter 8.
            }


            void templateScreenTouchMove( void *_ptr )
            {
                    The code for this function is identical to Chapter 8.
            }


            void templateScreenAccelerometer( void *_ptr )
            {
            }
```

Blender Basics

This appendix is intended to help people with no experience using Blender understand the basics of working with Blender to the point where they can follow the tutorials in this book. You should be aware that becoming skilled at Blender can take a lot of practice and study, and this appendix does not presume to be a replacement for the numerous books and tutorials available for Blender. If you plan to continue with 3D asset creation, you'll certainly want to investigate further Blender resources.

The exporter script bundled with SIO2 1.4 runs in Blender 2.49. Although by the time you read this, Blender 2.5 will likely have been released with considerable changes made to the interface and animation system, be aware that until a Blender 2.5 exporter is made available for SIO2, you must use Blender 2.49 for your SIO2-related work.

This appendix is not a step-by-step tutorial. The details of how to carry out the tasks relevant to the examples in the book can be found written in step-by-step fashion in the chapters themselves. If you have a minimum of Blender experience, you should be able to skip this appendix with no problems.

- **Interface and navigation**
- **Modeling**
- **Materials and textures**
- **Animation**

Interface and Navigation

Blender is an application for the creation of 3D animated movies and games. It includes functionality for modeling, texturing, lighting, rendering, rigging, posing, animation, physics simulation and dynamics, video and audio editing, compositing, game prototyping, and Python scripting. All this functionality is compartmentalized into window types. There are only a few window types that you work with in this book.

Windows and Headers

When you start up Blender, by default you will see a work area similar to the one shown in Figure A.1. The colors and icons may look different depending on your individual interface settings, but the overall layout of the screen should be recognizable. The window taking up most of the upper half of the desktop is the 3D viewport. The window taking up the

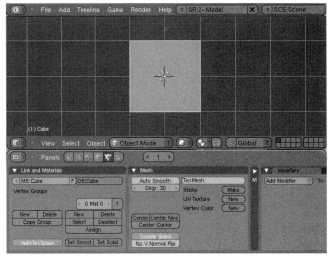

bottom half is the buttons area. There is actually a third window at the top of the work area, but only its header is visible. This is the area for setting preferences, but you don't deal with that in this book. You can read all about user preferences in my book *Mastering Blender* (Sybex, 2009).

Each window is general purpose. Other Blender functionality can be accessed by changing the window type of a particular window. This is done using the drop-down menu in the corner of the window's header, as shown in Figure A.2. In addition to the 3D viewport and the buttons area, you use the UV/Image Editor, the Text Editor, the Action Editor, and the NLA (nonlinear animation) Editor over the course of this book.

The arrangement of the work area is also customizable. You can divide the work area into as many windows as you like by splitting individual windows as shown in Figure A.3. Do this by right-clicking on a window border that is perpendicular to the way you would like to split the window and choosing Split Area from the pop-up menu that comes up.

Two areas can also be joined together, as shown in Figure A.4. To do this, right-click on the border between the two areas you would like to join and select Join Areas.

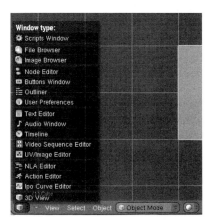

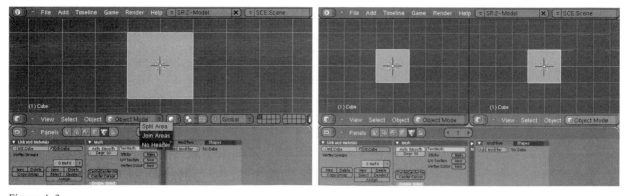

Figure A.3

Splitting a window area

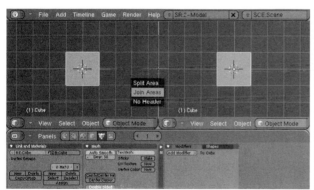

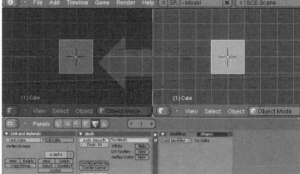

Figure A.4

Joining two areas

Layers

Objects in the 3D viewport can be organized into *layers*. These layers are not analogous to the use of the term in 2D software, and there is no real sense of one of them lying over the next. In fact, they are more like display groups. If you have Blender set to display Layer 1, only objects on that layer will be displayed. The layers are represented in the header of the 3D viewport by two side-by-side 5×2 grids of small square buttons. By default, the layer button in the upper-left corner of the grid is selected, indicating that only Layer 1 is set to display.

You can send an object to a different layer as shown in Figure A.5 by selecting the object and pressing thc M key. When you do this, a grid similar to the one in the header will pop up and you can click one layer button (or more than one while holding down the Shift key), followed by OK. If you send the object to a layer that is not set to display, the object will seem to disappear. If you set the destination layer to be displayed using the layer buttons in the header, you will be able to see it.

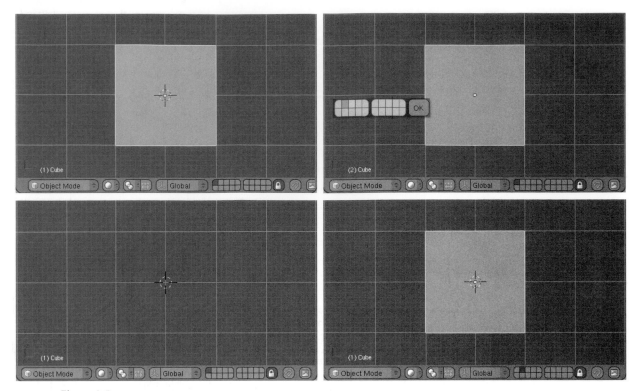

Figure A.5

Sending an object to a different layer

Navigating 3D Space

Objects reside in the 3D space with values for their x-, y-, and z-coordinates determining their locations. To work efficiently with objects, it is necessary to be able to quickly and easily navigate the 3D space and the objects in it.

The default Blender scene consists of a lamp, a camera, and a mesh cube as shown in Figure A.6.

Figure A.6

The cube, lamp, and camera in the default 3D space

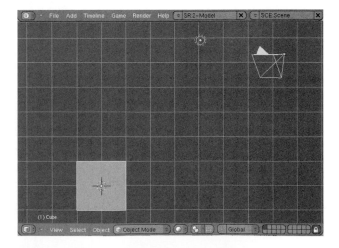

Rotating, Panning, and Zooming in Space

To move the user view around in the 3D space, you can rotate, pan, or zoom. Rotating is done by holding the middle mouse button (MMB) if you're using a three-button mouse or Alt+left mouse button (LMB) if you're using a two-button mouse and moving the mouse. Panning is done by holding Shift+MMB (or Shift+Alt+LMB) and moving the mouse. Zooming is done by holding Ctrl+MMB (or Ctrl+Alt+LMB) and moving the mouse.

Using the Number Pad Keys

The number pad keys enable you to quickly change the view. The main number pad keys for controlling the viewpoint are 1, 3, 7, 0, and 5. Number pad key 1 puts the space in front view with the camera along the y-axis (as shown in the image labeled *a* in Figure A.7), number pad key 3 puts the space in side view with the camera along the x-axis(as shown in the image labeled *b* in Figure A.7), number pad key 7 puts the space in top view along the z-axis(as shown in the image labeled *c* in Figure A.7), and number pad key 0 puts the scene in Camera view (as shown in the image labeled *d* in Figure A.7).

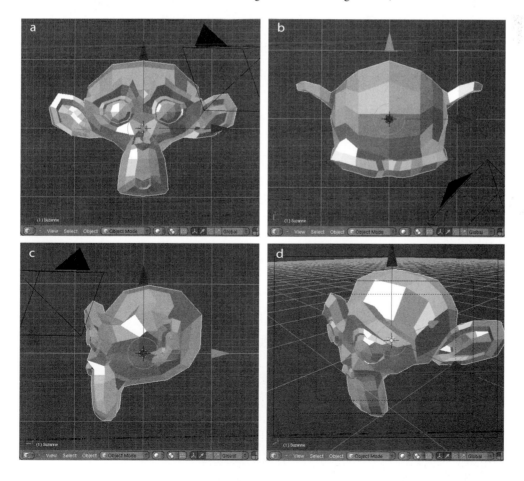

Figure A.7

Front (a), top (b), side (c), and camera (d) views

Number pad key 5 toggles between the orthographic (the top image in Figure A.8) and perspective and view (the bottom image in Figure A.8).

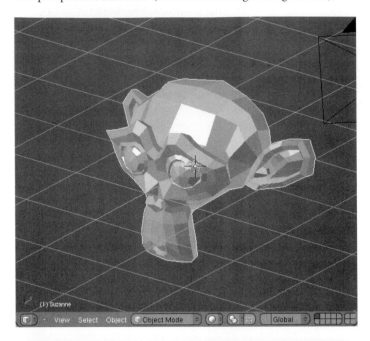

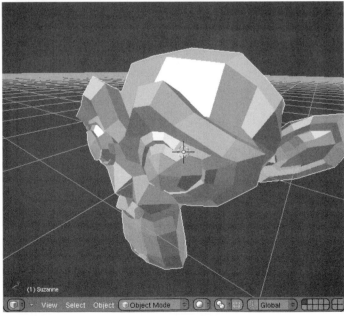

The 3D Cursor

The 3D cursor is shown in Figure A.9. The cursor has a number of uses, but you will use it chiefly to snap objects or other things to specific positions. The Snap menu can be accessed using Shift+S and is shown in Figure A.10. The entries in that menu are the options you have for snapping.

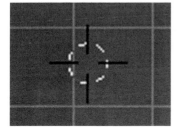

Snap
Selection –> Grid
Selection –> Cursor
Selection –> Center
Cursor –> Selection
Cursor –> Grid
Cursor –> Active

Figure A.9

The 3D cursor

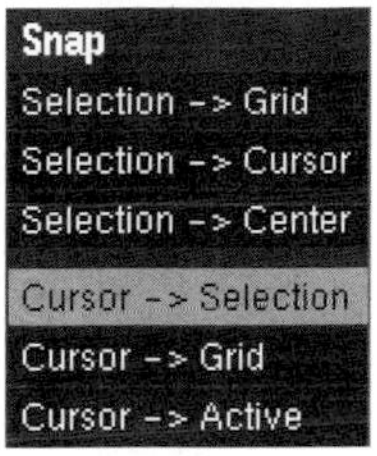

Figure A.10

The Snap menu

Modeling

For the purposes of this book, all modeling is carried out using polygon meshes, usually with a fairly low polygon count. Blender has other options for modeling, but you don't use them in this book.

Objects and Object Mode

Everything that can have a location in 3D space is an object, including lights and cameras, as you saw previously. Modeling specifically deals with mesh objects, whose vertices, edges, and faces can be edited. The kinds of operations you can carry out on such objects depend on the mode selected in the drop-down menu in the 3D viewport header. For operations that deal with the object-level characteristics of objects, you must be in Object mode. In Object mode, mesh objects, curves, lamps, cameras, and any other possible object types are treated the same. You cannot access object-internal data such as vertex position. Mainly you can translate, rotate, and scale the model itself.

Selecting

Selecting objects is done with the right mouse button (RMB) in Blender. Holding the Shift key while clicking the RMB will enable you to select multiple objects, otherwise the most recently clicked object will be the only one selected.

You can use a box-select tool by pressing the B key, holding the LMB down, and dragging the mouse to create a rectangular shape around the objects you want to select.

Pressing the A key toggles between the selection of all the objects or none of the objects.

3D Transforms

You can translate, rotate, and scale 3D objects in Object mode. The most straightforward way to do this is to use the hotkeys G, R, and S respectively to grab (translate), rotate, and scale the objects, as shown in the images in Figure A.11, labeled with the corresponding hotkey.

Figure A.11

Composite illustrations showing translation, rotation, and scaling

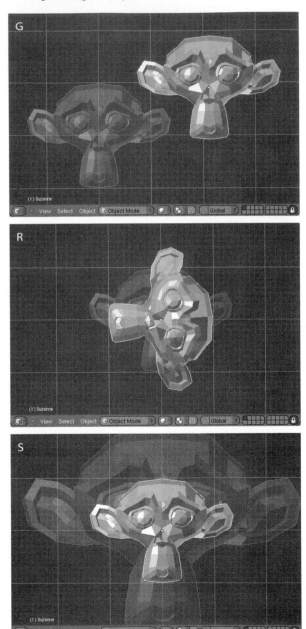

You can constrain any transform to an axis by pressing the key of the name of the axis (X, Y, or Z) after beginning the transform. For example, to rotate around the z-axis as shown in Figure A.12, press the R key followed by the Z key.

Figure A.12
Rotation around the z-axis

Transforming objects is an important and necessary part of working with 3D content in Blender. Object transforms enable you to move and rotate the camera and lights and to place objects in relation to each other—actions that are often necessary as you work through this book (although location and rotation values can also be edited manually). However, you need to be careful about using Object transforms on mesh objects when working with content intended to be used with SIO2 or other game engines (including the BGE). In particular, the object's scale should always be 1, meaning that you should either do all of your resizing directly on the vertex data in Edit mode

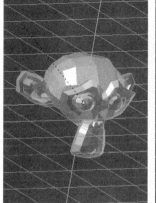

(see the following section on Edit mode) or apply any scaling done to the mesh by using Ctrl+A and selecting Scale to ObData. Working with an object whose scale is not 1 can have undesirable consequences, particularly if physics simulation or collisions are involved.

Figure A.13
Deleting a cube object

Deleting and Adding Objects

You can delete an object by selecting it and pressing the X key and then confirming that you want to delete it with the confirmation box shown in Figure A.13. You can add an object to the 3D space by pressing the spacebar and choosing the object you want to add from the pop-up menu that appears, as shown in Figure A.14. The new object will be placed at the location where the 3D cursor is.

Figure A.14
Adding a Monkey object

Meshes and Edit Mode

You can enter Edit mode by either selecting it from the drop-down menu in the 3D viewport header or simply pressing the Tab key with a mesh object selected. When you are in Edit mode, the vertex data is available to edit

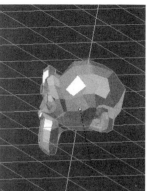

and you can make changes to a mesh's vertices, edges, and faces. You cannot select other objects when you are in Edit mode. For this, you need to return to Object mode by pressing Tab a second time.

Selecting

Selection in Edit mode is analogous to selection in Object mode. By default, you can select vertices. (Other options exist to select edges or faces, which you can read about in *Mastering Blender*, but for the purposes of this book vertex selection is sufficient.) You select a single vertex by right-clicking on it. Multiple vertices can be selected by holding Shift while you right-click the vertices.

As in Object mode, you can use the box-select option by pressing the B key and dragging your mouse over a rectangular area. All vertices within the area will be selected. You have one further option, a paintbrush-style select tool, which is activated by pressing the B key twice. When you activate this tool, a circle will appear onscreen. If you hold the LMB and drag the mouse, the vertices within this circle will be selected and you can use this as you would use a paintbrush tool to "paint" an area of selected vertices.

Pressing the A key will toggle between the selection of all vertices and none of the vertices.

3D Transforms

Transforms on vertices or groups of vertices are analogous to transforms on objects. Translation, rotation, and scaling are accomplished by using the G, R and S keys, respectively, just as in Object mode. Individual vertices do not have scale or rotation data, so scaling and rotation will have no effect on single vertices, but when multiple vertices are selected, scaling and rotation work as expected. Figure A.15 is a composite illustration showing a two-vertex edge being rotated.

As in Object mode, all transforms can be constrained to a single axis by pressing the appropriate axis key (X, Y, or Z) following G, R, or S.

Figure A.15

Rotating an edge

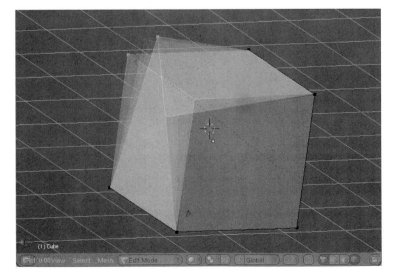

To scale objects that you intend to use with the SIO2 game engine, you should select all vertices with the A key and scale with the S key. Assuming the default pivot points, this will result in the same shape and size as scaling in Object mode, but it will leave the Object scale value at 1.

Mesh Modeling Tools

Blender has a large number of tools at your disposal for mesh modeling. Many of the main tools can be found in the Edit buttons area when in Edit mode, as shown in Figure A.16. In this book, only a few of these tools are discussed, and usually they are accessed via keyboard shortcuts rather than through the buttons. For an in-depth look at mesh modeling in Blender, particularly as it pertains to character modeling, you can refer to my book *Introducing Character Animation with Blender* (Sybex, 2007).

Figure A.16

The Edit buttons area

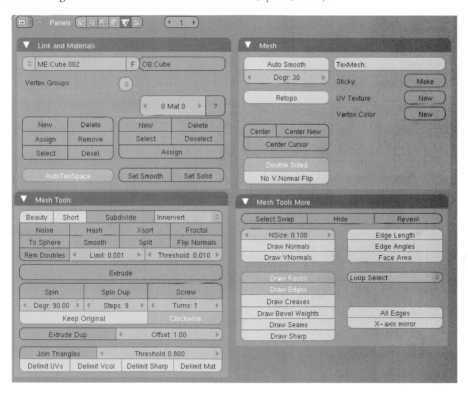

Pressing the W key while the mouse pointer is over the 3D viewport in Edit mode brings up the Specials menu shown in Figure A.17. This menu contains a variety of useful mesh modeling tools, including Subdivide, which subdivides the mesh into a higher-resolution mesh; Merge, which merges multiple vertices into a single vertex; Smooth, which smooths the overall shape of a selected area of a mesh; Remove Doubles, which merges any vertices that share the same location or are very near each other; and Flip Normals, which reverses the direction of faces for the calculation of reflection and shading.

Figure A.17

Selecting
Subdivide from
the Specials menu

Pressing the K key will bring up the Loop/Cut Menu shown in Figure A.18. This menu has options for adding geometry to a mesh in a way that's analogous to cutting the mesh.

Figure A.18

The Loop/Cut Menu

Figure A.17

Selecting
Subdivide from
the Specials menu

Proportional Editing

By default, if you operate on a vertex or vertices in a mesh, only those selected vertices will be affected by the operation. Sometimes this is not what you want. In cases when neighboring vertices should also be influenced by the operation, you can use the proportional editing tool. This can be activated from the drop-down menu in the 3D Viewport header as shown in Figure A.19. The proportional editing tool causes an editing operation to influence neighboring vertices so that the influence of the operation drops off with distance. The specific pattern of this influence falloff is selected in the Falloff drop-down menu directly to the right of the Proportional menu, shown in Figure A.20. There are seven options for the shape of the falloff.

Figure A.19

Activating proportional editing

Figure A.20

Setting the falloff

With proportional editing activated and using a default Smooth falloff, moving a single vertex on a mesh results in an edit like the one shown in Figure A.21. The light gray circle indicates the area of influence of the operation. The size of this influence can be changed using the mouse wheel if available or by using the + and – keys if no mouse wheel is available.

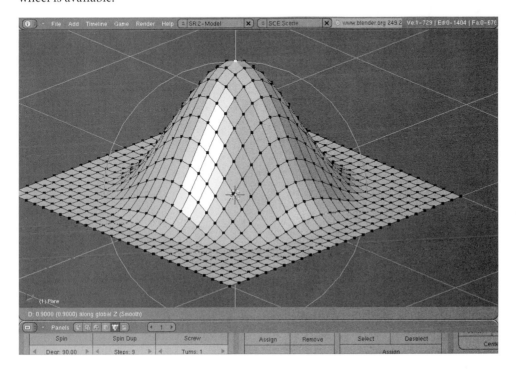

Figure A.21

Editing the mesh with proportional editing

Normals

Normals indicate the direction that a mesh face faces. In the default shaded view in Blender, the distinction between the front and the back of a mesh face is not visible, but there is a distinction, and it is relevant when working with real-time lighting. If you work with real-time lighting in SIO2, you may need to check the direction of your normals while modeling or troubleshooting. You can activate the drawing of normals in Edit mode by selecting Draw Normals from the Mesh Tools More panel of the Edit buttons as shown in Figure A.22. Figure A.23 shows a mesh sphere with normals drawn. Drawing normals has no effect on rendering or the appearance of an object in the game engine.

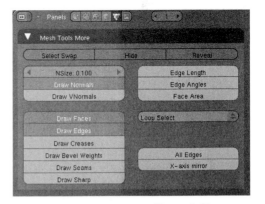

Figure A.22

Activating the Draw Normals option

Figure A.23

**A sphere with
visible normals**

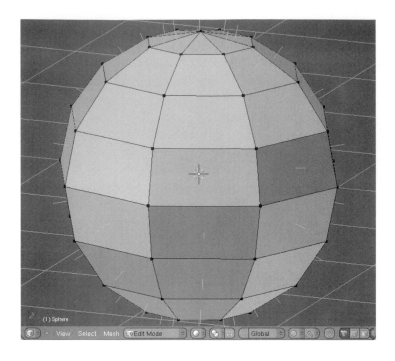

Figure A.23

**A sphere with
visible normals**

Armatures and Rigging

Figure A.24

Adding an armature

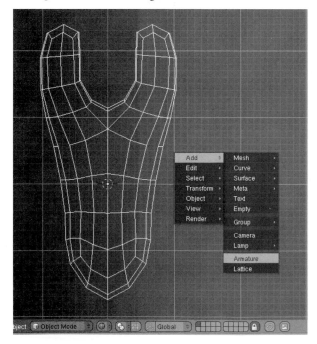

Character animation in Blender is done by creating skeleton-like *armatures* and associating them with a mesh in such a way that each bone in the armature influences a particular group of vertices. When the armature is animated, the appropriate mesh vertices move in relation to each other, resulting in deformations of the mesh. The SIO2 engine does not use armatures directly; rather, it exports the vertex location data from Blender so that the deformations can be reproduced. Animations to be exported in this way must be stored in Blender *actions*, which are described later in this appendix.

Once you have a modeled mesh ready for rigging, you add an armature in Object mode, just as you would add another object. Snap the 3D cursor to the mesh object's center by selecting the object, pressing Shift+S, and choosing Cursor To Selection from the snap options. Add the armature by pressing the spacebar and choosing Add → Armature from the pop-up menu, as shown in Figure A.24.

This will result in a new armature object with a single bone as shown in Figure A.25. In the Armature panel of the Edit buttons, select X-Axis Mirror and X-Ray from the Editing Options section at the top of the panel, as shown in Figure A.26. The X-Axis Mirror option enables you to edit the armature in a symmetrical way. The X-Ray option ensures that the armature remains visible even when the mesh around it is opaque.

Just as with meshes, armature objects can be manipulated in Object mode and their structure can be edited in Edit mode. Enter Edit mode with the Tab key to edit the armature. New bones are created from the tips of existing bones using extrusion. Normal, single-bone extrusion is done with the E key. Mirrored extrusion, in which two mirrored bones are extruded from the end of a single bone, is done with Shift+E. This is shown in Figure A.27. After a single mirrored extrusion, subsequent extrusions from the mirrored bones are done using the E key and their effect is mirrored, as shown in Figure A.28.

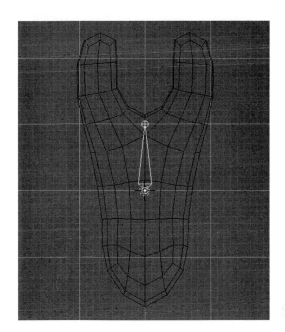

Figure A.25

A new armature with a single bone

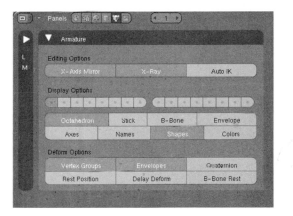

Figure A.26

Armature editing options

When the armature is complete, you must parent the mesh object to the armature using *armature parenting* in order for it to influence the mesh deformation. In Object mode, select the object first and then Shift+RMB on the armature to select it as well. Press Ctrl+P to parent the mesh object to the armature and choose Armature from the options, as shown in Figure A.29. When you do this, a menu appears and you can choose how you want to set up your vertex groups. Choose Bone Heat here, as shown in Figure A.30.

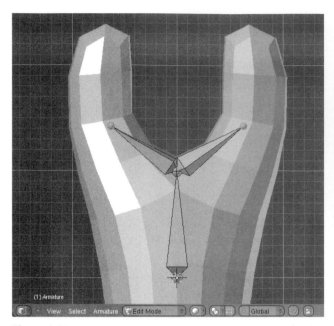

Figure A.27

Mirror extruding two new bones

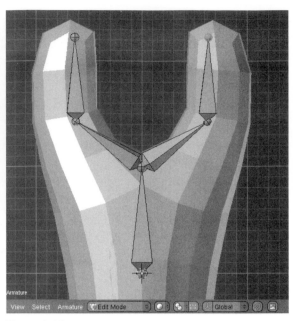

Figure A.28

Extruding two more bones

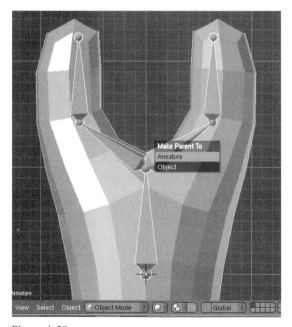

Figure A.29

Armature parenting

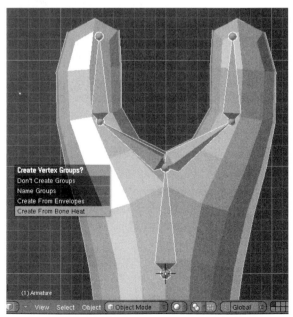

Figure A.30

Using the heat-based weighting feature

In addition to Object mode and Edit mode, a third mode is pertinent to armatures: Pose mode. Pose mode enables you to pose the armature by moving, rotating, or scaling bones in a way that does not change the basic pose of the armature and enables you to animate it. Enter Pose mode by selecting it from the Mode drop-down menu as shown in Figure A.31. In Pose mode, you can move, rotate, or scale bones, and the transform will be carried out on the relevant part of the mesh, as shown in Figure A.32.

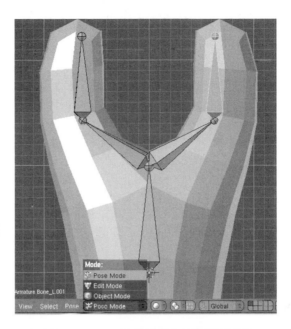

Figure A.31
Entering Pose mode

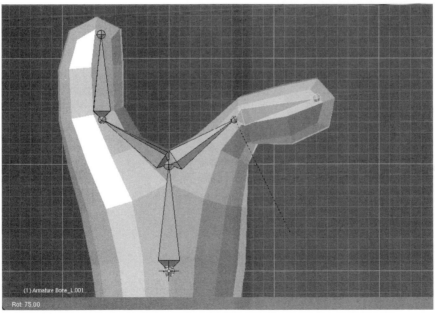

Figure A.32
Posing the armature

Materials and Textures

Materials and textures give 3D objects their visible surface qualities. Materials on their own can be used to set the object's color and reflective properties. Textures are used to add more detail. Often, textures override materials with respect to color. A material is always necessary, however, because textures must be associated with a material on the object in order to be used by SIO2.

There are a number of ways that objects can be textured in Blender, but the method pertinent to this book is to map 2D images to the surface of the 3D object. Using typical CG terminology, any 2D image mapped to the surface of a 3D object is a texture, even if it is affecting only the color of the object.

Materials

A material can be created by clicking the New button in the right side of the Link And Materials panel in the buttons area, shown in Figure A.33.

Be careful about clicking the New button on the Materials panel to create a material. Another identically named New button on the left side of this panel creates a new vertex group, although you don't use this button in the exercises in this book. The vertex groups you use in this book are automatically generated by the rigging process.

Figure A.33

The Link And Materials button panel before and after creating a first material

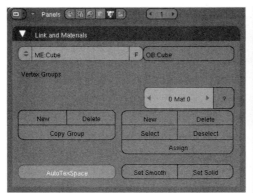

Once you have created a material for an object, you can enter the Material buttons area and see some of the tabs available for working with materials, as shown in Figure A.34. The Links And Pipeline tab, the Material tab, and the Texture tab all make appearances in this book, and their relevant functionality is discussed in the chapters where they appear.

The top two channels on the Texture tab in the Material buttons area are the only channels that SIO2 uses. When you click the Add New button on this tab, a new texture is created and associated with the active texture channel. After doing this, you can see the details of the texture in the Texture buttons area, as shown in Figure A.35 for a newly created texture. The texture type has not yet been selected, so there's not much information here. The texture type is selected using the Texture Type drop-down menu. In this book, only the Image texture type is used.

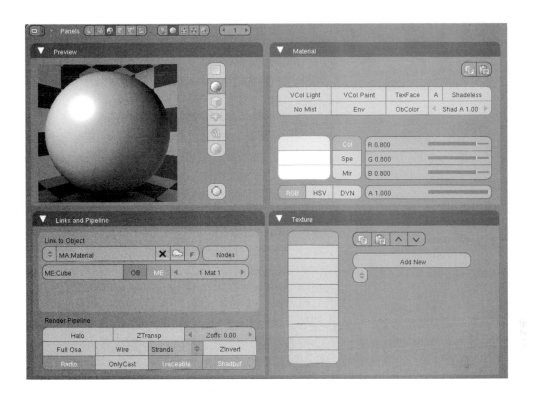

Figure A.34

Some important tabs in the Material buttons area

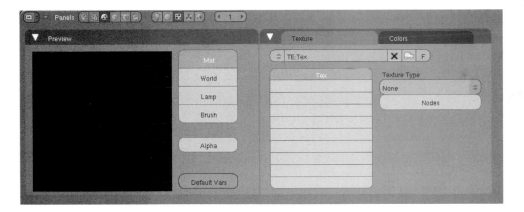

Figure A.35

Texture buttons for a new texture

Once a texture has been created, some new tabs become accessible in the Material buttons area. These new tabs relate to how the texture maps to the object and what surface characteristics it affects. The Material buttons tabs concerned with texture mapping are shown in Figure A.36. The relevant functionality here is all discussed in depth in the tutorials throughout the book.

Figure A.36

**Texture mapping
settings in the Mate-
rial buttons area**

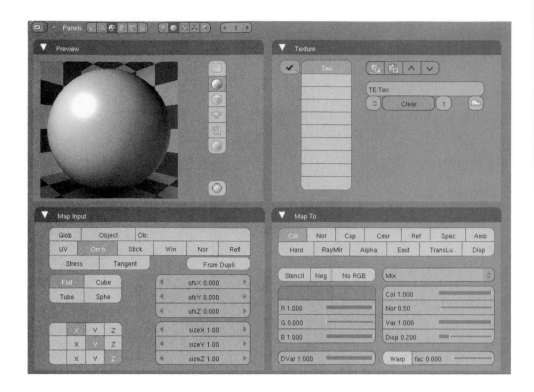

UV Texturing

The mapping transformation from the 2D image texture to the 3D surface is determined
by the selection you make in the top portion of the Map Input tab on the Material buttons area. By default this is set to Orco, but you use UV in this book. UV mapping maps a
2D texture to a grid defined over the surface of the 3D object. The coordinates of this grid
are the u- and v-coordinates, as distinct from the x- and y-coordinates of the image or the
x-, y-, and z-coordinates of the 3D space. UV mapping enables the maximum amount of
user control over where parts of the texture are mapped onto parts of the 3D surface.

Unwrapping and Mapping

UV mapping is done by first *unwrapping* the 3D mesh, which involves calculating the surface of the mesh as a two-dimensional pattern such that the overall geometric distortion
is minimized. Just as in the case of peeling an orange or representing clothing as material
patterns, it is necessary to cut the surface into some pattern of seams so that the shape
can be neatly spread onto a 2D surface. This is done by first selecting an edge or sequence
of edges as shown in Figure A.37 and creating a seam by pressing Ctrl+E and selecting
Mark Seam as shown in Figure A.38. Seams appear highlighted in orange.

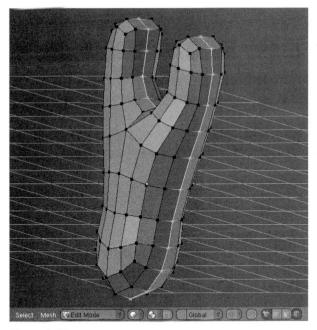

Figure A.37
Selecting an edge loop for a seam

Figure A.38
Creating a seam

Texture Settings

To create a UV texture on a mesh, you need to add a UV mapping by clicking the New button to the right of the UV Texture label on the Mesh panel of the Edit buttons, shown in Figure A.39. Although the label says UV Texture, this is somewhat misleading because this step needs to be done only once for any number of textures, provided the mapping is the same. Multiple UV mappings are used to bake from one mapping to another, but you do not use them in this book's exercises.

Figure A.39
The buttons for adding a UV texture

To prepare to unwrap a mesh, you need to open a UV/Image Editor window. Enter Edit mode and select all of the vertices of the mesh with the A key. If you have created a UV mapping as instructed, you will see a blue square that covers the entire image area in the UV/Image Editor window as shown in Figure A.40 (use your imagination regarding the color, but trust me, it's blue). This is actually the stacked quads of the mesh, in the state of having not yet been unwrapped.

Figure A.40

**Preparing
to unwrap**

Figure A.40

**Preparing
to unwrap**

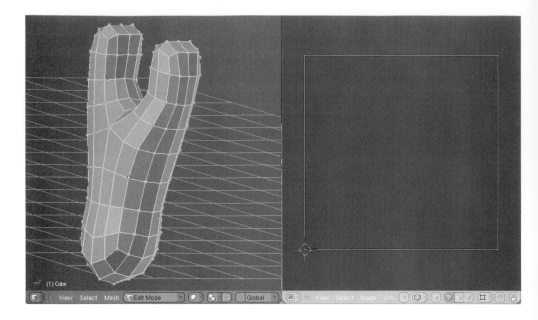

You unwrap the mesh by pressing the E key over the UV/Image Editor window. The resulting pattern will look something like the one shown in Figure A.41. Notice that this pattern represents the surface of the mesh object split in two pieces along the seam made previously.

Figure A.41

**Unwrapping
the mesh**

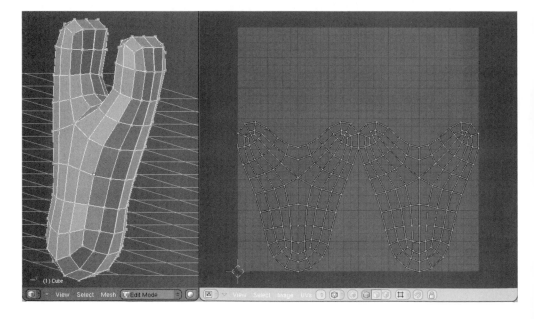

You create a new image by selecting New from the Image menu in the header of the UV/Image Editor, as shown in Figure A.42. You set the dimensions of the new image and determine whether it includes a default test grid pattern in the dialog box shown in Figure A.43. If you do not choose UV Test Grid in this

Figure A.42

Creating a new image

dialog box, the resulting image will be solid black. If you do choose UV Test Grid, the image will appear as shown in Figure A.44. The texture will be visible in the 3D viewport if Textured is chosen in the Draw Type drop-down menu in the 3D viewport header. Note that this object has only been textured and therefore is not yet ready to be exported for use

Figure A.43

Settings for the new image

in SIO2. The texture needs to be placed on a texture channel in a material for the object in order to be recognized by the SIO2 exporter. You learn how to do this in the relevant chapters of the book.

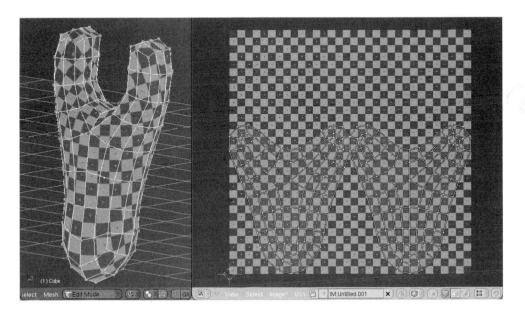

Figure A.44

The UV test grid image

Texture Baking

Texture baking is a close relative of rendering, which is the process of calculating a final detailed image based on all available 3D object, material, and lighting data. In the case of texture baking, the "rendered" image is made directly onto the surface texture of an object. Shadows, ambient occlusion, and other lighting effects can be baked onto an image and subsequently represented simply as an unshaded solid texture. This is a very common trick in game creation because of the demands of real-time rendering. The details of how to bake textures can be found in the relevant exercises in this book.

Animation

Blender is a very powerful tool for creating 3D animations. SIO2 enables you to make use of a great deal of Blender animation functionality in creating your iPhone game assets.

Ipo Curves

All animation in Blender is represented in terms of value changes over time, which in turn are represented by curves called Ipo (originally a shortening of *interpolation*) curves. The examples in this book do not use Ipos directly in SIO2, but once you understand how SIO2 works, you can refer to the tutorials and the SIO2 code to understand how to work with Ipos in SIO2. The SIO2 Meditation Garden contains some excellent examples of how Ipo curves can be used in SIO2.

Although this book does not deal with working with Ipos in SIO2, they are fundamental to animation in Blender, so it is worth taking a look at them in that context.

To work with Ipo curves, you should have an Ipo Curve Editor window open so you can see what you're doing. Values that can be animated—such as the location, rotation, and scale of an object—can be keyed for the current frame, causing a keyframe to be positioned on the relevant Ipo curves. To create a keyframe, press the I key in the 3D viewport, and then select the values you want to key from the Insert Key menu as shown in Figure A.45. When you have done this, colored horizontal lines representing Ipo curves will appear in the Ipo Curve Editor. The curves are flat because they represent only a single value. Move to another frame by pressing the right and left arrow keys (to advance forward or backward by 1 frame) or the up and down arrow keys (to advance forward or backward by 10 frames). Change the location, rotation, or scale; and add another keyframe, as shown in Figure A.46. The result is an animation curve representing the changing keyed values as shown in Figure A.47.

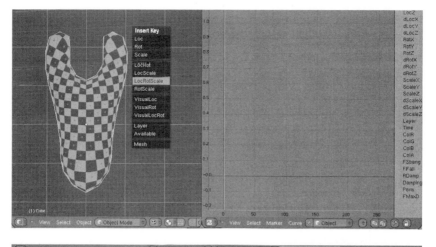

Figure A.45

Keying location, rotation, and scale

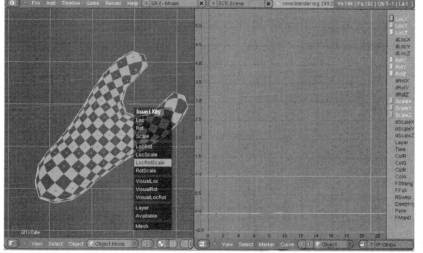

Figure A.46

Keying values for another frame

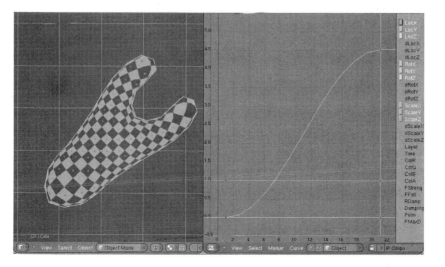

Figure A.47

The animation curve

Actions and Nonlinear Animation

When you do armature animation, Ipos are also created for each bone, although it is usually not necessary for you to work directly with Ipos. A better way to organize armature animations is in the Action Editor. This provides a simpler interface to working with keyframes on multiple bones. In the Action Editor, you create actions. These actions can then be combined in a nonlinear manner in the NLA (nonlinear animation) Editor. Keyframes and actions in the NLA Editor can be selected with the right mouse button or with the box-select tool (accessed by pressing B), which is analogous to how objects, vertices, and other entities are selected elsewhere.

Working with actions and the NLA Editor is central to using Blender character animation tools in SIO2 and is covered in depth in Chapter 8.

Key Concepts for Graphics Programming

As you study the tutorials and become familiar with the SIO2 pipeline, you will encounter a variety of topics in fundamental computer graphics programming that are beyond the scope of this book to explore thoroughly. This appendix is intended to provide a supplemental description of some core concepts to enable you to get the most out of the text and to give you a sense of what you should focus on in your further studies of graphics programming. The material in this appendix is not crucial to following the text, but understanding it should deepen your understanding of the tutorials and the code they cover.

- Coordinate systems, matrices, and transformations
- Transformations by matrix multiplication
- Matrices and OpenGL

Coordinate Systems, Matrices, and Transformations

All 3D entities exist in relation to one or more 3D coordinate systems. A coordinate system is a three-dimensional space defined by three orthogonal axes, typically labeled x, y, and z, which extend in both positive and negative directions and meet at a common zero point, known as the *origin* of the coordinate system. The coordinate system represents a *space*, and any point in the space can be described precisely by using three coordinates to represent the point's position with respect to the x-, y-, and z-axes. This is illustrated in Figure B.1, where the point is located at $x = 1$, $y = 2$, and $z = 3$, written (1, 2, 3). Objects in a three-dimensional space are built up of points in this way (the objects discussed in this book are generally polygon meshes, and the points are represented as vertices).

Figure B.1

A point in a coordinate system whose coordinates are (1, 2, 3}

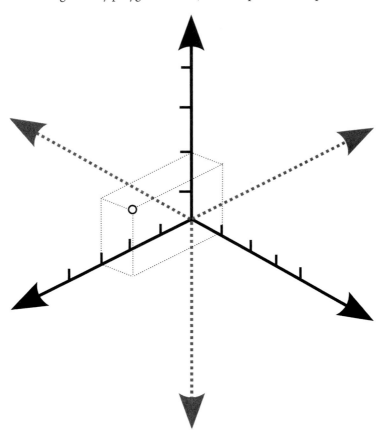

Matrix Notation

Matrices are tools for organizing numbers and operations that enable complex operations to be carried out on collections of values in a simple and compact way. It's not an exaggeration to say that matrices are what make most of modern computer graphics possible, so if you plan to go further in graphics programming, an introductory textbook on linear algebra is highly recommended.

For reasons that will become clear in the next few sections, the coordinates of points are often written in matrix form. In this form, the x, y, and z values are written vertically, between square brackets. A point in 3D space can be written as a vector, using a 3×1 matrix like this:

$$\begin{bmatrix} x \\ y \\ z \end{bmatrix}$$

However, this isn't quite how it's done. For computer graphics applications, a *homogeneous coordinate system* is used in which an extra, fourth "dimension" is added, typically with a value of 1. The full significance of the fourth coordinate is beyond the scope of this book, but one of its main purposes is to facilitate and generalize the use of transformation matrices, as you will see shortly. Using homogeneous coordinates, the point where $x = 1, y = 2, x = 3$ is written as a vector as follows:

$$\begin{bmatrix} A_1 \\ A_2 \\ A_3 \end{bmatrix} \begin{bmatrix} B_1 & B_2 & B_3 \end{bmatrix} = A_1B_1 + A_2B_2 + A_3B_3$$

Transformations

Computer graphics involves more than simply placing points or objects in space. In addition, operations called *transformations* are necessary that take points as input and yield new points in space as output. Transformations are fundamental in most areas of computer graphics, but for the present, it is enough to talk about two basic uses for transformations: transforming objects' spatial properties such as location, rotation, and scale and projecting a scene from the 3D space of the virtual graphical world to a 2D plane that will ultimately be sent to the screen.

Model/View Transformation

To represent the movement or change of objects, transformations are required that will take each point of the object and alter its location so that the object changes appropriately in space. For example, an object's location (translation) can be changed by adding a three-dimensional vector to each of the points in the object, which displaces the whole object according to the vector. Scaling an object is a matter of proportionally increasing each point's distance from a common center. An object is rotated by a specific angle around an axis by updating each point on the rotation plane according to the cosine and sine of the angle.

It is possible to think of these transformations as describing a relationship between two spaces. In particular, you can envision a coordinate space for the viewpoint (analogous to the camera in Blender) and a separate coordinate space for the scene you are viewing. In Figure B.2, you can see an illustration of these two coordinate spaces, with one offset along one axis from the other in such a way that the object should be visible from the viewpoint. Note that if only these two coordinate systems exist, the position of each coordinate system is meaningful only in reference to the other one. This means that there is no real difference between, for example, moving the model in a positive direction along an axis and moving the viewpoint in a negative direction along the same axis. You can think of the relationship between the coordinate systems in either way. Sometimes it will be most intuitive to think in terms of moving the model coordinate system; other times it will be most intuitive to think of moving the view coordinate system. Likewise, rotating the model coordinate system clockwise as shown in Figure B.3 is equivalent to rotating the view coordinate system counterclockwise. You can easily see that the resulting image from the point of view of the camera will be the same.

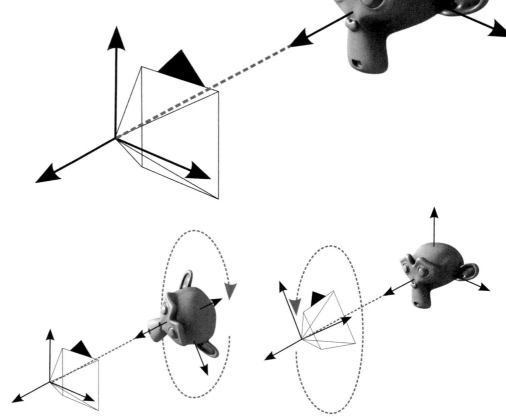

Figure B.2

A view coordinate space and a model coordinate space

Figure B.3

Two ways to think of rotation

As you will see in more detail shortly, it is possible to think of any arbitrary number of transformations performed in sequence (translation, rotation, scale, and so on) as a single complex transformation. In this way, the relationship between the model coordinate system and the view coordinate system can be expressed as one single transformation called the *model/view transformation*. By changing the parameters of the model/view transformation, you can draw objects in different areas of the screen, make them move, and change the camera view.

Projection Transformation

An important part of 3D computer graphics is the process of mapping, or *projecting* points from the virtual 3D environment to a 2D plane so that the scene can be converted to pixels. Once again, this can be accomplished by using a complex transformation to define a relationship between two coordinate systems: the 3D space that the camera sees, known as the *view volume*, and the 2D area of the *image plane*.

When viewing 3D spaces in perspective, the field of view farther away from the viewpoint is wider than the field of view near the viewpoint, just as in real life. This is why you can see an entire mountain from miles away but you can occlude your entire field of vision with a magazine held close to your face. Because objects of the same size take up proportionately different areas of the field of view depending on their distance from the viewpoint, things appear smaller in the distance. Depending on the parameters of your projection matrix, the angle that determines the field of view can vary in width. A very wide angle will produce an effect like a fish-eye lens, and a very narrow angle will approach a parallel or orthogonal view, where objects in the distance are rendered the same size as objects nearby.

In computer graphics, front and back *clipping panes* are also defined to determine the nearest and farthest distances from the viewpoint to be rendered. Objects nearer to the viewpoint than the front clipping pane and farther from the viewpoint than the back clipping pane are ignored. All together, these parameters define the view volume, which is shaped as a truncated pyramid (or *frustum*) as shown in Figure B.4.

A simplified illustration of the sequence of transformations from the view volume space to the final 2D image can be seen

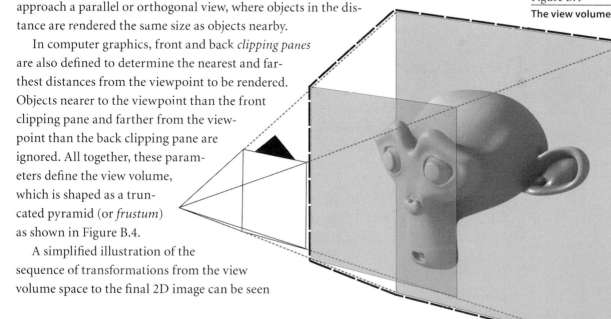

Figure B.4

The view volume

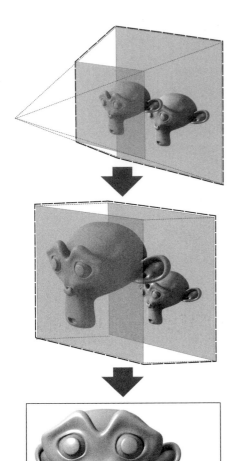

in Figure B.5. First, a transformation is used to map the points in the frustum to an orthogonal space. The frustum is scaled along its depth axis so that the near plane and the far plane are the same size. This results in nearer objects being scaled up relative to farther objects. From there, a transformation can be used to map the orthogonal 3D space to the 2D image plane. The width and height of the orthogonal space map to the width and height of the image plane, and the depth in the 3D space is used to determine which elements are rendered and which are hidden in the event that one element is directly in front of another.

In the case of orthogonal projection, the original view volume is orthogonal, so there is no scaling transformation between the frustum and orthogonal space. The view volume can be mapped directly onto the image plane.

Transformations by Matrix Multiplication

The method described previously of representing points in space using four-dimensional homogeneous coordinates yields some very powerful tools. When points are represented this way, it is possible to represent any graphical transformation with a single 4×4 matrix. Multiplying the matrix by a point will yield the corresponding point in the transformed space. Furthermore, because matrix multiplication is transitive, it is possible for any number of transformation matrices to be multiplied to yield another single 4×4 matrix that embodies all of the transformations of its factor matrices in one complex transformation. A single matrix can be used to scale, rotate, translate, or skew a space, or any combination of these. It is possible to scale a space proportionate to its depth (as must be done to transform the frustum to an orthogonal space) or to carry out any other necessary transformation operations.

Figure B.5

Transformations from view volume to perspective image

Multiplying Matrices

To understand how matrix transformations are carried out, it is necessary to understand how matrices work, in particular how they are multiplied. And to understand how matrices are multiplied, it is necessary to understand how to multiply *vectors*. Vectors are structures of ordered numbers that make up matrices.

Properly speaking, there are two kinds of vector multiplication, and the specific kind that is pertinent to this discussion is the calculation of the *inner product*. In this appendix, the term *multiplication* will always refer to this kind of vector multiplication.

The inner product can be calculated for two vectors with the same number of elements. Simply put, the inner product is the sum of the products of the corresponding elements of the two vectors. This is illustrated in the following equation:

$$\begin{bmatrix} A_1 \\ A_2 \\ A_3 \end{bmatrix} \begin{bmatrix} B_1 & B_2 & B_3 \end{bmatrix} = A_1 B_1 + A_2 B_2 + A_3 B_3$$

In this equation, the first vector is written in vertical notation and the second is written in horizontal notation, which will help to make the discussion of matrices clearer. The important thing is the ordering of the elements. As you can see, the result is the sum of the products of the elements of both vectors, considered in order. Note that the resulting product is not a vector but rather an ordinary number, or *scalar*. Note also that this kind of multiplication is not defined for vectors that have different numbers of elements.

Once you know how to derive a single number as the inner product of two vectors, you have the basic mechanism for multiplying matrices. Matrices are ordered collections of vectors. When you multiply two matrices, the product is a new matrix in which each number is the inner product of the corresponding row in the first matrix and the corresponding column in the second matrix, as shown in the following equation:

$$\begin{bmatrix} A_{11} & A_{12} \\ A_{21} & A_{22} \\ A_{31} & A_{33} \end{bmatrix} \begin{bmatrix} B_{11} & B_{21} & B_{31} \\ B_{12} & B_{22} & B_{21} \end{bmatrix} = \begin{bmatrix} A_1 B_1 & A_1 B_2 & A_1 B_3 \\ A_2 B_1 & A_2 B_2 & A_2 B_3 \\ A_3 B_1 & A_3 B_2 & A_3 B_3 \end{bmatrix}$$

An intuitive way to visualize the same equation is shown here:

$$\begin{bmatrix} B_{11} & B_{21} & B_{31} \\ B_{12} & B_{22} & B_{21} \end{bmatrix}$$
$$\begin{bmatrix} A_{11} & A_{12} \\ A_{21} & A_{22} \\ A_{31} & A_{33} \end{bmatrix} \begin{bmatrix} A_1 B_1 & A_1 B_2 & A_1 B_3 \\ A_2 B_1 & A_2 B_2 & A_2 B_3 \\ A_3 B_1 & A_3 B_2 & A_3 B_3 \end{bmatrix}$$

In this graphic, the B matrix is shown positioned above the product matrix so that its columns line up with the columns of the product. You can easily see how the scalar product of each pair of vectors in the two matrices is positioned in the product matrix.

You can also see that the rules of vector multiplication imply that the number of columns in the first matrix must be equal to the number of rows in the second matrix so that each pair of vectors can be multiplied. The number of rows in the first matrix and the number of columns in the second matrix need not be the same, and the matrices do not need to have matching numbers of rows or columns. The resulting product matrix will have the same number of rows as the first matrix and the same number of columns as the second matrix.

Another thing to take note of is that AB ≠ BA. You can see this very easily in the previous example simply by noticing the fact that if B precedes A, the resulting product matrix is a 2×2 matrix instead of a 3×3 matrix. In fact, the inequality holds even if the dimensions of the two matrices are the same. In math terminology, matrix multiplication is not commutative. You don't have to worry about oddly shaped matrices in graphics programming. You will most likely only ever be dealing with 4×4 matrices, but you need to be aware that the order of operations matters.

Another property of matrix multiplication is that (AB)C = A(BC). This is the property of transitivity, and it holds for matrix multiplications. This means that any number of matrices can be multiplied in advance and if you multiply the product with another matrix, the result will be the same as if the new matrix had been included in the original product. This is very important because it means that complex transformations such as combinations of rotation, scaling, and translation can be encoded into a single 4×4 matrix simply by multiplying the individual matrices for each transformation. This property is what makes much of contemporary computer graphics possible.

Matrix Transformations

So how do matrices encode transformations? To understand this, it's best to start in two dimensions and to discard the extra homogeneous coordinate. A 2D position can be described by a vector of two elements. What's the best way to translate a vector position? It might seem at first glance that the simplest way to do this is to simply add another vector. For example, if you want to move something 2 units along the x-axis and 2 units along the y-axis, you could simply add a <2, 2> vector as shown here:

$$\begin{bmatrix} 1 \\ 3 \end{bmatrix} + \begin{bmatrix} 2 \\ 2 \end{bmatrix} = \begin{bmatrix} 3 \\ 5 \end{bmatrix}$$

This transforms the position <1, 3> to the position <3, 5>, which is the correct translation. If all you ever wanted to do was move things from one position to another, this kind of vector addition would be sufficient. You could simply add the same vector to all the points in the object.

But what if you want to scale or rotate points rather than translate them? In these cases, vector addition is not sufficient. In the case of scaling, you want to increase the distance of each point in the object from some center point by some factor. This implies that scaling requires multiplication. But vector multiplication clearly is not what you need; it doesn't even yield a new vector as a product, but rather a scalar.

Scaling of 2D vectors can be accomplished using a 2×2 transformation matrix. With a matrix, you can control exactly what value each element of the vector is multiplied by, as you can see from this example:

$$\begin{bmatrix} 2 & 0 \\ 0 & 2 \end{bmatrix} \begin{bmatrix} 1 \\ 3 \end{bmatrix} = \begin{bmatrix} 2 \\ 6 \end{bmatrix}$$

In this example, the point <1, 3> is scaled by 2 along each axis, yielding the point <2, 6>.

Another aspect of matrix transformations such as this is that the original values of both axes may be included in the calculation of the new values for each axis. In the simple scaling example, the zero values in the upper-right and lower-left positions reflect the fact that the two axes' values do not influence the outcome of the other. However, there are many cases in which they might. Rotation is one such example. To rotate a point around an origin by a particular angle, the x- and y-coordinates of the new point are both calculated based upon the x- and y-coordinates of the original point, combined with the sine and cosine values of the angle. This can be expressed in matrix form like this:

$$\begin{bmatrix} \cos\theta & -\sin\theta \\ \sin\theta & \cos\theta \end{bmatrix} \begin{bmatrix} x \\ y \end{bmatrix} = \begin{bmatrix} x' \\ y' \end{bmatrix}$$

You can test this yourself by plugging in some numerical values and graphing the results on a 2D graph.

This is fine as an example, but it's not a sufficiently general way to carry out matrix transformations for computer graphics. For one thing, it would be nice to be able to take advantage of the previously mentioned property of transitivity to be able to represent multiple transformations with a single matrix. At the moment, though, translation is being carried out by vector addition, not matrix multiplication, so it can't be included in such complex transformations. Furthermore, there's no general way to represent 2D vector addition as a 2×2 matrix multiplication operation.

This is one of the reasons the method of homogeneous coordinates is used. Using an extra coordinate, it is possible to represent translation as a matrix multiplication operation. Vectors representing 2D points are made up of the x-, y-, and homogeneous coordinate, which for the purposes of this explanation will have a value of 1. The same translation shown previously using addition is shown here using matrix multiplication:

$$\begin{bmatrix} 1 & 0 & 2 \\ 0 & 1 & 2 \\ 0 & 0 & 1 \end{bmatrix} \begin{bmatrix} 1 \\ 3 \\ 1 \end{bmatrix} = \begin{bmatrix} 3 \\ 5 \\ 1 \end{bmatrix}$$

This also translates a two-dimensional point two units along the y-axis and two units along the x-axis. In this case, however, the 3×3 matrix can be multiplied by other 3×3 matrices representing other transformations to result in a complex transformation. Any transformation that can be accomplished with 2×2 matrix multiplication can also be accomplished with 3×3 matrix multiplication with homogeneous coordinates. The example of scaling shown previously is shown here with homogeneous coordinates:

$$\begin{bmatrix} 1 & 0 & 2 \\ 0 & 1 & 2 \\ 0 & 0 & 1 \end{bmatrix} \begin{bmatrix} 1 \\ 3 \\ 1 \end{bmatrix} = \begin{bmatrix} 3 \\ 5 \\ 1 \end{bmatrix}$$

3D Matrix Transformations

Matrix transformations in 3D space are a straightforward extension of the 2D transformations presented here. 3D rotation around an axis is calculated in the same way as 2D rotation, with the rotation axis held fixed. For example, rotation around the y-axis would be represented like this:

$$\begin{bmatrix} \cos\theta & 0 & -\sin\theta & 0 \\ 0 & 1 & 0 & 0 \\ \sin\theta & 0 & \cos\theta & 0 \\ 0 & 0 & 0 & 1 \end{bmatrix} \begin{bmatrix} x \\ y \\ z \\ w \end{bmatrix} = \begin{bmatrix} x' \\ y' \\ z' \\ w' \end{bmatrix}$$

Arbitrary rotation in space can be represented as the product of three matrices representing component rotations around each axis. Of course, this product is also a 4×4 matrix.

An important matrix to know about is the *identity* matrix. The identity matrix is the matrix that, when multiplied by any vector, yields the same vector. The identity matrix has 1s in a diagonal line from the upper-left corner to the lower-right corner and 0s in all other positions, like this:

$$\begin{bmatrix} 1 & 0 & 0 & 0 \\ 0 & 1 & 0 & 0 \\ 0 & 0 & 1 & 0 \\ 0 & 0 & 0 & 1 \end{bmatrix}$$

It should be clear that the product of any four-element vector multiplied by this matrix will be the same as the original vector.

Projection-related transformations—such as the transformation between the orthogonal world space and the perspective view volume and the transformation between the view volume and the 2D image plane—are also accomplished using the same kind of 4×4 matrix multiplication.

The most explicit example of a matrix transformation in this book is in Chapter 8, where the shadow object is created by flattening a copy of the shadow-casting object with a single matrix transformation and coloring it black. If you study the matrix in that chapter, you should be able to figure out why the values of the matrix result in a shadowlike object. It should also become clearer why that technique of shadow creation can work only for shadows cast on planar surfaces.

Less explicitly described matrix transformations occur throughout this book. If you've understood this appendix, it should be clearer to you what is meant by applying a transformation, and you should have a deeper understanding of why the order of transformations matters.

Matrices and OpenGL

In the OpenGL|ES programming environment, matrices are encountered frequently. For the most part, you will deal with matrices by using built-in GL functions that enable you to work with matrices in an intuitive way, without having to deal directly with numerical values. Nevertheless, knowing the basics about matrix math is important for understanding matrix operations in OpenGL|ES.

OpenGL|ES holds several transformation matrices in memory at a time. The GL_MODELVIEW matrix represents the complex transformation to be applied to objects in a scene. When you want to rotate an object, you use the GL_MODELVIEW matrix to create a rotation between the frames of reference of the model and the view, as discussed previously in this chapter. The other pertinent matrix that OpenGL|ES holds in memory is the GL_PROJECTION matrix. This matrix encodes the relationship between the virtual 3D space and the 2D image that is ultimately created.

OpenGL|ES operates as a *state machine*. This means that the behaviors of GL functions are dependent upon the current state of the system when the function is called. For this reason, matrix operation functions are general and can be applied to either the GL_MODELVIEW matrix or the GL_PROJECTION matrix, depending on the state in which the function is called. The state that controls which matrix is operated on is the matrix mode state, and this is set with the function glMatrixMode(). In the code samples, you will see that the render function in the SIO2 template begins with the line glMatrixMode (GL_MODELVIEW);. This prepares GL to apply matrix operations to the model/view matrix. Subsequent matrix operations will be applied to the model/view matrix until the matrix mode is changed again by another call to glMatrixMode().

The next line in the template render function is a good example of a function that is applied to a matrix. It consists of a call to the glLoadIdentity() function. This function loads the identity matrix as the model/view matrix. This effectively resets the matrix so that it represents no transformation.

Unfortunately, it is beyond the scope of this appendix to go into further detail about GL matrix functions. There are numerous books about computer graphics programming with OpenGL and you should refer to one of them for further information on this topic.

SIO2 Reference

This appendix provides information for use in your further study of SIO2.

- SIO2 learning resources
- The .sio2 file format
- SIO2 flag values
- SIO2 functions

SIO2 Learning Resources

If you've followed the tutorials in this book, by now you have learned a lot about how to exploit the graphical power of SIO2. However, there is more to an engaging game or 3D application than just interacting with 3D assets and graphics. The atmosphere of the game or application is enhanced by ambient sound and sound effects, the game play is guided by levels and screens, data such as high scores or player identities must be made persistent, and controls and interface elements must be created to give the user the best possible playing experience. Depending on the game or application, network connectivity may even be necessary. Many of these topics are beyond the scope of this book, but fortunately, the official SIO2 distribution package comes complete with an extremely informative set of tutorials, as you've already seen.

Official SIO2 Tutorials and Code Samples

The SIO2 tutorials are in the form of heavily annotated Xcode projects, some of which also have accompanying videos available for viewing online. Generally, the videos deal with the Blender side of content creation and exporting, and the corresponding Xcode project assumes that you followed the video tutorial to export the necessary .sio2 file.

The tutorials are comprehensive and the information is dense, but with the background you have gained from this book, you should not have difficulty following them. However, due to the density of the information and the way it's organized between videos and complete Xcode projects, it's helpful to have an overview of the tutorials to tell you exactly where to look for specific functionality. Here is a brief list of the contents of the official SIO2 tutorials.

Tutorial 1 covers the basics of starting up and rendering a scene with SIO2. The content of this tutorial overlaps the material in Chapter 2 of this book. No Blender content is presented at this point.

Tutorial 2 introduces a basic Blender scene with a single object, Suzanne the monkey. You build and execute this tutorial in Chapter 1 and see most of its content throughout other chapters. It tells you how to export a scene and how to use vertex painting to color an object without material or texture.

Tutorial 3 contains material that you are not exposed to in this book, in particular regarding mixing and blending materials. You learn the basics of handling materials and textures in this book, but Tutorial 3 shows you how to use multiple textures in conjunction with vertex colors and how these techniques can be used to achieve lighting effects.

Tutorial 4 creates an immersive world with many of the characteristics of the world you create in Chapter 6 of this book. Billboards are dealt with in greater detail than they are in Chapter 6, and an interesting technique for creating simple, fast real-time shadows for planar surfaces is shown.

Tutorial 5 goes into working with text and fonts in considerably more detail than you learn about in Chapter 5 of this book. In this tutorial, you work with multiple different fonts to discover how to resize fonts on the fly and position them in any way you wish on the screen.

Tutorial 6.1 introduces physical simulation and rigid bodies, expanding on that aspect of Chapter 6 in this book. This tutorial also discusses instancing and color-based picking, which is introduced in this book in Chapter 2 and Chapter 6. In Tutorial 6.1, you learn how a set of instances or the parent object of the instances can be picked.

Tutorial 6.2 uses essentially the same content as Tutorial 6.1, but it does things in a different, more sophisticated way. This tutorial introduces threading for physics to improve performance, a topic that is not touched on at all in this book. Also, an alternate form of picking is introduced that makes use of the Bullet physics library, and a method for picking up and dragging objects is presented.

Tutorial 7 describes how to use movie files as animated textures, which is not addressed at all in this book.

Tutorial 8 delves into real-time lighting. The main points of this tutorial are introduced in the discussion of lighting in Chapter 3 of this book, but the topic is dealt with in more detail. Multiple mobile lights of varying colors are used.

Tutorial 9 explores alternate ways of controlling the first-person camera using the iPhone's accelerometer. This tutorial also introduces using ambient and 3D positional sound. This tutorial also shows you how to use your own custom properties set from Blender and how to use the SIO2 parser to retrieve them, a very useful function for game creation.

Tutorial 10 focuses on integrating Lua scripting into your apps. SIO2 enables you to have almost unlimited control over the content of your game by means of the Lua scripting interface.

Tutorial 11 covers the use of a handy Python script for baking rendered textures and shadow maps that is included in the official SIO2 package. This offers an alternative to some of the baking approaches described in this book.

Tutorial 12 covers the SIO2 particle system. Flames, fountains, snow, smoke, and sparkling shooting stars are all demonstrated in this tutorial. By picking apart the sample code, you will be able to figure out how to implement a wide variety of particle effects. The SIO2 particle system is completely separate from Blender particle functionality, so there's no Blender component to creating these particle effects.

Tutorials 13.1 and 13.2 cover networking with SIO2. The `SIO2socket` structure enables you to develop client/server and multiplayer apps. As an example, this pair of tutorials shows you how to communicate wirelessly between your device and the OS X iPhone simulator.

Tutorial 14 contains a lot of material, some of which is touched on in chapters in this book, but much of it is not. Keyframe animation, object parenting, rigid body physics, and collision detection are dealt with as well as a number of interesting atmospheric effects, including sun flares and fog.

Tutorial 15 covers some of the same material as Chapter 8 of this book, in terms of character animation and action controls. However, this tutorial takes things further by making the character into a collision object that can interact physically with its environment. Ambient sound is also covered in this tutorial.

Tutorial 16 covers soft-body physics in SIO2.

Tutorial 17 goes into detail about how to create an official SIO2 splash screen. If you use SIO2 without the Indie Certificate to create an application available on iTunes, you should follow this tutorial.

I highly recommend all of the tutorials. The comments in the code contain numerous useful tips and will help you deepen your understanding of SIO2 greatly. Taken together, these tutorials contain all the information you need to push the interactive 3D capabilities of the iPhone to their limits with SIO2.

Transcending Your Limits with SIO2 Meditation Garden

A terrific resource for learning advanced SIO2 techniques is the SIO2 Meditation Garden. The app itself is available from the iTunes App Store, but the full project directory with all the assets, graphics, .blend files, and code is available for sale from the official SIO2 website at http://sio2interactive.com. The cost of the whole package is about a hundred dollars, which is well worth the investment if you plan to get serious about creating games with SIO2. The Meditation Garden uses sophisticated asset- and state-management techniques that will enable you to take what you've learned in this book and apply it to creating powerful, responsive games that scale well. Diving into this well-organized and heavily annotated code is guaranteed to make you a stronger SIO2 developer. Furthermore, buying the Meditation Garden package helps support SIO2 development and keep the whole project advancing and improving.

Shooting to Score with Hoops Frenzy

The SIO2 Hoops Frenzy app project is another tutorial package available from the SIO2 website. However, it is a slightly more complex project than Meditation Garden in terms of interactivity and game play. Hoops Frenzy uses rigid body physics and instancing to create an arcade-style basketball game, complete with scorekeeping, skill levels, physics debugging, and a variety of other useful game-play functions.

Powering Up with SIO2 Backyard War

For those interested in creating even more complex games, the multilevel first-person shooter Backyard War is the ideal resource for further study. Like Meditation Garden and Hoops Frenzy, the full project—including all code, textures, .blend files, and other assets—is available for sale to serious game creators on the SIO2 website. Backyard War features dynamic-level rendering using Lua scripting, non-player character artificial intelligence, complex game states and game logic, physics debugging, and optimizations for minimal memory use. See the SIO2 website for a complete overview of the topics covered in this extensive tutorial app.

The SIO2 Forum

In addition to these resources, the SIO2 forum at `http://forum.sio2interactive.com/` is a good place to ask questions and discuss SIO2 development. If you get stuck on something in this book or the tutorials, you can use this forum to get help. If you don't need help, consider joining the forum to help others benefit from your knowledge!

The *.sio2* File Format

This section provides an overview of the information contained in the SIO2 v1.4 File Format Specification document that's included with the standard SIO2 v1.4 distribution package. Check that document for more detail and notes.

The .sio2 file format holds data for use in the SIO2 programming environment. At the highest level, the .sio2 file is basically a renamed ZIP file. If you delete the .sio2 filename extension and replace it with .zip, you can uncompress the file just as you would an ordinary ZIP file. Likewise, you can create an .sio2 file by zipping a directory and changing the filename extension to .sio2. Most often, the data in a .sio2 file is generated by the Blender Python exporter. In this case, the file format consists of a local filesystem containing nine directories, each of which contains a collection of plain-text files representing assets to be used in the game environment. The exceptions are the image directory, which contains image files, and the sound directory, which contains the .ogg files.

The directories are as follows:

```
action
camera
image
ipo
lamp
material
object
script
sound
```

The following tables list properties and values for the SIO2 entities represented in the .sio2 file. The format of the data for each item in each text file is based on the struct format in C. The first table gives an overview of the basic data type notation that is used in the subsequent tables. The remaining tables list the properties and their associated values in the Token column (on the left) and the meaning of the properties in the Description column (on the right).

SIO2TYPE

%f	Floating-point value
%d	Integer value
%s	String value (restricted to 64 characters)
%c	Unsigned char value
%h	Unsigned short value

SIO2CAMERA

camera("%s"){}

TOKEN	DESCRIPTION
l(%f %f %f)	The location of the camera
r(%f %f %f)	The rotation of the camera
d(%f %f %f)	The normalized direction vector of the camera
f(%f)	The angle of the camera lens (field of view)
cs(%f)	The camera clip start value (zNear)
ce(%f)	The camera clip end value (zFar)
ip("%s")	The internal name of the Ipo that is linked to the camera

SIO2MATERIAL

material("%s"){}

TOKEN	DESCRIPTION
tfl0(%d)	The texture image binary flags for channel 0. See the SIO2_IMAGE_FLAGS table in the next section of this appendix for more information.
tfi0(%f)	The value of the mipmap filter for channel 0 (ranges from 0.0 to 2.0).
t0("%s")	The internal name of the texture image assigned to channel 0.
tfl1(%d)	The texture image binary flags for channel 1. See the SIO2_IMAGE_FLAGS table for more information.
tfi1(%f)	The value of the mipmap filter for channel 1 (ranges from 0.0 to 2.0).
t1("%s")	The internal name of the texture image assigned to channel 0.
sfl(%d)	The sound buffer binary flags attached to the current material.
sb("%s")	The internal sound buffer name attached to the material.
d(%f %f %f)	The diffuse color of the material (ranges from 0.0 to 1.0).
sp(%f %f %f)	The specular color of the material (ranges from 0.0 to 1.0).
a(%f)	The alpha value of the material (ranges from 0.0 to 1.0).
sh(%f)	The shininess component (ranges from 0.0 to 128.0).
fr(%f)	The material friction for physics (ranges from 0.0 to 100.0).

TOKEN	DESCRIPTION
re(%f)	The elasticity of the material (ranges from 0.0 to 1.0).
al(%f)	The alpha level threshold for alpha testing (ranges from 0.0 to 1.0). Only fragments (pixel data) with values greater than this value will be rendered onscreen.
b(%c)	The material's blending code. See the SIO2_MATERIAL_BLEND table in the next section of this appendix for the value range.

SIO2LAMP

lamp("%s"){}

TOKEN	DESCRIPTION
t(%c)	The lamp type. See the SIO2_LAMP_TYPE table in the next section of this appendix for more information.
fl(%d)	The lamp flags. See the SIO2_LAMP_FLAGS table in the next section of this appendix for more information.
l(%f %f %f)	The location of the lamp.
d(%f %f %f)	The lamp direction vector based on the negative z-axis.
c(%f %f %f)	The lamp color in RGB values; clamped between 0.0 and 1.0.
n(%f)	The energy factor of the light source; clamped between 0.0 and 10.0.
ds(%f)	The distance of the lamp radius.
f(%f)	The angle of the spotlight beam in degrees.
sb(%f)	The softness of the spotlight edges. Only used with SIO2_LAMP_SPOT.
at1(%f)	The linear distance attenuation for a linear or quadratic weighted lamp. This value should be between 0.0 and 1.0.
at2(%f)	The quadratic distance attenuation for a linear or quadratic weighted lamp. This value should be between 0.0 and 1.0.
ip("%s")	The internal Ipo object name linked to the lamp.

SIO2OBJECT

object("%s"){}

TOKEN	DESCRIPTION
l(%f %f %f)	The location of the object's pivot point.
r(%f %f %f)	The rotation of the object in degrees.
s(%f %f %f)	The scale of the object.
ra(%f)	The bounding sphere radius of the object.
fl(%d)	The binary flags for the object. See the SIO2_OBJECT_FLAGS table in the next section of this appendix for more information.
b(%d)	The physics bound type for dynamic, rigid, and soft body objects. See the SIO2_PHYSIC_BOUNDS table in the next section of this appendix for more information.
ma(%f)	The mass of the object for physics simulation.
da(%f)	The damping factor for physics objects; clamped between 0.0 and 1.0.
rd(%f)	The rotation damping factor for physics objects; clamped between 0.0 and 1.0.
mr(%f)	The collision margin for rigid body objects; clamped between 0.0 and 1.0.
di(%f %f %f)	The dimensions of the maximum value of the bounding box of the object.

continues

continued

TOKEN	DESCRIPTION
ip("%s")	The Ipo object name that is linked to the object.
ls("%f")	Linear stiffness for soft bodies. This value ranges from 0.0 to 1.0.
sm("%f")	The amount of the soft body shape maintained during simulation. This value ranges from 0.0 to 1.0.
ci("%c")	Specifies the number of cluster iterations.
pi("%f")	Specifies the number of position solver iterations.
in("%s")	The object instance name.
vb(%d %d %d %d %d)	The size and offset distances in bytes of the VBO and its offsets. The values should be ordered as shown in the SIO2_OBJECT_VBO_OFFSET table in the next section of this appendix.
v(%f %f %f)	Represents a single vertex location.
c(%c %c %c)	Represents a single vertex color.
n(%f %f %f)	Represents a single face normal vector.
u0(%f %f)	Represents a single UV coordinate mapping for texture channel 0.
u1(%f %f)	Represents a single UV coordinate mapping for texture channel 1.
ng(%d)	The number of vertex groups defined on the object. (The properties that follow the token provide details of the vertex groups themselves.)
g("%s")	Represents a single vertex group and its name. (The following properties provide details about this vertex group.)
mt("%s")	The internal material name associated with this vertex group.
ni(%d %d)	The number of vertex indices necessary to draw the current vertex group.
i(%h %h %h)	A set of vertex indices for drawing a face within the current vertex group.

SIO2ACTION

action("%s"){}

TOKEN	DESCRIPTION
nf(%d %d)	The number of frames in the action and the size of each frame in bytes.
f(%d)	The frame number. Frame vertices and normals are listed in sequence after each frame number.
fv(%f %f %f)	A single vertex for the current frame.
fn(%f %f %f)	A single normal vector for the current frame.

SIO2IPO

ipo("%s"){}

TOKEN	DESCRIPTION
lx("%f %f %f %f")	The LocX point set of the current Ipo curve.
ly("%f %f %f %f")	The LocY point set of the current Ipo curve.
lz("%f %f %f %f")	The LocZ point set of the current Ipo curve.
rx("%f %f %f %f")	The RotX point set of the current Ipo curve.
ry("%f %f %f %f")	The RotY point set of the current Ipo curve.
rz("%f %f %f %f")	The RotZ point set of the current Ipo curve.
sx("%f %f %f %f")	The SclX point set of the current Ipo curve.

TOKEN	DESCRIPTION
sy("%f %f %f %f")	The Sc1Y point set of the current Ipo curve.
sz("%f %f %f %f")	The Sc1Z point set of the current Ipo curve.
i(%c)	The interpolation mode of this curve. See the SIO2_IPO_CURVE_INTERPOLATION_TYPE table in the next section for more information.
e(%c)	The extrapolation mode of the curve. See the SIO2_IPO_CURVE_EXTRAPOLATION_TYPE table in the next section for more information.

SIO2 Flag Values

This section gives the specifications for the flags used by different SIO2 image types. This information can also be found in the SIO2 v1.4 File Format Specification document included with the standard SIO2 v1.4 distribution package.

SIO2_IMAGE_FLAGS

NAME	VALUE	DESCRIPTION
SIO2_IMAGE_MIPMAP	(1 << 0)	Controls whether or not the image will have mipmaps based on the SIO2 image filtering type.
SIO2_IMAGE_CLAMP	(1 << 1)	Clamps the UV coordinates to a range of 0.0 to 1.0. When this is activated, repeating textures are disabled.

SIO2_SOUND_FLAGS

NAME	VALUE	DESCRIPTION
SIO2_SOUND_AUTOPLAY	(1 << 0)	Starts the sound playing automatically as soon as the sound source ID is generated
SIO2_SOUND_LOOP	(1 << 0)	Loops the sound playback
SIO2_SOUND_AMBIENT	(1 << 2)	Specifies whether or not this sound will be used as ambient music
SIO2_SOUND_FX	(1 << 3)	Specifies that the sound source will be used as a positional (3D) sound

SIO2_LAMP_TYPE

NAME	VALUE	DESCRIPTION
SIO2_LAMP_LAMP	0	Creates an omnidirectional point light source
SIO2_LAMP_SUN	1	Creates a constant direction, parallel light source
SIO2_LAMP_SPOT	2	Creates a directional cone (spot) light source
SIO2_LAMP_HEMI	3	Creates a 180-degree constant light source
SIO2_LAMP_AREA	4	Creates a directional area light source

SIO2_LAMP_FLAGS

NAME	VALUE	DESCRIPTION
SIO2_LAMP_NO_DIFFUSE	(1 << 0)	Causes the diffuse color to be omitted and the default value of the implementation to be used
SIO2_LAMP_NO_SPECULAR	(1 << 1)	Causes the specular color to be omitted and the default value of the implementation to be used

SIO2_IPO_CURVE_INTERPOLATION_TYPE

NAME	VALUE	DESCRIPTION
CONSTANT	0	Sets the curve interpolation constant from the current knot to the next knot
LINEAR	1	Sets the curve to be linearly interpreted between adjacent knots
BEZIER	2	Sets the curve to be interpolated as a cubic Bezier curve between adjacent knots

SIO2_IPO_CURVE_EXTRAPOLATION_TYPE

NAME	VALUE	DESCRIPTION
CONSTANT	0	Sets the curve to be constant beyond the first and last knots
EXTRAPOLATION	1	Sets the curve to maintain the same slope beyond the first and last knots
CYCLIC	2	Sets the curve values to repeat beyond the first and last knots
CYCLIC_EXTRAPOLATION	3	Sets the curve values to repeat beyond the first and last knots, while retaining continuity

SIO2_MATERIAL_BLEND

NAME	VALUE	DESCRIPTION
SIO2_MATERIAL_MIX	0	The default material blending mode; equivalent to no blending
SIO2_MATERIAL_MULTIPLY	1	Color multiplication
SIO2_MATERIAL_ADD	2	Color addition
SIO2_MATERIAL_SUBTRACT	3	Subtracts the source alpha and destination color by one
SIO2_MATERIAL_DIVIDE	4	Color division
SIO2_MATERIAL_DARKEN	5	Not supported
SIO2_MATERIAL_DIFFERENCE	6	Subtracts the source and destination color values from 1, inverting them
SIO2_MATERIAL_LIGHTEN	7	Not supported
SIO2_MATERIAL_SCREEN	8	Adds the source color to the destination color
SIO2_MATERIAL_OVERLAY	9	Not supported
SIO2_MATERIAL_HUE	10	Not supported
SIO2_MATERIAL_SATURATION	11	Not supported
SIO2_MATERIAL_VALUE	12	Not supported
SIO2_MATERIAL_COLOR	13	Standard alpha blending based on the source alpha and the destination color

SIO2_OBJECT_FLAGS

NAME	VALUE	DESCRIPTION
SIO2_OBJECT_ACTOR	(1 << 0)	Determines if the object is a physical object
SIO2_OBJECT_GHOST	(1 << 1)	Sets the object to be part of the physics simulation but not to respond to contact
SIO2_OBJECT_DYNAMIC	(1 << 2)	Tags the object as a rigid body but without rolling physics
SIO2_OBJECT_RIGIDBODY	(1 << 3)	Tags the object as a rigid body with rolling physics
SIO2_OBJECT_SOFTBODY	(1 << 4)	Tags the object as a soft body
SIO2_OBJECT_BILLBOARD	(1 << 5)	Sets the object to be a billboard that rotates on the z-axis
SIO2_OBJECT_HALO	(1 << 6)	Sets the object to be a billboard that rotates on both the x- and z-axes
SIO2_OBJECT_TWOSIDE	(1 << 7)	Tags the object to render both its back face and front face
SIO2_OBJECT_NOSLEEPING	(1 << 8)	Keeps physics simulation activated even if objects are at rest
SIO2_OBJECT_SHADOW	(1 << 9)	Specifies that the object can cast a shadow
SIO2_OBJECT_DYNAMIC_DRAW	(1 << 10)	Specifies that the object's vertices will dynamically change at runtime
SIO2_OBJECT_INVISIBLE	(1 << 11)	Prevents an object from being rendered on screen

SIO2_PHYSIC_BOUNDS

NAME	VALUE	DESCRIPTION
SIO2_PHYSIC_BOX	0	Creates a box physics object
SIO2_PHYSIC_SPHERE	1	Creates a sphere physics object
SIO2_PHYSIC_CYLINDER	2	Creates a cylinder physics object
SIO2_PHYSIC_CONE	3	Creates a cone physics object
SIO2_PHYSIC_TRIANGLEMESH	4	Creates a triangle-based shape similar to the original geometry
SIO2_PHYSIC_CONVEXHULL	5	Creates a point cloud based on the shape that consists of the unique vertices of an object

SIO2_OBJECT_VBO_OFFSET

NAME	VALUE	DESCRIPTION
SIO2_OBJECT_SIZE	0	The total size of the VBO in bytes
SIO2_OBJECT_VCOLOR	1	The offset in bytes where the first vertex color starts (if not 0)
SIO2_OBJECT_NORMALS	2	The offset in bytes where the normals data starts (if not 0)
SIO2_OBJECT_TEXUV0	3	The offset in bytes where the UV data for channel 0 starts (if not 0)
SIO2_OBJECT_TEXUV1	4	The offset in bytes where the UV data for channel 0 starts (if not 0)

SIO2 Functions

This section provides a list of the functions of SIO2. Many of the most-common functions are described in detail throughout the book as they come up in the text, but this list gives a more-complete overview of the functions available to you. There is not enough space to go into detail about each one; however, you should be able to get a good sense of their functionality from the function names, the arguments, and the return data types. Be sure to also refer to the Doxygen documentation bundled with the SIO2 installation package. You can unzip it and navigate the API in your browser.

You can search the source code in Xcode for the function names to read their definitions.

```
SIO2action *sio2ActionFree(SIO2action *action)
SIO2action *sio2ActionInit(char *name)
unsigned char sio2ActionLoad(char *root, char *tok, char *val)
void sio2ActiveTexture(GLenum texture)
void sio2AlphaFunc(GLenum func, GLclampf ref)
void sio2BindBuffer(GLenum target, GLuint buffer)
void sio2BindTexture(GLenum target, GLuint texture)
void sio2BlendFunc(GLenum sfactor, GLenum dfactor)
void sio2BufferData(GLenum target, GLsizeptr size,
                    const GLvoid *data, GLenum usage)
void sio2BufferSubData(GLenum target, GLintptr offset,
                    GLsizeiptr size, const GLvoid *data)
unsigned char sio2CameraCubeInFrustum(
                    SIO2camera *camera, vec3 *v1, vec3 *v2)
unsigned char sio2CameraCubeIntersectFrustum(
                    SIO2camera *camera, vec3 *v1, vec3 *v2)
SIO2camera *sio2CameraFree(SIO2camera *camera)
unsigned char sio2CameraGeometryInFrustum(
                    SIO2camera *camera, unsigned int *nvert,
                    float *vert)
void sio2CameraGetModelviewMatrix(SIO2camera *camera)
void sio2CameraGetProjectionMatrix (SIO2camera *camera)
SIO2camera *sio2CameraInit( char *camera_name )
unsigned char sio2CameraLoad(char *root, char *token, char *value)
unsigned char sio2CameraPointInFrustum(SIO2camera *camera, vec3 *v)
void sio2CameraRender(SIO2 camera *camera)
float sio2CameraSphereDistInFrustum(SIO2camera *camera, vec3 *v, float *r)
unsigned char sio2CameraSphereInFrustum(SIO2camera *camera,
                                        vec3 *v, float *r)
unsigned char sio2CameraSphereIntersectFrustum(SIO2camera *camera,
                                        vec3 *v1, vec3 *v2)
void sio2CameraUpdateFrustum(SIO2camera *camera)
void sio2CameraUpdateListener(SIO2camera *camera)
void sio2Clear(GLbitfield mask)
```

```
void sio2ClearColor(GLclampf red, GLclampf green,
                    GLclampf blue, GLclampf alpha)
void sio2ClearDepthf(GLclampf depth)
void sio2ClearStencil(GLint s)
void sio2ClientActiveTexture (GLenum texture)
void sio2ClipPlanef(GLenum plane, const GLfloat *equation)
col4 *sio2Col4Free(col4 *c)
col4 *sio2Col4Init(void)
void sio2Color4f(GLfloat red, GLfloat green, GLfloat blue, GLfloat alpha)
void sio2Color4ub (GLubyte red, GLubyte green, GLubyte blue, GLubyte alpha)
void sio2ColorMask(GLboolean red, GLboolean green,
                   GLboolean blue, GLboolean alpha)
void sio2ColorPointer(GLint size, GLenum type,
                      GLsizei stride, const GLvoid *pointer)
void sio2CompressedTexImage2D(GLenum target, GLint level,
                              GLenum internalformat,
                              GLsizei width, GLsizei height,
                              GLint border, GLsizei imageSize,
                              const GLvoid *data)
void sio2CompressedTexSubImage2D(GLenum target, GLint level,
                                 GLint xoffset, GLint yoffset,
                                 GLsizei width, GLsizei height,
                                 GLenum format, GLsizei imageSize,
                                 const GLvoid *data)
void sio2CopyTexImage2D(GLenum target, GLint level,
                        GLenum internalformat, GLint x, GLint y,
                        GLsizei width, GLsizei height, GLint border)
void sio2CopyTexSubImage2D(GLenum target, GLint level,
                           GLint xoffset, GLint yoffset,
                           GLint x, GLint y, GLsizei width,
                           GLsizei height)
float sio2CubicBezier(float t, float a, float b, float c, float d)
void sio2CullFace(GLenum mode)
void sio2CurrentPaletteMatrixOES(GLuint matrixpaletteindex)
void sio2DeleteBuffers(GLsizei n, const GLuint *buffers)
void sio2DeleteTextures(GLsizei n, const GLuint *textures)
void sio2DepthFunc(GLenum func)
void sio2DepthMask(GLboolean flag)
void sio2DepthRangef(GLclampf zNear, GLclampf zFar)
void sio2Disable(GLenum cap)
void sio2DisableClientState(GLenum array)
void sio2DrawArrays(GLenum mode, GLint first, GLsizei count)
void sio2DrawElements(GLenum mode, GLsizei count,
                      GLenum type, const GLvoid *indices)
void sio2DrawTexfOES(GLfloat x, GLfloat y, GLfloat z,
                     GLfloat width, GLfloat height)
```

```
void sio2DrawTexfvOES(const GLfloat *coords)
void sio2EmitterCreate(SIO2emitter *emitter,
                       SIO2material, *material,
                       SIO2particlecreation *particle_creation,
                       SIO2particlerender *particle_render,
                       vec3 loc, vec3 dir, vec3 att,
                       unsigned int maxp, float pps, float rad)
SIO2emitter *sio2EmitterFree(SIO2emitter *emitter)
SIO2emitter *sio2EmitterInit(char *emitter_name)
SIO2emitter *sio2EmitterPause(SIO2emitter *emitter)
SIO2emitter *sio2EmitterPlay(SIO2emitter *emitter)
void sio2EmitterRender(SIO2emitter *emitter,
                       SIO2window *window,
                       unsigned char usematrix)
void sio2EmitterResetParticles(SIO2emitter *emitter)
void sio2EmitterSetupParticles(SIO2emitter *emitter)
SIO2emitter *sio2EmitterStop(SIO2emitter *emitter)
void sio2Enable(GLenum cap)
void sio2EnableClientState(GLenum array)
sio2EnableState()
void sio2ErrorAL(const char *fname, const char *funct, unsigned int line)
void sio2ErrorGL(const char *fname, const char *funct, unsigned int line)
int sio2ExecLUA(char *code)
void sio2ExtractPath(char *fname, char *ppath, char *aname)
void sio2Finish(void)
void sio2Flush(void)
void sio2Fogf(GLenum pname, GLfloat param)
void sio2Fogfv(GLenum pname, const GLfloat *params)
void sio2FontBuild(SIO2font *font)
void sio2FontCreate(SIO2font *font, SIO2material *material,
                    unsigned char n_char, unsigned char c_offset,
                    float size, float space)
SIO2font *sio2FontInit(const char *font_name)
unsigned char sio2FontPrint(SIO2font *font, unsigned char use_matrix,
                            const char *fmt)
void sio2FontReset(void)
SIO2frame *sio2FrameFree(SIO2frame *frame)
SIO2frame *sio2FrameInit(unsigned int frame, unsigned int size)
void sio2FrameSetCallback(SIO2frame *frame,
                          SIO2framecallback *frame_callback)
void sio2FrontFace(GLenum mode)
void sio2Frustumf(GLfloat left, GLfloat right,
                  GLfloat bottom, GLfloat top,
                  GLfloat zNear, GLfloat zFar)
void sio2GenBuffers(GLsizei n, GLuint *buffers)
void sio2GenColorIndex(unsigned int index, col4 *col)
```

```
void sio2GenTextures(GLsizei n, GLuint *textures)
float sio2GetAngleX(vec3 *v)
float sio2GetAngleZ(vec3 *v)
void sio2GetBooleanv(GLenum pname, GLboolean *params)
void sio2GetBufferParameteriv(GLenum target, GLenum pname, GLint *params)
void sio2GetClipPlanef(GLenum pname, GLfloat *equation)
unsigned int sio2GetElapsedTime(void)
void sio2GetFace(unsigned int f)
void sio2GetFloatv(GLenum pname, GLfloat *params)
void sio2GetIntegerv(GLenum pname, GLint *params)
void sio2GetLightfv(GLenum light, GLenum pname, GLfloat *params)
void sio2GetLightParam(unsigned int lp)
void sio2GetMaterialfv(GLenum face, GLenum pname, GLfloat *params)
unsigned int sio2GetMicroTime(void)
unsigned int sio2GetNextPow2(unsigned int s)
void sio2GetPointerv(GLenum pname, void **params)
void sio2GetState(unsigned int f)
const GLubyte *sio2GetString(GLenum name)
void sio2GetTexEnvfv(GLenum env, GLenum pname, GLfloat *params)
void sio2GetTexEnviv(GLenum env, GLenum pname, GLint *params)
void sio2GetTexParameterfv(GLenum target, Glenum pname, GLfloat *params)
void sio2GetTexParameteriv(GLenum target, GLenum pname, GLint *params)
void sio2GetTexture(unsigned int t)
void sio2Hint(GLenum target, GLenum mode)
void sio2ImageBlur(SIO2image *image)
void sio2ImageFlip(SIO2image *image)
void sio2ImageGenId(SIO2image *image, unsigned int flags, float filter)
SIO2image *sio2ImageInit(const char image_name)
void sio2ImageLoad(SIO2image *image, SIO2stream *stream)
void sio2ImageLoadJPEG(SIO2image *image, SIO2stream *stream)
void sio2ImageLoadPNG(SIO2image *image, SIO2stream *stream)
void sio2ImageLoadTGA(SIO2image *image, SIO2stream *stream)
void sio2ImageRGBAtoBGRA(SIO2image *image)
void sio2ImageRender(SIO2image *image)
void sio2ImageScale(SIO2image *image, unsigned int width,
                    unsigned int height)
void sio2ImageSetAlpha(SIO2image *image0, SIO2image *image1)
sio2Init() Initialize the SIO2 global variable
void sio2InitAL(void)
void sio2InitGL(void)
void sio2InitLUA(void)
void sio2InitWidget(void)
SIO2ipocurve *sio2IpoCurveFree(SIO2ipocurve *ipocurve)
SIO2ipocurve *sio2IpoCurveInit(void)
float sio2IpoCurveGetRatio(SIO2ipocurve *ipocurve)
float sio2IpoCurveRender(SIO2ipocurve *ipocurve, SIO2window *window)
```

```
float sio2IpoCurveReset(SIO2ipocurve *ipocurve)
void sio2IpoCurveSetPointCallback(SIO2ipocurve *ipocurve,
                                  SIO2pointcallback *pointcallback,
                                  unsigned int point_callback)
SIO2ipo *sio2IpoFree(SIO2ipo *ipo)
SIO2ipo *sio2IpoInit(char *name)
void sio2IpoPause(SIO2ipo *ipo)
void sio2IpoPlay(SIO2ipo *ipo)
void sio2IpoRender(SIO2ipo *ipo, SIO2window *window)
void sio2IpoReset(SIO2ipo *ipo, SIO2transform *transform)
void sio2IpoStop(SIO2ipo *ipo)
GLboolean sio2IsBuffer(GLuint buffer)
GLboolean sio2IsEnabled(GLuint cap)
unsigned char sio2IsPow2(int size)
GLboolean sio2IsTexture(GLuint texture)
void sio2LampEnableLight(void)
SIO2lamp *sio2LampFree(SIO2lamp *lamp)
SIO2lamp *sio2LampInit(char *name)
unsigned char sio2LampLoad(char *root, char *toc, char val)
unsigned char sio2LampRender(SIO2lamp *lamp, unsigned char index)
void sio2LampReset(void)
void sio2LampResetLight(void)
void sio2LampSetAmbient(vec4 *col)
void sio2Lightf(GLenum light, GLenum pname, GLfloat param)
void sio2Lightfv(GLenum light, GLenum pname, const GLfloat *params)
void sio2LightModelf(GLenum pname, GLfloat param)
void sio2LightModelfv(GLenum pname, const GLfloat *params)
void sio2LineWidth(GLfloat width)
void sio2LoadIdentity(void)
void sio2LoadMatrixf(const GLfloat *m)
void sio2LogicOp(GLenum opcode)
void sio2LoadPaletteFromModelViewMatrixOES(void)
void sio2LookAt(vec3 eye, vec3 center, vec3 up)
void *sio2MapBuffer(unsigned int id, int type)
void sio2Materialf(GLenum face, GLenum pname, GLfloat param)
void sio2Materialfv(GLenum face, GLenum pname, const GLfloat *params)
SIO2material *sio2MaterialFree(SIO2material *material)
SIO2material *sio2MaterialInit(const char *name)
void sio2MaterialLoad(char *root, char *tok, char *val)
void sio2MaterialRender(SIO2material *material)
void sio2MaterialReset(void)
void sio2MaterialResetImages(SIO2material *material)
void sio2MatrixIndexPointerOES(GLint size, GLenum type,
                               GLsizei stride,
                               const GLvoid *pointer)
```

```
void sio2MatrixMode(GLenum mode)
sio2Md2BuildAction()
sio2Md2ClearAllAction()
sio2Md2Free()
sio2Md2Init()
sio2Md2Load()
sio2Md2Play()
sio2Md2Render()
sio2Md2SetAction()
sio2Md2SetFps()
sio2Md2SetNextAction()
void sio2MistCreate(SIO2mist *mist, vec4 *col,
                    float dens, float mode,
                    float cstart, float cend)
SIO2mist *sioMistFree(SIO2mist *mist)
SIO2mist *sio2MistInit(char *name)
void sio2MistRender(SIO2mist *mist)
void sio2MistReset(void)
void sio2MultiTexCoord4f(GLenum target, GLfloat s,
                         GLfloat t, GLfloat r, GLfloat q)
void sio2MultMatrixf(const GLfloat *m)
void sio2Normal3f(GLfloat nx, GLfloat ny, GLfloat nz)
void sio2NormalPointer(GLenum type, GLsizei stride, const GLvoid *pointer)
sio2Normalize()
void sio2ObjectBillboard(SIO2object *object, vec3 v)
sio2ObjectBindAllMatrix()
sio2ObjectBindMatrix()
void sio2ObjectBindSound(SIO2object *object)
void sio2ObjectBindVBO(SIO2object *object, unsigned char use_material)
sio2ObjectBuildAction()
sio2ObjectClearAllAction()
void sio2ObjectCopyPhysicAttributes(SIO2object *object0,
                                     SIO2object *object1)
void sio2ObjectDisableObjectCollisionCallback(SIO2object *object)
sio2ObjectDuplicate()
void sio2ObjectEnableObjectCollisionCallback(SIO2object *object)
SIO2object *sio2ObjectFree(SIO2object *object)
void sio2ObjectGenId(SIO2object *object)
unsigned int sio2ObjectGetNumVert(SIO2object *object)
SIO2object *sio2ObjectHardCopy(SIO2object *object, char *name)
SIO2object *sio2ObjectInit(char *name)
void sio2ObjectInitAnimationAttributes(SIO2object *object)
void sio2ObjectInitPhysicAttributes(SIO2object *object)
unsigned char sio2ObjectLoad(char *root, char *tok, char *val)
void sio2ObjectPause(SIO2object *object)
void sio2ObjectPlay(SIO2object *object, unsigned char loop)
```

```
unsigned char sio2ObjectRender(SIO2object *object,
                                        SIO2window *window,
                                        SIO2camera *camera,
                                        unsigned char use_material,
                                        unsigned char use_matrix)
void sio2ObjectRenderAction(SIO2object *object, SIO2window *window)
void sio2ObjectReset(void)
void sio2ObjectSetAction(SIO2object *object, SIO2action *action,
                            float interp, float fps)
void sio2ObjectSetFrame(SIO2object *object, unsigned int frame)
unsigned char sio2ObjectSetNextAction(SIO2object *object,
                                        SIO2action *action,
                                        float interp, float fps)
SIO2object *sio2ObjectSoftCopy(SIO2object *object, char *name)
void sio2ObjectStop(SIO2object *object)
void sio2ObjectUpdateTimeRatio(SIO2object *object)
void sio2ObjectUpdateType(SIO2object *object)
size_t sio2OggRead(void *ptr, size_t size, size_t read, void *stream)
int sio2OggSeek(void *stream, ogg_int64_t offset, int stride)
sio2Orbit()
void sioOrthof(GLfloat left, GLfloat right, GLfloat bottom,
                GLfloat top, GLfloat zNear, GLfloat zFar)
SIO2particle *sio2ParticleFree(SIO2particle *particle)
SIO2particle *sio2ParticleInit(void)
void sio2Perspective(float fovy, float aspect, float zNear, float zFar)
void sio2PhysicAddCamera(SIO2physic *physic_object, SIO2camera *camera)
void sio2PhysicAddObject(SIO2physic *physic_object, SIO2object *object)
void sio2PhysicAddRigidBody(SIO2physic *physic_object, SIO2object *object)
void sio2PhysicAddSoftBody(SIO2physic *physic_object, SIO2object *object)
bool sio2PhysicCollisionCallback(btManifoldPoint, &cp,
                                        const btCollisionObject *colObj0,
                                        int partId0, int index0,
                                        const btCollisionObject *colObj1,
                                        int partId1, int index1)
SIO2physic *sio2PhysicFree(SIO2physic *physic_object)
SIO2physic *sio2PhysicInit(char *name)
void sio2PhysicPause(SIO2physic *physic_object)
void sio2PhysicPlay(SIO2physic *physic_object)
void sio2PhysicRemoveAllObjects(SIO2physic *physic_object)
void sio2PhysicRemoveCamera(SIO2physic *physic_object, SIO2camera *camera)
void sio2PhysicRemoveObject(SIO2physic *physic_object, SIO2object *object)
void sio2PhysicRender(SIO2physic *physic_object, float timestep, int pass)
void sio2PhysicResetAll(SIO2physic *physic_object)
void sio2PhysicResetCamera(SIO2physic *physic_object, SIO2camera *camera)
void sio2PhysicResetObject(SIO2physic *physic_object, SIO2object *object)
void sio2PhysicResetRigidBody(SIO2physic *physic_object,
                                SIO2object *object)
```

```
void sio2PhysicSetGravity(SIO2physic *physic_object, vec3 *gravity)
void sio2PhysicStop(SIO2physic *physic_object)
void sio2PixelStorei(GLenum pname, GLint param)
void sio2PointParameterf(GLenum pname, GLfloat param)
void sio2PointParameterfv(GLenum pname, const GLfloat *params)
void sio2PointSize(GLfloat size)
void sio2PointSizePointerOES(GLenum type, GLsizei stride,
                             const GLvoid *pointer)
void sio2PolygonOffset(GLfloat factor GLfloat units)
void sio2PopMatrix(void)
void sio2PushMatrix(void)
unsigned char sio2Project(float objx, float objy,
                          float objz, float model[16],
                          float proj[16], int viewport[4],
                          float *winx, float *winy, float *winz)
unsigned int sio2Randomui(unsigned int max)
void sio2ReadPixels(GLint x, GLint y, GLsizei width, GLsizei
                    height, GLenum format, GLenum type,
                    GLvoid *pixels)
float sio2RGBtoFloat(unsigned char c)
void sio2ResetListener(void)
void sio2ResetLUA(void)
void sio2ResetState(void)
void sio2ResourceAdd(SIO2resource *resource, unsigned char type, void *ptr)
void sio2ResourceAddEntry(SIO2resource *resource,
                          const char str, SIO2parsercallback *root,
                          SIO2parsercallback *custom)
void sio2ResourceBindAllImages(SIO2resource *resource)
void sio2ResourceBindAllInstances(SIO2resource *resource)
void sio2ResourceBindAllIpos(SIO2resource *resource)
void sio2ResourceBindAllMaterials(SIO2resource *resource)
void sio2ResourceBindAllPhysicObjects(SIO2resource *resource,
                                      SIO2physic *physic_object)
void sio2ResourceBindAllSoundBuffers(SIO2resource *resource)
void sio2ResourceBindAllSounds(SIO2resource *resource)
void sio2ResourceBindCameraIpo(SIO2resource *resource, SIO2camera *camera)
void sio2ResourceBindImage(SIO2resource *resource, SIO2material *material)
void sio2ResourceBindInstance(SIO2resource *resource, SIO2object *object)
void sio2ResourceBindLampIpo(SIO2resource *resource, SIO2lamp *lamp)
void sio2ResourceBindObjectIpo(SIO2resource *resource, SIO2object *object)
void sio2ResourceBindSoundBuffer(SIO2resource *resource,
                                 SIO2material *material)
void sio2ResourceClose(SIO2resource *resource)
void sio2ResourceCreateDictionary(SIO2resource *resource)
void sio2ResourceCull(SIO2resource *resource, SIO2camera *camera)
void sio2ResourceDel(SIO2resource *resource, unsigned char type, void *ptr)
```

```
void sio2ResourceDispatchEvents(SIO2resource *resource,
                                SIO2window *window,
                                unsigned char type,
                                unsigned char state)
SIO2stream *sio2ResourceDispatchStream(SIO2resource *resource,
                                       SIO2stream *stream)
void sio2ResourceExtract(SIO2resource *resource, char *password)
unsigned char sio2ResourceExtractFile(SIO2resource *resource,
                                      SIO2stream *stream,
                                      const char *fname,
                                      char *password)
SIO2resource *sio2ResourceFree(SIO2resource *resource)
void sio2ResourceGenId(SIO2resource *resource)
void *sio2ResourceGet(SIO2resource *resource,
                      unsigned char type, char *name)
SIO2action *sio2ResourceGetAction(SIO2resource *resource, char name)
SIO2camera *sio2ResourceGetCamera(SIO2resource *resource, char name)
SIO2emitter *sio2ResourceGetEmitter(SIO2resource *resource, char name)
SIO2font sio2ResourceGetFont(SIO2resource *resource, char name)
SIO2image *sio2ResourceGetImage(SIO2resource *resource, char name)
SIO2ipo *sio2ResourceGetIpo(SIO2resource *resource, char name)
SIO2lamp *sio2ResourceGetLamp(SIO2resource *resource, char name)
SIO2material *sio2ResourceGetMaterial(SIO2resource *resource, char name)
SIO2mist *sio2ResourceGetMist(SIO2resource *resource, char name)
SIO2object *sio2ResourceGetObject(SIO2resource *resource, char name)
SIO2physic sio2ResourceGetPhysic(SIO2resource *resource, char name)
SIO2script *sio2ResourceGetScript(SIO2resource *resource, char name)
SIO2sensor sio2ResourceGetSensor(SIO2resource *resource, char name)
SIO2sound *sio2ResourceGetSound(SIO2resource *resource, char name)
SIO2soundbuffer *sio2ResourceGetSoundbuffer(
                                SIO2resource *resource,
                                char name)
SIO2timer sio2ResourceGetTimer(SIO2resource *resource, char name)
unsigned int sio2ResourceGetVRAMSize(SIO2resource *resource)
SIO2resource *sio2ResourceInit(char *name)
unsigned char sio2ResourceOpen(SIO2resource *resource,
                               const char *fname,
                               unsigned char rel)
void sio2ResourceRender(SIO2resource *resource,
                        SIO2window *window,
                        SIO2camera *camera, int mask)
sio2ResourceResetState()
SIO2object *sio2ResourceSelect3D(SIO2resource *resource,
                                 SIO2camera *camera,
                                 SIO2window *window, vec2 *v)
void sio2ResourceSetAmbientVolume(SIO2resource *resource,
                                  SIO2window *window)
```

```
void sio2ResourceSetFxVolume(SIO2resource *resource, SIO2window *window)
void sio2ResourceUnload(SIO2resource *resource, unsigned char type)
void sio2ResourceUnloadAll(SIO2resource *resource)
void sio2ResourceUpdateAllWidgetBoundaries(SIO2resource *resource,
                                                SIO2window *window)
void sio2Rotate3D(vec3 v1, float ax, float az, float d, vec3 v2)
void sio2Rotatef(GLfloat ansio2e, GLfloat x, GLfloat y, GLfloat z)
float sio2RoundAngle(float angle)
void sio2SampleCoverage(GLclampf value, GLboolean invert)
void sio2Scalef(GLfloat x, Glfloat y, GLfloat z)
void sio2Scissor(GLint x, GLint y, GLsizei width, GLsizei height)
unsigned char sio2ScriptCompile(SIO2script *script)
SIO2script *sio2ScriptFree(SIO2script *script)
void sio2ScriptGetError(SIO2script *script)
SIO2Script *sio2ScriptInit(char *name)
unsigned char sio2ScriptLoad(SIO2script *script, SIO2stream *stream)
void sio2SensorEvaluate(SIO2sensor *sensor)
SIO2sensor *sio2SensorFree(SIO2sensor *sensor)
SIO2sensor *sio2SensorInitCollision(char name,
                            SIO2object *object0,
                            SIO2object *object1,
                            SIO2sensorcollision *sensor_collision)
SIO2sensor *sio2SensorInitContact(char name,
                            SIO2sensorcontact *sensor_contact)
SIO2sensor *sio2SensorInitDistance(char name, SIO2object *object0,
                                    SIO2object *object1, float
threshold,
                                    SIO2sensordistance *sensor_
distance)
SIO2sensor *sio2SensorInitRay(char name, vec3 from, vec3 to,
                                SIO2physic *physic,
                                SIO2sensorray *sensor_ray)
void sio2ShadeModel(GLenum mode)
void sio2ShutdownAL(void)
void sio2ShutdownLUA(void)
void sio2ShutdownWidget(void)
sio2Shutdown()
void sio2Sleep(unsigned int ms)
int sio2SocketAccept(SIO2socket *socket)
unsigned char sio2SocketConnect(SIO2socket *socket, char *ip,
                                    unsigned short *port)
void sio2SocketDisconnect(SIO2socket *socket)
SIO2socket *sio2SocketFree(SIO2socket *socket)
SIO2socket *sio2SocketInit(void)
unsigned char sio2SocketListen(SIO2socket *socket,
                                unsigned short port,
                                unsigned short maxc)
```

```
int sio2SocketReceive(SIO2socket *socket)
void sio2SocketSetOpt(SIO2socket *socket)
unsigned char sio2SocketSend(SIO2socket *socket, char *buf)
SIO2soundbuffer *sio2SoundBufferFree(SIO2soundbuffer *sound_buffer)
SIO2stream *sio2SoundBufferGenId(SIO2soundbuffer *sound_buffer,
                                 unsigned char streamed)
SIO2soundbuffer *sio2SoundBufferInit(char *name)
void sio2SoundBufferLoad(SIO2soundbuffer *sound_buffer, SIO2stream stream)
unsigned char sio2SoundBufferStream(SIO2soundbuffer *sound_buffer,
                                    unsigned int buffer)
SIO2sound *sio2SoundFree(SIO2sound *sound)
void sio2SoundGenId(SIO2sound *sound, SIO2soundbuffer *sound_buffer,
                    unsigned int flags)
SIO2sound *sio2SoundInit(char *name)
void sio2SoundPause(SIO2sound *sound)
void sio2SoundPlay(SIO2sound *sound)
void sio2SoundRewind(SIO2sound *sound)
void sio2SoundSetAmbient(SIO2sound *sound)
void sio2SoundSetDefault(SIO2sound *sound)
void sio2SoundSetFx(SIO2sound *sound, vec3 *pos, float rad)
void sio2SoundSetSpeed(SIO2sound *sound, float speed)
void sio2SoundSetVolume(SIO2sound *sound, float volume)
void sio2SoundStop(SIO2sound *sound)
void sio2SoundUpdateState(SIO2sound *sound)
void sio2SoundUpdateStream(SIO2sound *sound)
unsigned char sio2StateDisable(SIO2state *state, unsigned int mask)
unsigned char sio2StateEnable(SIO2state *state, unsigned int mask)
SIO2state *sio2StateFree(SIO2state *state)
SIO2state *sio2StateInit(void)
unsigned char sio2StateSetActiveTexture(SIO2state *state, int texture)
void sio2StateSetAlphaFunc(SIO2state *state, float v)
void sio2StateSetBlendMode(SIO2state *state, unsigned char blend)
unsigned char sio2StateSetClientActiveTexture(SIO2state *state,
                                              int texture)
void sio2StateSetColor(SIO2state *state, vec4 color)
void sio2StencilFunc(GLenum func, GLint ref, GLuint mask)
void sio2StencilMask(GLuint mask)
void sio2StencilOp(GLenum fail, GLenum zfail, GLenum zpass)
SIO2stream *sio2StreamClose(SIO2stream *stream)
SIO2stream sio2StreamEOF(SIO2stream *stream)
SIO2stream *sio2StreamInit(const char *fname)
SIO2stream *sio2StreamOpen(char *fname, unsigned char rel)
SIO2stream *sio2StreamOpenText(char *fname, unsigned char rel)
void sio2StreamParse(SIO2stream *stream, unsigned int n_entry,
                     SIO2entry *entry)
```

unsigned int **sio2StreamRead**(SIO2stream *stream*, void *ptr*,
                                                unsigned int *size_t*)

void ***sio2StreamReadPtr**(SIO2stream *stream*, unsigned int *size_t*)

int **sio2StringScanf**(char *str*, const char *fmt*)

void **sio2TexCoordPointer**(GLint *size*, GLenum *type*,
                                                GLsizei *stride*, const GLvoid *pointer*)

void **sio2TexEnvf**(GLenum *target*, GLenum *pname*, GLfloat *param*)

void **sio2TexEnvi**(GLenum *target*, GLenum *pname*, GLint *param*)

void **sio2TexEnvfv**(GLenum *target*, GLenum *pname*, const GLfloat *params*)

void **sio2TexEnviv**(GLenum *target*, GLenum *pname*, const GLint *params*)

void **sio2TexImage2D**(GLenum *target*, GLint *level*, GLint *internalformat*,
                                GLsizei *width*, GLsizei *height*, GLint *border*,
                                GLenum *format*, GLenum *type*, const GLvoid *pixels*)

void **sio2TexParameterf**(GLenum *target*, GLenum *pname*, GLfloat *param*)

void **sio2TexParameteri**(GLenum *target*, GLenum *pname*, GLint *param*)

void **sio2TexParameterfv**(GLenum *target*, GLenum *pname*, const GLfloat *params*)

void **sio2TexParameteriv**(GLenum *target*, GLenum *pname*, const GLint *params*)

void **sio2TexSubImage2D**(GLenum *target*, GLint *level*, GLint *xoffset*,
                                GLint *yoffset*, GLsizei *width*, GLsizei *height*,
                                GLenum *format*, GLenum *type*, const GLvoid *pixels*)

void **sio2ThreadCreate**(SIO2thread *thread*, SIO2threadcallback *thread_callback*,
                                        void *userdata*, int *priority*)

SIO2thread ***sio2threadFree**(SIO2thread *thread*)

SIO2thread ***sio2threadInit**(void)

void **sio2ThreadPause**(SIO2thread *thread*)

void **sio2ThreadPlay**(SIO2thread *thread*)

void **sio2ThreadRun**(void *ptr*)

void **sio2ThreadStop**(SIO2thread *thread*)

void **sio2TimerCreate**(SIO2timer *timer*, SIO2window *window*,
                                SIO2timercallback *timer_callback*,
                                unsigned int *interval*)

void **sio2TimerEvaluate**(SIO2timer *timer*)

SIO2timer ***sio2TimerFree**(SIO2timer *timer*)

SIO2timer ***sio2TimerInit**(char *name*)

void **sio2TimerPause**(SIO2timer *timer*)

void **sio2TimerPlay**(SIO2timer *timer*)

void **sio2TimerStop**(SIO2timer *timer*)

void **sio2TransformApply**(SIO2transform *transform*)

void **sio2TransformBindMatrix**(SIO2transform *transform*)

void **sio2TransformCopy**(SIO2transform *transform1*,
                                    SIO2transform *transform2*)

SIO2transform ***sio2TransformFree**(SIO2transform *transform*)

SIO2transform ***sio2TransformInit**(void)

void **sio2TransformRender**(SIO2transform *transform*)

```
void sio2TransformRotateX(SIO2transform *transform, float rotx)
void sio2TransformRotateZ(SIO2transform *transform, float rotz)
void sio2TransformSetDir(SIO2transform *transform, vec3 *dir)
void sio2TransformSetMatrix(SIO2transform *transform, float *mat)
void sio2TransformSetLoc(SIO2transform *transform, vec3 *loc)
void sio2TransformSetRot(SIO2transform *transform, vec3 *rot)
void sio2TransformSetScl(SIO2transform *transform, vec3 scl)
void sio2Translatef(GLfloat x, GLfloat y, GLfloat z)
void *sio2UnmapBuffer(unsigned int id, int type)
unsigned char sio2UnProject(float winx, float winy,
                                  float winz, float model[16],
                                  float projection [16], int viewport[4],
                                  float *objx, float *objy, float *objz)
sio2Vec3Diff()
vec2 *sio2Vec2Free(vec2 *v)
vec2 *sio2Vec2Init(void)
vec3 *sio2Vec3Free(vec3 *v)
vec3 *sio2Vec3Init(void)
vec4 *sio2Vec4Free(vec4 *v)
vec4 *sio2Vec4Init(void)
SIO2vertexgroup *sio2VertexGroupFree(SIO2vertexgroup *vertexgroup)
SIO2vertexgroup *sio2VertexGroupInit(char *name)
void sio2VertexGroupGenId(SIO2vertexgroup *vertexgroup)
void sio2VertexGroupLoad(SIO2vertexgroup *vertexgroup, SIO2stream *stream)
void sio2VertexGroupRender(SIO2vertexgroup *vertexgroup,
                                  unsigned char *use_material)
void sio2VertexPointer(GLint size, GLenum type, GLsizei stride,
                             const GLvoid *pointer)
unsigned char *sio2VideoBufferStream(SIO2video *video)
SIO2video *sio2VideoFree(SIO2video *video)
unsigned char sio2VideoGetImage(SIO2video *video,
                                       SIO2image *image, int flags,
                                       float filter)
SIO2video *sio2VideoInit(char *name)
void sio2VideoLoad(SIO2video *video, SIO2stream *stream)
void sio2VideoPause(SIO2video *video)
void sio2VideoPlay(SIO2video *video, unsigned char loop)
void sio2VideoQueueBuffers(SIO2video *video)
void sio2VideoStop(SIO2video *video)
void sio2Viewport(GLint x, GLint y, GLsizei width, GLsizei height)
void sio2WeightPointerOES(GLint size, GLenum type,
                                GLsizei stride, const GLvoid *pointer)
void sio2WidgetDebug(SIO2widget *widget)
SIO2widget *sio2WidgetFree(SIO2widget *widget)
SIO2widget *sio2WidgetInit(char *name)
```

```
unsigned char sio2WidgetRender(SIO2widget *widget,
                               SIO2window *window,
                               unsigned char use_matrix)
void sio2WidgetReset(void)
unsigned char sio2WidgetUpdateBoundary(SIO2widget *widget,
                                       SIO2window *window)
sio2WindowAddTouch()
void sio2WindowDebugTouch(SIO2window *window)
void sio2WindowEnter2D(SIO2window *window, float cstart, float cend)
void sio2WindowEnterLandscape2D(SIO2window *window)
void sio2WindowEnterLandscape3D(void)
SIO2window *sio2WindowFree(SIO2window *window)
void sio2WindowGetViewportMatrix(SIO2window *window)
SIO2window *sio2WindowInit(void)
void sio2WindowLeave2D(void)
void sio2WindowLeaveLandscape2D(SIO2window *window)
void sio2WindowLeaveLandscape3D(void)
sio2WindowResetTouch()
void sio2WindowSetAccelerometerSensitivity(SIO2window *window,
                                           float smooth)
void sio2WindowShutdown(SIO2window *window,
                        SIO2windowshutdown *window_shutdown)
void sio2WindowSwapBuffers(SIO2window *window)
sio2WindowUpdate()
void sio2WindowUpdateViewport(SIO2window *window, int x,
                              int y, int w, int h)
```

Index